422

ABORı

10

ABORIGINAL SOVEREIGNTY

Reflections on race, state and nation

HENRY REYNOLDS

ALLEN & UNWIN

First published in 1996 by
Allen & Unwin Pty Ltd
9 Atchison Street, St Leonards, NSW 2065
Phone: (61 2) 9901 4088
Fax: (61 2) 9906 2218
E-mail: 100252.103@compuserve.com

National Library of Australia
Cataloguing-in-Publication entry:

Reynolds, Henry, 1938– .
    Aboriginal sovereignty: reflections on race, state and nation.

    Includes index.
    ISBN 1 86373 969 6.

    1. Native title (Australia). 2. Aborigines, Australian—
    Land tenure. 3. Aborigines, Australian—Legal status,
    laws, etc. 4. Aborigines, Australian—Government
    relations. 5. Aborigines, Australian—Politics and
    government. 6. Australia—Colonization—History.
    I. Title.

323.119915

Set in 12/12.5pt Bembo and Garamond by DOCUPRO, Sydney
Printed by Australian Print Group, Maryborough, Victoria

10 9 8 7 6 5 4 3 2 1

CONTENTS

IN MEMORY OF

EDWARD KOIKI MABO

1936–1992

ACKNOWLEDGEMENTS

THE RESEARCH ON WHICH THIS BOOK is based was made possible by grants provided by both James Cook University and the Australian Research Council. Staff in many libraries in numerous Australian cities have provided irreplaceable professional assistance. My colleagues at James Cook University have, as ever, been supportive and patient with the inconveniences caused by my peripatetic life-style. May Carlson, in particular, has had to deal with innumerable callers seeking an absentee staff member. I owe particular thanks to my typist Val Hicks, who turned muddled hand-written pages into professional and polished text.

I have benefitted from contact with many colleagues, particularly those who have supplemented my inadequate grasp of the law. In particular, I would like to mention Garth Nettheim in Australia and my Canadian colleagues Brian Slattery, Patrick Macklem and Kent McNeill, who have been pioneers in the field of indigenous people and the law. Marilyn Lake shared ideas and articles, and read and commented on an early version of the manuscript. John Iremonger provided the early stimulus and encouragement for the nascent ideas which grew into the book.

My family have, as ever, been both tolerant and supportive of my obsessions. Rebecca Reynolds translated extracts from nineteenth century French books on international law. John and Anna Reynolds engaged me in often vigorous debate about the central ideas of the book and their possible outcomes. Margaret Reynolds has heard the arguments embodied in the book many times over, was a supportive reader of the manuscript and, as always, provided the contact with the practical world of politics which has helped convert academic argument into cogent social comment.

INTRODUCTION

A FUNDAMENTAL MORAL PROBLEM which arose from the European settlement of Australia was foreshadowed long before Cook sailed along the east coast of the continent. One hundred and fifty years earlier the English savant Francis Bacon wrote in his essay *On Plantations*: 'I like a plantation in a pure soil, that is, where people are not displanted to the end to plant in others, for else it is rather an extirpation than a plantation'.[1]

Australia was not 'a pure soil' in 1788. For generations indigenous Australians were 'displanted to the end to plant in' European settlers. All too often colonisation on those terms resulted, as Bacon foresaw, in the extirpation of the Aborigines and the destruction of their society.

British colonisation began in the belief that the continent was largely uninhabited, which was the advice provided to the government by men like Banks and Matra who had been with Cook on the *Endeavour*. Like Dampier before them Banks and Matra were convinced that fish were the only possible consistent source of sustenance in Australia. In 1688 Dampier had concluded that the Aborigines of the north-west coast needed to efficiently harvest the sea 'or else they must fast; For the Earth affords them no food at all'.[2] Eighty-two years later and on the far side of the continent Banks made the same assumption, believing that while the coastline was 'thinly inhabited even to admiration' it could be assumed that the vast interior was 'totally uninhabited'.[3] Matra thought that the Aborigines' 'animal existence' was 'almost entirely sustained by catching fish'.[4] It was a belief that was brought back to Australia in 1788. The marine captain Watkin Tench reported that while the members of the First Fleet had found the land around Sydney Harbour 'more populous than it was generally believed to be in Europe' there was 'every reason to conclude from our researches', as well as from the 'manner of living practices by the natives', that the interior was uninhabited.[5]

Policy was framed in the belief that the colony would be planted in a pure soil, that the British would be the first legal occupants of the land and that the Crown would be the first sovereign. As the most popular international law text of the era, Emerich de Vattel's *The Law of Nations*, explained:

> When a Nation takes possession of a country which belongs to no-one, it is considered as acquiring *sovereignty* over it as well as *ownership*; for, being free and independent, it cannot intend, when it settles a territory, to leave to others the right to rule it, nor any other right which belongs to sovereignty.[6]

The British settlers quickly had to adjust their ideas once they gained experience in Australia. The interior was not empty; there was no land without owners. Everywhere the British travelled resident clans were in possession. No matter how far back from the coast they went the story was the same; Aborigines flourished in places where white people starved or died of thirst.

The advantages of assuming the absence of people were so great, however, that legal doctrine continued to depict Australia as a colony acquired by occupation of a *terra nullius*, although once the demographic picture became clear the theoretical justification changed course. The indigenous people were there all right, the new story ran, but they were too primitive to be regarded as the actual owners and sovereigns. They ranged over the land rather than inhabiting it. They had no social or political organisation which Europeans could recognise and respect.

Terra nullius changed its legal clothes but lived vigorously on. A hundred years after the arrival of the First Fleet the Privy Council's Lord Watson determined in *Cooper v Stuart* that Australia had been 'practically uninhabited' in 1788.[7] It was a decision which Justice Blackburn declared binding when he found the Yirrkala people had no common law rights to the traditional lands in the Gove Land Rights case in 1971.[8] It is possible therefore to draw a direct line from observations made from the quarter-deck of the *Endeavour* in 1770, through the Privy Council decision in *Cooper v Stuart* in 1889 and on to Blackburn's judgement in the Northern Territory Supreme Court in 1971.

Having found that Australia was not an empty land many colonists expected the Aborigines to eventually 'die out'. The doctrine of *terra nullius* might not accurately account for the past but it could point the way to the future. The catastrophic fall in the Aboriginal population as a result of disease, deprivation and violence suggested that indigenous demographic decline would resolve the vexed question of prior ownership once and for all.

The cultural merging of the indigenous and immigrant communities has been foreshadowed and planned for at varying times since the early years of settlement. It has invariably been seen as requiring the adaption of Aboriginal people to introduced patterns of thought and behaviour. They were to become 'civilised', to adopt the 'Australian way of life'. Either way, the expectation was that Aboriginality would ebb away through a process of ethnocide, either chosen or imposed.

By the 1970s however, it was clear to the wider community that Aboriginal society was not being absorbed or assimilated. Instead, the opposite was occurring. 'We Have Survived', the banners proudly proclaimed in the marches and demonstrations of the period. When the Aboriginal political movement dramatically advanced across the national stage the prime objective was land rights—the attempt to reverse the decision taken at the birth of colonial society to treat the continent as a *terra nullius*. Two hundred years of history was being challenged—the theories of Sir Joseph Banks as well as the legal doctrine of Lord Watson. Self-serving Eurocentric jurisprudence was being called to account.

Aboriginal prior ownership of land was conceded both in legislation, particularly in the Northern Territory and South Australia, and, above all, in the High Court's Mabo judgement in 1992 which declared that the Aborigines had owned and possessed their traditional lands when the Europeans arrived and that in some places native title would certainly still survive.

An Australian court had finally contradicted the Privy Council's assertion of 1889 that there had been no land ownership or tenure in 1788. But the Privy Council was only partially corrected. The High Court accepted as settled law the British assertion of sovereignty in 1788. From that time forth there was only one sovereign and one system of law in Australia.

No treaties were ever negotiated like the hundreds signed with indigenous people in North America, Africa and New Zealand. There was no recognition or acceptance in Australia that remnant sovereignty survived annexation permitting autonomy or local self-government. The Aborigines were never allowed the status of domestic dependent nations accorded to the Indian tribes in the United States following the famous Supreme Court judgements of Chief Justice Marshall in *Worcester v Georgia*, 1830, and the *Cherokee Nation v The State of Georgia*, 1831. Nor was there any acceptance of customary law—and, in effect, of legal pluralism—which occurred throughout the rest of the Empire in the eighteenth and nineteenth centuries.

All this did not happen because the law itself lacked flexibility. It was accepted doctrine that the common law applied in colonies of settlement only to the extent appropriate for a new society. What is more, the common law embraced local customary law—the *lex loci* as it was known—in the British Isles itself and continued to do so as it was carried to all parts of the world.

The Australian colonists behaved as though their society was simply an extension of metropolitan Britain. They felt no need to adapt to the presence of indigenous people—they lived out the legend of *terra nullius*. Aboriginal culture, laws, customs and interests could be ignored. Central to this view was the cultural condescension and racial contempt that was immured in the legal and constitutional foundations. It is a legacy which distinguished Australian society, one we live with still and must learn to live down.

It matters to us because we will inevitably have to reconcile our national politics and law with the growing body of international jurisprudence about the rights and interest of indigenous people. Meanwhile, Aborigines and Islanders expand their horizons and increase their contacts. Their cause relates to and gathers strength from the re-assertion of ethnic identities all over the world. In 1975, when Aboriginal issues were being pushed to the forefront of national politics, the American scholars Nathan Glazer and Daniel Patrick Moynihan wrote of ethnic groups that:

> Formerly seen as *survivals* from an earlier age, to be treated variously with annoyance, toleration, or mild celebration, we now have a growing sense that they may be *forms* of social life that are capable of reviving and transforming themselves [emphasis in original].[9]

Twenty years later the relations between ethnic groups and national minorities on the one hand and the states which make up the international system on the other are central to world politics. In a recent article in the *Times Literary Supplement*, D. Papinean referred to 'that most pressing of contemporary problems—which people have the right to draw a line around themselves and constitute a sovereign state'.[10] The international jurist Richard Falk argued in a book on *The Rights of Indigenous People in International Law* published in 1987 that:

> We need to understand the extent to which there exists in all parts of the world now, an awareness that one of the great current problems of world order, is the plight of what I would call entrapped nations, nations that are entrapped within the structure and framework of the sovereign state. An enormous juristic fraud has been perpetrated on modern political consciousness by confusing national identity with the power political reality of state sovereignty. The whole idea of what it means to be a national has been converted

through a formal juristic device into a legal status that the state confers, which, for the majority of people living in the world, does not correspond with their ethnic, psychological, and political reality. Their sense of what it means to belong to a collectivity, however one describes it, whether in tribal terms or in national terms, is often at odds with a network of imposed obligations owed to the sovereign state. Rather than a sense of loyalty associated with the natural sentiment of nationality, there exists a condition of political alienation in a variety of forms. Such circumstances pertain, to varying degree, to virtually every region of the world. The sooner that links and coalitions and bonds are forged between all those who are trying to struggle against the coercive mechanism of the state . . . the sooner will we be able to liberate the entrapped nations of the world.[11]

Australia is now grappling with a problem which, in one form or another, is found worldwide. It will exercise our minds for a generation or more to come. Its roots lie deep in the past; present and future policies must, therefore, be informed by what has happened over the last 200 years.

Central to these matters is the question of sovereignty and the sprawling issues of political, legal and constitutional power and authority. It confronts the wayfarer as a dense, variegated thicket which must be carefully and patiently negotiated. Before we have finished some progress may have been made across what, for Australia, is lightly explored terrain. So where should our journey begin? With what questions should we take our bearings?

Did the Aborigines exercise political and legal dominion over Australia before the coming of the Europeans? Were the tribes actually nations, albeit very small ones? Could they have been recognised as such in European law in the later eighteenth century and early nineteenth century? Or was that out of the question? If the tribes were small nations exercising at least a rudimentary form of sovereignty how did they lose it and when? On the other hand, was the continent a *terra nullius* in relation to sovereignty, a legal vacuum? Was British sovereignty, therefore, original rather than derivative?

For a long time now international law has provided for three ways for the acquisition of sovereignty: by conquest, by cession and by occupation. Australian courts have always opted for occupation but does the theory fit the facts of history as we know them? And if so, when did British authority override and extinguish Aboriginal sovereignty and indigenous law? Was it done on the instant on those four occasions when the British formally annexed parts of the continent in 1788, 1824, 1829 and 1879? Or did it happen in a slow, piecemeal fashion as settlement was pushed out over the land surface? Did Aboriginal law disappear suddenly and completely? Was there one system of law in colonial Australia or many? If Aboriginal law and authority were slowly eroded away has some residual sovereignty survived among people still on their own land and maintaining customary law? If, as the High Court decided in Mabo, it is necessary to extinguish land rights in a clear and plain manner, is the same test required for the acquisition of sovereignty? Did this happen? Or was the assumption that because there was no sovereignty here in the first place nothing was required of the annexing power? Will Australia ever come to accept, as Canadian authorities have done, that indigenous people have an inherent right to self-government stemming from their prior occupation of the continent?

How do these questions relate to contemporary Aboriginal demands for recognition of customary law, for self-government and for political autonomy? Are current developments aspects of the global process of decolonisation working its way out, belatedly, in a distinctive Australian way? Will Aboriginal communities seek their own special status in the federal system? Will they ever attempt to secede from Australia? Where, indeed, will it all end? Can Australia accept the idea of the separation of nation and state which has been conflated since Federation? Can we come to terms with the idea that there is more than one nation within the state and that in this way Australia is like most countries in the world?

Many of these questions are unfamiliar ones—and disturbing ones as well. They lead us into a whole new territory of discourse and contention. But they must be dealt with because they have deep roots in our history and are implicated in many of the changes which are preparing the way for our plunge into the twenty-first century. Can Australia transcend its colonial heritage and at the same time find a distinctive local answer to that ubiquitous contemporary problem: the deeply troubled relation between a large number of nations and a small number of states?

Our capacity to deal with these questions is inhibited by the lack of discussion in the nation's courts. Whenever the issue of sovereignty is raised Australian judges have determined that the matter is not just closed but is beyond serious enquiry. They do so for two reasons. Extensions of sovereignty, the conventional argument runs, are matters of international, not domestic law and are, therefore, beyond the reach of Australian courts. A linked view is that acquisition of territory is a prerogative of the Crown which cannot be questioned by the courts. While these interpretations may be sound in law they mean that Australian judges dodge some of the most important legal—and moral and political—issues confronting us. The tendency of courts to hide behind what is known as the act of state doctrine has recently been sharply criticised by the Canadian legal scholar Brian Slattery who wrote:

> Whatever the merits of this argument in other contexts, it is doubtful whether it should induce modern Canadian or American courts to accept fictitious accounts of the manner in which their countries came into being, accounts that accept even the most extravagant imperial claims at face value and ignore the historical presence and viewpoints of indigenous peoples. When it comes to reconstructing the legal history of their own countries, courts cannot take refuge in the act of state doctrine without forfeiting their moral authority and acting as passive instruments of colonial rule. In this context, the act of state doctrine is mischievous and should be modified.[12]

Central to the issue of sovereignty is the question of the status and nature of traditional society and whether it had become what eighteenth-century European jurists called a civil—as opposed to a natural—society regulated by a system of laws which people generally obeyed and was, as a consequence, the bearer and wielder of sovereignty. Much turns on that question. The discussion below considers the issue in relation to European international law but before we venture in that direction it is important to understand that Aborigines made the same distinctions as the eighteenth-century Europeans, as some of their myths and legends show. Particularly pertinent were the stories about the introduction of law to the Worora people in the central Kimberley region between the Glenelg and Prince Regent rivers:

> Way back in the dreamtime when the earth was made, men and women were also made. They had a lot of children and when they grew up they just married each other and had more children. They ate raw meat, fruit and berries. As yet people did not have fire sticks; people only used fire when they were lucky enough to get fire from lightning, when it struck trees and fire kept on burning. People then lived lawlessly. They ate food and meat without having to cook it; they lived like animals. There were no relationships.
>
> A man by the name of Ngunyarri thought about making sacred art and totems. He lived alone with his mother who was old and blind and who stayed most of the time in camp looking after the first lot of art that her son had done. One day when Ngunyarri went out to do more carvings a man from a neighbouring tribe, called Webalma, came around and saw this old lady all alone with all the totems. He asked her who had done them. She answered, 'My son, Ngunyarri, goes out every day and does all this handiwork'. Knowing that she could not see, he stole some of the art and took it off back to his tribal land. On arriving there he sent out smoke signals to other tribes. There they gathered and had a big meeting and discussed how things should continue from that day. At this meeting leaders and elders were formed to make a council. Among these were Wodoi and Jungun (or Jungunja). These two men discussed their marriages. Jungen married his daughters and so did Wodoi, and both of them saw that it was not right to marry their own daughter. So these two men agreed that their two tribes should intermarry.
>
> Meanwhile when Ngunyarri returned to his camp his mother suddenly realised that his beautiful art was missing. He asked his old mother what had happened and she told

him about Webalma, the man who had visited her after he had left to do more work. (Webalma happened to be hunting when he came across the camp of the old lady and her son). So Ngunyarri left his mother and went to look for the thief and his stolen totem.

When he reached the people in their land he asked for the art and the thief, but the leaders said to Ngunyarri, 'That piece of art has made us set up rules and laws and made us form leaders and elders, and it has been shown to all the tribes of other lands'. So Ngunyarri thought, 'I will go back and make some more art and handiwork seeing that it was so worthwhile and so useful to all the tribes and will be from generation to generation'.

Since then men lived by laws and rules. Leaders were formed to control the tribes of people of the lands. They also discussed marriages. So Wodoi and Jungen were the first leaders of all the people.[13]

Despite the gulf between Aboriginal and eighteenth-century British society this legend is remarkably similar in important ways to the accounts written by classical European jurists of the historical transition from a state of nature to civil society and nationhood. Aboriginal society had made that transition with clear and ultimately inescapable consequences for Australian jurisprudence which our courts have, as yet, refused to face up to, for as Emerich de Vattel wrote in his *The Law of Nations* in 1758:

The territory which a Nation inhabits, whether the Nation moved into it as a body, or *whether the families scattered over the territory came together* to form a civil society, forms a national settlement, to which the Nation has a private and exclusive right. [*emphasis added*][14]

1

TERRA NULLIUS AND SOVEREIGNTY

UNTIL RECENTLY *TERRA NULLIUS* was an obscure legal term known only to a few experts. Over the last few years however, it has become the focal point for an intense national debate about property and sovereignty, law and morality; about the past, the present and the future. But while the term was little known in the community at large the idea of a land without owners dominated Australian legal thinking from the earliest years of settlement until the recent Mabo judgement. Up until then *terra nullius* had played a central role in determining the legal, political and constitutional relations between the European settlers and their descendants and the indigenous people of Australia. It is deeply implicated in Australia's current quest for a new identity and destiny in a post-colonial, post-Cold War world. While the legacy of *terra nullius* survives the country will remain shackled to its colonial past.

In the case of *Mabo v Queensland, no. 2*, the judges had to choose between arguments put by the Murray Islander Eddie Mabo and his associates on one hand and the Queensland Government on the other. Queensland advanced the case for *terra nullius* arguing that when, in 1879, in the name of the Queen the colonial government annexed the Murray Islands it gained both sovereignty and the ownership of all the property, that from that moment forward the Islanders were only in occupation of their land with permission of the

1

government, that in point of law they could have been driven into the sea at any time. The state's case was summarised by Justice Dawson who remarked that 'if the traditional land rights claimed by the plaintiffs ever existed, they were extinguished from the moment of annexation'.[1]

The six other judges came down on the side of Mabo determining that the Murray Islanders were entitled, as against the whole world, to possession, occupation, use and enjoyment of their traditional land. The Islanders had owned their land before 1879; they had not been dispossessed by the claim of sovereignty; nothing the Queensland Government had done between 1879 and 1992 had extinguished their native title. In rejecting the Queensland case Justice Brennan observed that: 'The fiction by which the rights and interests of indigenous inhabitants in land were treated as non-existent was justified by a policy which has no place in the contemporary law of this country.'[2]

In fact, the theory that the indigenous inhabitants of a 'settled' colony had no proprietary interest in the land depended on 'a discriminatory denigration of indigenous inhabitants, their social organization and customs'.[3] Brennan believed that 'an unjust and discriminatory doctrine' of that kind could no longer be accepted.[4]

The principles enunciated in relation to Murray Island applied to the rest of Australia, Justice Toohey observing:

Before proceeding further, one more point should be noted. While this case concerns the Meriam people, the legal issues fall to be determined according to fundamental principles of common law and colonial constitutional law applicable throughout Australia. The Meriam people are in culturally significant ways different from the Aboriginal peoples of Australia, who in turn differ from each other. But, as will be seen, no basic distinction need be made, for the purposes of determining what interests exist in ancestral lands of indigenous peoples of Australia, between the Meriam people and those who occupied and occupy the Australian mainland. The relevant principles are the same.[5]

The principles in question were that as a result of annexation the common law flowed into Australia and the Aborigines and Torres Strait Islanders became British subjects. The law recognised and embraced their native title although the Crown exercised what was called the radical title or eminent domain, which allowed it to extinguish the indigenous interest. The Aborigines did not lose their native title at the moment of annexation but in a piecemeal fashion over a long period. Those communities still living on Crown land and maintaining their cultural traditions were likely to still possess it.

But while the court demolished the concept of *terra nullius* in respect of property, it preserved it in relation to sovereignty. The plaintiffs did not question the legality of the annexation but the court affirmed it just the same. Justices Deane and Gaudron observed that 'it must be accepted in this Court' that the whole of the territory designated in Governor Phillip's commission was, from the formal declaration of annexation on 7 February 1788 'validly established as a settled British Colony'.[6] Referring to Murray Island their colleague Justice Dawson remarked that:

> The annexation of the Murray Islands is not now questioned. It was an act of state by which the Crown in right of the Colony of Queensland exerted sovereignty over the islands. Whatever the justification for the acquisition of territory by this means (and the sentiments of the nineteenth century by no means coincide with current thought), there can be no doubt that it was, and remains, legally effective.[7]

The Court followed established law in considering the question of sovereignty arguing that the Crown, while acting outside Britain itself and on the international stage, exercised prerogative powers which were beyond the reach of domestic—or municipal courts—as they are termed. This had been settled legal doctrine for a long time; British courts paying homage to the all powerful sovereign of English constitutional theory. In 1906 the King's Bench declared that the extension of territory was:

> essentially an exercise of sovereign power, and hence cannot be challenged, controlled, or interfered with by municipal

courts. Its sanction is not that of law, but that of sovereign power, and, whatever it be, municipal courts must accept it, as it is, without question.[8]

In a case in 1927 the courts determined that even the proper extent of territorial sovereignty was a matter which the courts could not question. In fact, any definite statement 'from the proper representative of the Crown as to the territory of the Crown must be treated as conclusive. A conflict is not to be contemplated between the courts and the executive on such a matter'.[9]

These principles were re-affirmed in Australia by the High Court in the so-called Sea and Submerged Sea Case in 1975, Justice Gibbs arguing that the acquisition of territory by a sovereign state for the first time was 'an act of state which cannot be challenged, controlled or interfered with by the Courts of that State'.[10]

It would, then, have been futile for Mabo and his associates to question the claim of sovereignty over their island in 1879. Justice Brennan explained that the law was such that it precluded any contest between the executive and judicial branches of government as to whether a territory was or was not within the 'Queen's Domain'. These issues were 'not justiceable in the municipal courts'.[11]

Such a doctrine may well make life easier for the judiciary. It makes it very hard however, for anyone questioning the legality of the British annexation of Australia, an issue raised most notably in the case *Coe v the Commonwealth* in 1979. Paul Coe sought to sue the Commonwealth of Australia on behalf of the 'Aboriginal community and nation of Australia'.[12] He presented the court with a long and detailed statement of claim which included the following points:

- From time immemorial prior to 1770 the aboriginal nation had enjoyed exclusive sovereignty over the whole of the continent now known as Australia.
- The aboriginal people have had from time immemorial a complex social, religious, cultural and legal system under which individuals and tribes had proprietary and/or possessory rights, privileges, interests, claims and

4

entitlements to particular areas of land subject to usufructuary rights in other aboriginal people. Some of the
aboriginal people still exercise these rights.

- Clans, tribes and groups of aboriginal people travelled
widely over the said continent now known as Australia
developing a system of interlocking rights and responsibilities making contact with other tribes and larger
groups of aboriginal people thus forming a sovereign
aboriginal nation.

- The whole of the said continent now known as Australia
was held by the said aboriginal nation from time immemorial for the use and benefit of all members of the
said nation and particular proprietory [*sic*] possessory
and usufructuary rights in no way separated from the
sovereignty of the said aboriginal nation.[13]

Having provided an account of traditional Australia Coe then
turned his attention to the British:

- On or about a day in April 1770 Captain James Cook
R.N. at Kurnell wrongfully proclaimed sovereignty and
dominion over the east coast of the continent now
known as Australia for and on behalf of King George
III for and on behalf of what is now the secondnamed
Defendant.

- On or about the 26th day of January, 1788 Captain
Arthur Phillip, R.N. wrongfully claimed possession and
occupation for the said King George III on behalf of
what is now the secondnamed Defendant of that area
of land extending from Cape York to the southern coast
of Tasmania and embracing all the land inland from the
Pacific Ocean to the west as far as the 135th longitude
including that area of land now occupied by the
firstnamed Defendant at the Commonwealth Offices,
Sydney, Commonwealth Bank Building, Martin Place,
Sydney.

- The claims of Captain Cook, Captain Phillip and others
on behalf of King George III and his heirs and successors
were contrary to the rights, privileges, interests, claims
and entitlements of the aboriginal people both individually and in tribes and of the aboriginal community and
nation . . .[14]

Coe's claims were decisively rejected. Justice Jacobs determined that the questions at issue were not matters of domestic laws but of the 'law of nations'. Indeed they were not 'cognisable in a court exercising jurisdiction under that sovereignty which is sought to be challenged'.[15] Justice Gibbs was both more expansive and more dismissive. He argued that if Coe's statement of claim intended

> to suggest either that the legal foundation of the Commonwealth is insecure, or that the powers of the Parliament are more limited than is provided in the Constitution, or that there is an aboriginal nation which has sovereignty over Australia, it cannot be supported. In fact, we were told in argument, it is intended to claim that there is an aboriginal nation which has sovereignty over its own people, notwithstanding that they remain citizens of the Commonwealth; in other words, it is sought to treat the aboriginal people of Australia as a domestic dependent nation, to use the expression which Marshall C.J. applied to the Cherokee Nation of Indians: *Cherokee Nation v. State of Georgia* (1831). However, the history of the relationships between the white settlers and the aboriginal peoples has not been the same in Australia and in the United States, and it is not possible to say, as was said by Marshall C.J. of the Cherokee Nation, that the aboriginal people of Australia are organized as a 'distinct political society separated from others', or that they have been uniformly treated as a state. The judgments in that case therefore provide no assistance in determining the position in Australia. The aboriginal people are subject to the laws of the Commonwealth and of the States or Territories in which they respectively reside. They have no legislative, executive or judicial organs by which sovereignty might be exercised. If such organs existed, they would have no powers, except such as the laws of the Commonwealth or of a State or Territory, might confer upon them. The contention that there is in Australia an aboriginal nation exercising sovereignty, even of a limited kind is quite impossible in law to maintain.[16]

The Coe family attempted to establish their case a second time in 1993, arguing that the Wiradjuri people were a 'sovereign nation of people' or were alternatively a 'domestic dependant nation'[17] which was entitled to self-government and full rights over their traditional lands. Justice Mason was as dismissive as his brother judges had been fourteen years before. There was no sovereignty 'adverse to the Crown'[18] residing in the Aboriginal people of Australia, nor was there a limited kind of sovereignty 'embraced in the notion that they are "a domestic dependant nation" entitled to self government'.[19]

Claims of Aboriginal sovereignty have been made in a number of criminal cases. In *R. v Wedge* in 1976 it was argued by the defendant that the New South Wales courts had no jurisdiction because 'the Aboriginal people were and still are a sovereign people, and as such are not subject to English law'.[20] It was an argument with little appeal to Justice Rath who felt he was bound by precedent laid down in the nineteenth-century cases *R. v Murrell* in the Supreme Court of New South Wales in 1836 and *Cooper v Stuart* in the Privy Council in 1889. In *R. v Murrell* Justice Burton asserted that:

> although it might be granted that on the first taking possession of the Colony, the Aborigines were entitled to be recognized as free and independent, yet they were not in such a position with regard to strength to be considered free and independent tribes. They had no sovereignty.[21]

Burton's arguments, Rath believed, were 'as valid today as they were when judgement was given on 19/2/1836'.[22] Rath saw himself as working within an old legal tradition which had been settled for 140 years, one which totally disregarded Aboriginal customary law. As Lord Watson declared in *Cooper v Stuart* in 1889, in cases where a colony had been established by settlement 'there was only one sovereign, namely the King of England, and only one law, namely English law'.[23]

A similar decision was handed down by the High Court at the end of 1994 in the case of *Walker v NSW*. The plaintiff Dennis Walker appealed against a charge he was facing on the grounds that the Australian parliaments lacked the power to legislate in a manner affecting Aboriginal people without their request and consent. Chief Justice Mason dismissed the proposition that 'sovereignty resided in the Aboriginal people'. The Parliament of New South Wales had power to make laws for the 'peace, welfare and good government of New South Wales in all cases whatsoever'. The proposition that those laws could not apply 'to particular inhabitants or particular conduct occurring within the State must be rejected'.[24]

In the Mabo decision the High Court judges told the legal story of Australia in a new way. According to the old story, when the British arrived in New South Wales the Crown became both the sovereign authority and the actual proprietor of the land over the eastern half of the continent and over the remainder as a result of succeeding claims of sovereignty in 1824, 1829 and 1879. The post-Mabo story is different. The claim of sovereignty only delivered the radical title of the land, the incoming common law recognising the native title of indigenous people who retained a legal interest in their homelands until they were formally extinguished by government. The new story overturns the judgement of Chief Justice Stephen in the important case of *Attorney-General v Brown* in 1847 that the Crown was the absolute owner of the land because there was 'no other proprietor of such lands'.[25] Justice Brennan argued that:

> The proposition that, when the Crown assumed sovereignty over an Australian colony, it became the universal and absolute beneficial owner of all the land therein, invites critical examination. If the conclusion at which Stephen C.J. arrived in *Attorney-General v. Brown* be right, the interests of indigenous inhabitants in colonial land were extinguished so soon as British subjects settled in a colony, though the indigenous inhabitants had neither ceded their lands to the Crown nor suffered them to be taken as the spoils of conquest. According to the cases, the common law itself took from indigenous inhabitants any right to occupy their traditional land, exposed them to deprivation of the religious, cultural and economic sustenance which the land provides, vested the land effectively in the control of the Imperial authorities without any right to compensation and made the indigenous inhabitants intruders in their own homes and mendicants for a place to live. Judged by any civilized standards, such a law is unjust and its claim to be part of the common law to be applied in contemporary Australia must be questioned.[26]

The old story had the advantage of simplicity and consistency. Either Aboriginal sovereignty and property rights didn't exist prior to the arrival of the First Fleet or they disappeared all together in one apocalyptic moment on 7 February 1788 when New South Wales was formally annexed. The common law came into a legal desert—one that had either always been there or, alternatively, had just been created, depending on which version of the story is followed.

The new story is more complicated. The Aborigines didn't lose their land rights in 1788 but they were stripped of their right to manage their own affairs and to live according to their own laws. So the old and the new stories overlap. In that apocalyptic moment on 7 February 1788, the new story runs, communities living across half a continent, hundreds of kilometres away from the tiny European encampment, lost their sovereignty although they weren't aware of that fact and may not have seen a white man for 50 or 100 years after the event. The law in relation to sovereignty remains as defined by Lord Watson in 1889 as Justice Rath explained in *R. v Wedge* in 1976:

> As Lord Watson said, in the case of a colony founded by settlement, the law of England . . . becomes from the outset the law of the Colony, and is administered by its tribunals. The law of England is the only law which those tribunals then recognize and apply. Thus it seems evident that, as New South Wales, in legal theory was founded by settlement, there was only one sovereign, namely the King of England, and only one law, namely English law.[27]

Law points in one direction, logic in the other. If, as the High Court determined, indigenous land rights and land law survived the arrival of the British why didn't other aspects of the local law? If property rights continued until they were extinguished in a clear and plain manner why didn't other elements of Aboriginal law, custom and politics? If interest in land ran on into the colonial period and beyond why didn't the right of internal self-government? If the doctrine of continuity, as it is called, operated in one case why didn't it work more generally?

If there were many Aboriginal nations exercising sovereignty and enforcing laws and custom before 1788 how did they lose their authority; and when? How did sovereignty which had existed for thousands of years simply disappear without military conquest or cession by means of treaties? Nineteenth-century jurists had a ready answer to these questions. Australia, they reasoned, was a place without settled inhabitants or settled law before 1788. Justice Burton argued in 1836 that the Aborigines 'had not attained at first settlement to such a position in point of numbers and civilization, and to such a form or Government and laws, as to be entitled to be recognized as so many sovereign states governed by laws of their own'.[28]

Do contemporary jurists still see traditional Australia in this light? The question was closely considered by Justice Blackburn in *Milerrpum v Nabalco* in 1971. He referred to a discussion in the Privy Council in 1921 in the case *In re Southern Rhodesia* which referred to the problem of evaluating the 'rights of aboriginal tribes'. Some tribes, their lordships declared, were 'so low in the scale of social organization that their usages and conceptions of rights and duties' could not be reconciled with 'the institutions and legal ideas of civilized society'.[29] Such a gulf, they declared, could not be bridged.

After hearing voluminous evidence about traditional Aboriginal society Blackburn was

> very clearly of opinion, upon the evidence, that the social rules and customs of the plaintiffs cannot possibly be dismissed as lying on the other side of an unbridgeable gulf. The evidence shows a subtle and elaborate system highly adapted to the country in which the people led their lives, which provided a stable order of society and was remarkably free from the vagaries of personal whim or influence. If ever a system could be called 'a government of laws, and not of men', it is that show in the evidence before me . . .
>
> What is shown by the evidence is, in my opinion, that the system of law was recognized as obligatory upon them by the members of a community which, in principle, is definable, in that it is the community of aboriginals which made ritual and economic use of the subject land.[30]

Blackburn's assessment was supported and given the imprimatur of the High Court in 1979 by Justice Murphy who explained in *Coe v the Commonwealth*:

> There is a wealth of historical material to support the claim that the aboriginal people had occupied Australia for many thousands of years; that although they were nomadic, the various tribal groups were attached to defined areas of land over which they passed and stayed from time to time in an established pattern; that they had a complex social and political organization; that their laws were settled and of great antiquity.[31]

In the opinion of both Blackburn and Murphy, then, the Aborigines exercised sovereignty prior to the arrival of the Europeans. Murphy concluded: 'Independent tribes, travelling over a territory or stopping in certain places, may exercise de-facto authority which prevents the territory being *terra nullius*.'[32]

In the Mabo judgement Justices Deane and Gaudron argued that:

> Under the laws of customs of the relevant locality, particular tribes or clans were, either on their own or with others, custodians of the areas of land from which they derived sustenance and from which they often took their tribal names. Their laws or customs were elaborate and obligatory. The boundaries of their traditional lands were likely to be long-standing and defined. The special relationship between a particular tribe or clan and its land was recognized by other tribes or groups within the relevant local native system and was reflected in differences in dialect over relatively short distances. In different ways and to varying degrees of intensity, they used their homelands for all the purposes of their lives: social, ritual, economic. They identified with them in a way which transcended common law notions of property or possession. As was the case in other British colonies, the claim to the land was ordinarily that of the tribe or other group, not that of an individual in his or her own right.[33]

Having absorbed the insights provided by modern anthropology it is far from certain that the High Court has allowed them to fully inform its jurisprudence. The judges have used them to overturn part of the legacy of *Cooper v Stuart* but not all of it. While they have rejected the assertion that there was no land law or tenure prior to settlement they have clung to the idea that there was no sovereignty, to the assertion that Australia, prior to 1788, was a land without settled inhabitants or settled law. In terms of law and political authority the Aborigines apparently still dwell on the far side of the Privy Council's great gulf between civilisation and savagery.

Justice Brennan was fully aware that at the very heart of the settled colony doctrine, which he helped re-affirm in Mabo, was the assessment that the indigenous people concerned were 'taken to be without laws, without a sovereign, and primitive in their social organization'. The central logic of the doctrine was that there was 'no recognized sovereign else the territory could have been acquired only by conquest or cession'.[34]

Is it possible to reject one half of the legacy of *Cooper v Stuart* relating to property and preserve the other one respecting sovereignty when both embody attitudes and beliefs considered unacceptable and unsupportable at the end of the twentieth century? Justice Brennan wrote: 'Whatever the justification advanced in earlier days for refusing to recognize the rights and interests in land of the indigenous inhabitants of settled colonies, an unjust and discriminatory doctrine of that kind can no longer be accepted.'[35]

It was unacceptable for international as well as domestic reasons. *Terra nullius* was out of step with international standards of human rights, on the one hand, and with fundamental values of common law on the other, because it entrenched a discriminatory rule based on 'the supposed position' of indigenous people on a 'scale of social organization'.[36]

In rejecting *terra nullius* as applied to property rights, Justice Brennan referred with approval to the comments made by his colleague Justice Deane in a case heard in 1985 to the effect that Australian law at the time had still not reached the 'stage of retreat from injustice' which American jurisprudence attained in the great judgement of Chief Justice John Marshall in *Johnson v McIntosh* in 1823 which provided the classic definition of native title. It could be said that after Mabo the High Court finally marched Australia up to 1823 but has gone no further. It has not reached the point attained by Marshall's Supreme Court in 1831 when, in *The Cherokee Nation v Georgia*, the Indians were defined as domestic dependent nations which retained significant rights of internal self-government because their sovereignty had been curtailed but not obliterated by the imposition of the overarching sovereignty of the US Federal Government. If the American analogy was to be pursued further, Australian law sits uneasily somewhere between 1823 and 1831. Logic provides momentum towards 1831, tradition holds it back.

The High Court's decision to recognise prior rights of property but not sovereignty lines Australian law up with the international lawyers writing at the high noon of imperialism. In 1904 John Westlake wrote in his study *International Law*:

> Because a native tribe is unable to supply a government suited to white men, and therefore cannot be credited with sovereignty it does not follow that it is not to be credited with rights of a simpler kind. Property is within the range of native intelligence, and at the moment when white sovereignty is acquired property may be held by natives or by whites to whom they have transferred it.[37]

Justice Brennan appreciated the problem inherent in the proposition that the interests of Aborigines in colonial land were extinguished as soon as the British arrived given that they had neither 'ceded their lands to the Crown nor suffered them to be taken as the spoils of conquest'.[38] The way around that difficulty was to determine that Aboriginal interests were not immediately extinguished and in some places have survived to the present day.

That doesn't resolve the question of sovereignty however. It becomes increasingly difficult to sustain the view that the Aborigines were traditionally without sovereignty. Neither our anthropological knowledge nor our contemporary values allow that position to be held indefinitely. This brings us to a fundamental problem at the heart of Australian jurisprudence. The doctrine of the settled colony only works if there literally was no sovereignty—no recognisable political or legal organisation at all—before 1788. And that proposition can only survive if underpinned by nineteenth-century ideas about 'primitive' people. If the opposite course is taken and prior Aboriginal sovereignty is recognised it is very difficult to explain how and when it disappeared without conquest or cession. It beggars belief to suggest that it disappeared over half a continent on that one day, 7 February 1788, when Britain formally annexed eastern Australia.

Two barriers stand in the way of a resolution of that jurisprudential tangle—and in the way of further advance along the road from injustice. One is frankly declared in Mabo, the other is implicit and unspoken. Australian courts regard as settled law the doctrine enunciated in the English courts about the inability to question the exercise of prerogative power when it comes to the extension of sovereignty. If the British Crown claimed sovereignty over various parts of Australia in 1788, 1824, 1829 and 1879 all the court can do is record that fact. They were acts of state which by their very nature could not be challenged, controlled or interfered with by Australian courts. It may be a view which is sound in law but it will not necessarily commend itself to the wider community. Questions of critical national importance are declared off limits. The court feels obliged to turn aside from the challenge of reconciling our law and our history, the Aborigines and the descendants of the settlers.

The second reason appears to be the view that any questioning of the settled colony doctrine would seriously 'fracture the skeleton or principle which gives the body of our law its shape and internal consistency'. Justice Brennan explained: 'The peace and order of Australian society is built on the legal system. It can be modified to bring it into conformity with contemporary notions of justice and human rights, but it cannot be destroyed.'[39]

In Mabo the High Court determined that law in relation to Aboriginal land rights must be brought into line with contemporary standards of justice and that it was possible to do so without undermining the legal system. If the two objectives had been incompatible then justice would have given way to stability. Justice Brennan argued that: 'However recognition by our common law of the rights and interests in land of the indigenous inhabitants of a settled colony would be precluded if the recognition were to fracture a skeletal principle of our legal system.'[40]

Application of the doctrine of continuity to Aboriginal sovereignty—even to the extent of recognising a right to some form of self-government—would, in the view of the court, lead to unacceptable trauma. What then should be done about injustice if it is ingrained in the bones of the system, if the skeleton itself is impregnated with values which come down to us from the era of European imperialism and white racism? Do diseased bones have to be saved from surgery at all costs?

For 200 years Australian law was secured to the rock of *terra nullius*. One pinioned arm represented property, the other sovereignty. With great courage the High Court recognised native title in the Mabo judgement and released one arm from its shackles. The other remains as firmly secured as ever and seems destined to remain there for some time but in the long run the situation will prove unstable. What is more, the resulting legal pose will become increasingly uncomfortable as time passes.

2

ASSESSMENT OF
ABORIGINAL SOCIETY

DURING THE LAST THIRTY YEARS Australian courts have had
access to large amounts of detailed anthropological information
which has both informed and helped shape their decisions. In
the past, jurists in Australia and Britain had less material to
work with but there has always been a clear relationship
between the law, current ethnography and contemporaneous
European attitudes. Theory and fact were often far apart with
judicial decisions more often grounded in prejudice than in
carefully sifted assessments of currently available information.
This would not matter too much were it not for the fact that
nineteenth-century legal decisions still influence contemporary
courts and mould their judgements.

Two cases stand out—*R v Murrell* in the New South Wales
Supreme Court in 1836 and *Cooper v Stuart* in the Privy
Council in 1889. In the first, Justice Burton determined that
Aborigines had no law and no sovereignty before 1788. In
the second, Lord Watson declared that Australia was a colony
of settlement because in 1788 it was 'a tract of territory
practically unoccupied without settled inhabitants or settled
law'.[1]

Were these reasonable assessments given the state of
European knowledge about Aboriginal society in 1836 and
1889 respectively or could—even should—the judges have
known better? Is our law founded on unavoidable misunder-

standing or wilful ignorance, on judicious assessment of known facts or on prejudice inspired by European racism and cultural arrogance? To investigate that question we should consider the state of European knowledge about the Aborigines, their culture and society, as it developed during the hundred or so years between the arrival of the First Fleet in 1788 and the early twentieth century.

How reasonable, then, were the assumptions made by Lord Watson in *Cooper v Stuart* that in 1788 Australia—

- was practically uninhabited
- was without 'settled inhabitants'
- had no 'settled law'
- had no land law or tenure
- had no political authority and no sovereignty.

To begin with it is necessary to consider what assumptions were made when the settlement of Australia was being planned in Britain and how they were changed by experience during the first years of occupation. Members of Cook's expedition of 1770 took back to Britain the belief that Australia was, indeed, 'practically uninhabited'. Sir Joseph Banks wrote and spoke most authoritatively on the subject. He noted in his journal in August 1770:

> Upon the whole New Holland, tho in every respect the most barren countrey I have seen, is not so bad but that between the productions of sea and Land a company of People who should have the misfortune of being ship-wrecked upon it might support themselves, even by the resources that we have seen. Undoubtedly a longer stay and visiting different parts would discover many more.
>
> This immense tract of Land, the largest known which does not bear the name of a continent, as it is considerably larger than all Europe, is thinly inhabited even to admiration, at least that part of it that we saw: we never but once saw so many as thirty Indians together and that was a family, Men and women and children, assembled upon a rock to see the ship pass by. At Sting-Rays bay where they evidently came down to fight us several times they never could muster above 14 or 15 fighting men, indeed in other places they

generally ran away from us, from whence it might be concluded that there were greater numbers than we saw, but their houses and sheds in the woods which we never faild to find convincd us of the smallness of their parties. We saw indeed only the sea coast: what the immense tract of inland country may produce is to us totaly unknown: we may have liberty to conjecture however that they are totaly uninhabited.[2]

Why did Banks make the critically important assumption that the unseen interior was likely to be totally uninhabited, literally a *terra nullius*? He believed that the sea had been universally found to be the:

chief source of supplys to Indians ignorant of the arts of cultivation: the wild produce of the Land alone seems scarce able to support them at all seasons, at least I do not remember to have read of any inland nation who did not cultivate the ground more or less, even the North Americans who were so well versd in hunting sowd their Maize. But should a people live inland who supported themselves by cultivation these inhabitants of the sea coast must certainly have learn'd to imitate them in some degree at least, otherwise their reason must be supposd to hold a rank little superior to that of monkies.[3]

As Banks saw it, if there was no cultivation on the coast there was likely to be none inland and without agriculture no-one could survive. His views were particularly important because he was considered to be the leading authority on Australia in the years before the first settlement. He gave advice to both government and to parliament telling the House of Commons Committee on the Return of Felons in 1779 that he thought there would be little opposition to a British landing party because 'during his Stay there' in 1770 he saw 'very few, and did not think there were above Fifty in all the neighbourhood, and had Reason to believe the Country was very thinly peopled'.[4] His evidence before the Committee on Transportation in 1785 was even more influential. He was asked:

Is the Coast in General or the particular part you have mentioned much inhabited?

There are very few Inhabitants.

Are they of a peaceable or hostile Disposition?

Though they seemed inclined to Hostilities they did not appear at all to be feared. We never saw more than 30 or 40 together.

It would have been reasonable to assume early in 1787 as the First Fleet was prepared for departure that Australia was 'practically uninhabited', that there was a small population on the coast but that the inland was a *terra nullius*. But that assumption did not stand up against actual experience; within a few days of arrival the assessments of Cook and Banks were challenged. Captain Watkin Tench noted that the British found the local Aborigines 'tolerably numerous' around Botany Bay and 'even at the harbour's mouth [they] had reason to conclude the country was more populous than Mr. Cook had thought it'.[5] When parties began to explore the reaches of Sydney Harbour it was realised that although the Aborigines spent much of their time in small hunting and foraging parties, as reported by the visitors of 1770, the total population was quite large. A First Fleeter noted in his journal of 5 February 1788.

There is something odd in their never being seen but in small [numbers] but by accident, tho' there is every reason to suppose they are numerous. Since our arrival at Port Jackson, during a survey of the harbour a body of near a hundred were seen drawn up with an unexpected degree of regularity.[6]

At much the same time Captain John Hunter found the Aborigines around the harbour 'very numerous', a circumstance which he was 'a little surprised to find after what had been said in the voyage of the *Endeavour*'.[7] By May the British had come across a party of 300, 'a striking proof of the numerousness of the natives', as Tench observed.[8] Governor Phillip reported to his superiors in Britain that he estimated that there were at least 1500 Aborigines resident within a radius of ten miles from the settlement—that is, there were more blacks around Sydney Harbour than there were Europeans on the First Fleet.[9] By the following year the reassessment of the indigenous population was being reported to the British public. In *An Authentic and Interesting Narrative of the Late Expedition to Botany Bay*, the anonymous author noted that Cook had only seen a few blacks and had 'therefore concluded that the country was thinly inhabited [but] in this manner he was much mistaken, as frequently tribes of three or four hundred came down together'.[10]

The experience around Sydney Cove was repeated all over the continent. The great exploring expeditions of the 1820s, 1830s and 1840s found Aborigines in possession of the land wherever they travelled. There was no land without owners. The explorer Edward Eyre wrote of his experiences in 1845:

> I have myself observed, that no part of the country is so utterly worthless, as not to have attractions sufficient occasionally to tempt the wandering savage into its recesses. In the arid, barren, naked plains of the north, with not a shrub to shelter him from the heat, and not a stick to burn for his fire . . . the native is found, and where, as far as I could ascertain, the whole country appears equally devoid of either animal or vegetable life.[11]

By the middle of the nineteenth century with over half the continent unexplored, including the tropical north, the settlers were uncertain about the overall size of the indigenous population. Rough censuses were carried out in particular districts; estimates were made of population densities. Governor Phillip assessed the numbers around Sydney; Governor Stirling did the same around Perth. Estimates made by scholars in Europe between 1804 and 1834 ranged from as low as 100 000 to as high as 5 000 000. Generally, estimates were over 1 000 000. The most thorough assessment of the available evidence was made by a subcommittee of London's Aborigines Protection Society in 1838. It concluded after examining 'every reasonable account and estimate' that the total population could not 'be stated as short of 1,400,000'.[12] This may have been too high but it was probably closer to present-day assessments than the figure of 300 000 accepted from 1930 until recently.

Dampier and Banks made the critical error of assuming that there was little food in Australia to sustain life away from the sea. The officers of the First Fleet gave up this idea reluctantly. During a journey inland in May 1788 Phillip was 'surprised to find temporary huts made by the natives far inland'. He fossicked around the ashes of Aboriginal fires but could find neither shells nor fish bones, leading him to the conclusion that the blacks must 'depend solely upon animals for food', a fact which contradicted the settlers' preconceptions.[13] Two months later Phillip saw smoke on the Blue Mountains and concluded that there could not be 'any doubt of there being inhabitants fifty miles inland'. He determined to travel there in order to clear up what was 'at present a mystery to me, how people who have not the least idea of cultivation can maintain themselves in the interior part of the country'.[14]

When the presence of inland Aborigines was impossible to overlook it was assumed they were merely stragglers driven away from coastal fishing grounds by more powerful enemies. But contact with more distant clans increased. In April 1791 Tench spoke to a man who told him that his people depended 'but little on fish' and that their principal support was derived from small animals and yams which they dug 'out of the earth'.[15] Later expeditions gradually increased the Europeans' knowledge of Aboriginal land use. By 1802 Francis Barrallier was able to provide a list of many varieties of food used by inland blacks who 'appeared to be good hunters'.[16]

During the first half of the nineteenth century the settlers gradually came to appreciate how extensive and varied were Aboriginal food sources, that almost everything edible was exploited at some time during a typical year. 'Prior to our coming among them', missionary Francis Tuckfield observed, 'every forest . . . every valley . . . every plain and sheet of water furnished its number of repasts at the proper season . . .'.[17] Settlers who sought to understand the traditional economy came to appreciate that it was based on sophisticated bushcraft and a profound understanding of the environment. The explorer and colonial Governor George Grey observed that in his own district, the Aborigine 'knows exactly what it produces, the proper time at which the several articles are in season, and the readiest means of procuring them'.[18] Edward Eyre realised that the Aborigines were dependent on 'the intimate knowledge they have of every nook and corner of the country they inhabit'. Of the desert groups he wrote:

> does a shower of rain fall, they know the very rock where a little water is most likely to be collected, the very hole where the longest grass grows, from which they may collect the spangles, and water is sometimes procured thus in very great abundance.[19]

The Europeans also came to appreciate that as well as exploiting their knowledge of the country the Aborigines managed the environment. As early as 1790 they were aware of the extensive use of fire and that it had a utilitarian purpose. John Hunter observed:

> They also, when in considerable numbers, set the country on fire for several miles extent; this, we have generally understood, is for the purpose of disturbing such animals as may be within reach of the conflagration; and thereby they have an opportunity of killing many. We have also had much reason to believe, that those fires were intended to clear that part of the country through which they have frequent occasion to travel, of the brush or underwood, from which they, being naked, suffer very great inconvenience. The fires, which we very frequently saw, particularly in the summertime, account also for an appearance, which, when we arrived here, we were much perplexed to understand the cause of; this was, that two-thirds of the trees in the woods were very much scorched with fire, some were burnt quite black, up to the very top: as to the cause of this appearance we differed much in our opinions; but it is now plain, that it has ever been occasioned by the fires, which the natives so frequently make, and which we have seen reach the highest branches of the trees: we sometimes, upon our arrival here, conjectured that it proceeded from lightning, but upon looking farther, it appeared too general amongst the woods to have been occasioned by such an accident.[20]

Knowledge of Aboriginal 'fire stick farming' accumulated during the 1830s, explorers and frontier settlers coming to realise that it had helped create the open grasslands which attracted the squatters with promise of ready-made pastures, that the environment was, in part, man-made. While travelling in central Queensland the German explorer Ludwig Leichhardt noted that:

> the natives seemed to have burned the grass systematically along every water-hole, in order to have them surrounded with young grass as soon as the rain sets in . . . Long strips of lately burnt grass were frequently observed extending for many miles along the creeks. The banks of small isolated water-holes in the forest were equally attended to . . . It is no doubt connected with a systematic management of their runs, to attract game to particular spots, in the same way that stockholders burn parts of theirs in proper seasons.[21]

By the middle of the nineteenth century the consequences of not burning the country regularly were becoming apparent. Thomas Mitchell noted that in the open forest around Sydney, where formerly a man could gallop without impediment and see 'whole miles before him', there were now thick forests of young trees.[22]

A critical assumption made about the Aborigines, both before and after settlement, was that they were nomadic, had no permanent homelands and therefore were not in effective possession of the land over which they wandered. It was an assessment with important legal implications. A correspondent wrote to the *Sydney Gazette* in 1824 arguing that there was no doubt about the 'lawfulness' of the British assuming possession of Australia because it had never been:

> the property of its original inhabitants . . . for the very notion of property, as applicable to territorial possession, did not exist among them. They had no civil polity, no regular organised frame of society, on the regulations of which the distinction of landed property depends. Which tribe, or which individual, could with propriety be considered as the proper owner of any particular district? Each tribe wandered about wheresoever inclination prompted, without ever

supposing that any one place belonged to it more than to another. They were the *inhabitants*, but not the *proprietors* of the land. This country then was to be regarded as an unappropriated remnant of common property; and, in taking possession of it, we did not invade another's right, for we only claimed that which before was unclaimed by any.[23]

But the officers of the First Fleet had learnt enough about traditional Aboriginal society within a few years of arrival to see the error in the assumption that tribes wandered wheresoever inclination prompted. They knew that the Aborigines around Sydney Harbour lived in clan or tribal groups, that each group had a homeland with known boundaries and that they took their name from their district and rarely moved outside it. Governor Phillip informed Lord Sydney in February 1790 that 'the natives lived in tribes, which are distinguished by the name of their chief, who probably takes his name from the district in which he resides'.[24] John Hunter arrived at a similar conclusion. 'We have reason to believe', he wrote, 'that the natives associate in tribes of many families together, and it appeared now they have one fixed residence, and the tribe takes its name from the place of their general residence'.[25]

Phillip was able to list the tribes and their homelands in his letter home to Britain:

About the north-west part of this harbour there is a tribe which is mentioned as being very powerful, either from their numbers or the abilities of their chief. The district is called Cammerra; the head of the tribe is named Cammerragal, by which name the men of that tribe are distinguished. A woman of this tribe is called a Cammerragalleon . . .

From the entrance of the harbour, along the south shore, to the cove adjoining this settlement the district is called Cadi, and the tribe Cadigal; the women, Cadigalleon.

The south side of the harbour from the above-mentioned cove to Rose Hill, which the natives call Parramatta, the district is called Wann, and the tribe, Wanngal.

The opposite shore is called Wallumetta, and the tribe, Wallumedegal.

> The other tribes which live near us are those of
> Gweagal, Noronggerragal, Borogegal, Gomerrigal, and
> Boromedegal.[26]

The settlers soon realised that tribal boundaries were of long
standing; differences of dialect were apparent over compara-
tively short distances; coastal blacks knew little about the
hinterland. Those who accompanied the earliest expeditions
inland saw country as new to them as it was to their European
travelling companions.[27] Aboriginal conflict was often about
territorial jurisdiction. 'Their battles', observed a First Fleeter
in July 1789, 'are sometimes concerning the right of fishing
or dwelling in some particular cove'.[28] When exploring parties
took Aboriginal guides into the interior they witnessed the
formal diplomatic exchanges necessary when entering the
territory of other tribes. In April 1791, Tench was travelling
inland with Boladeree and Colbee when he witnessed the
following exchange:

> Colbee no longer hesitated, but gave the signal of invitation,
> in a loud hollow cry. After some whooping, and shouting,
> on both sides a man, with a lighted stick in his hand,
> advanced near enough to converse with us. The first words,
> which we could distinctly understand were, 'I am Colbee,
> of the tribe of 'Cad-i-gal'. The stranger replied, 'I am
> Ber-ee-wan, of the tribe of Boorooberongal'. Boladeree
> informed him also of his name, and that they were white
> men and friends, who would give them something to eat.
> Still he seemed irresolute. Colbee therefore advanced to
> him, took him by the hand, and led him to us. By the light
> of the moon, we were introduced to this gentleman, all our
> names being repeated in form by our two masters of
> ceremonies, who said that we were Englishmen, and Bud-
> yee-yee [good], that we came from the coast, and that we
> were travelling inland.[29]

The assessment of the officers of the First Fleet about tribal
boundaries was supported by evidence gathered by settlers
in all parts of the continent during the first half of the
nineteenth century. In his book *Observations of the Colonies of
New South Wales and Van Diemens Land*, James Henderson
summed up the generally accepted view of Aboriginal

territoriality explaining that although the various tribes had no settled place of residence 'the limits of their respective hunting grounds appear to be distinctly recognized'.[30] The explorer George Grey believed that every Aborigine knew the limit of his own land and could 'point out the various objects which mark his boundary'.[31] The prominent cleric J.D. Lang concurred, arguing that boundaries were 'well known and generally respected by them'.[32] The Quaker missionary James Backhouse wrote after visiting Western Australia that it was

> quite clear that the natives . . . from Swan River to King George Sound, recognize their distinct hunting grounds as the private property of the different families, and that the boundaries are distinctly defined . . . they have their private property clearly distinguished into hunting grounds, the boundaries of which are definite, trees being often recognized by them as landmarks.[33]

The corollary of known boundaries and a keen sense of property which the colonists detected in Aboriginal society was a ready response to trespass. It was appreciated that tribes visited one another for formal ceremonies but that there was always a protocol involved. After joint corroborees tribes returned to their respective territory 'to pass which at other times is considered an act of aggression, or a signal of war'.[34] Grey discovered that the punishment for trespass was 'invariably death if taken in the fact, and at the very least an obstinate contest ensues'.[35] Henderson was witness to a large gathering of Aborigines to deal with a case of trespass because one tribe had 'in defiance of the national law, audaciously hunted Emus within the territories' of their neighbours and the 'latter came to demand reparation for the insult offered'.[36] European explorers were often conducted through the country by Aboriginal guides who performed formal ceremonies at tribal boundaries and passed the strangers on to their neighbours. Writing of his journey down the Murray, Sturt observed that the Aborigines 'sent ambassadors forward regularly from one tribe to another, in order to prepare for an approach'. The party, he noted in retrospect, had passed tribe after tribe 'under the protection of envoys'.[37] While describing his journey from

Port Phillip to the new colony of South Australia, Joseph Hawdon observed that 'in passing through the tribes of natives we were extremely fortunate in keeping a friendly intercourse with them by means of ambassadors sent from one tribe to another'.[38] After learning all he could about Aboriginal society, both by reading and direct observation, the expatriate Polish explorer Paul de Strzelecki wrote that:

> the foundation of their social edifice may, like that of civilized nations, be said to rest on an inherent sense of property. As strongly attached to that property, and to the rights which it involves, as any European political body, the tribes of Australia resort to precisely similar measures for protecting it, and seek redress and revenge for its violated laws through the same means as an European nation would if similarly situated.[39]

A few years earlier South Australia's Governor Gawler wrote to the prominent settler and philanthropist G.F. Angas that:

> The natives have . . . very distinct and well defined proprietary rights. These rights afford them protection from other tribes and bodily support—they hunt the game upon, catch the fish in and eat the roots of their own districts just as much as the English gentleman kills the deer and sheep upon or the fish in his private park. The property is equally positive and well defined.[40]

The combination of constant movement with strong attachment to territory was commented on by the pioneer missionary William Walker who wrote in 1821 that the Aborigines:

> possess some tract of country which they call their own; but, even on this, although it may afford them animals and fish, they will not be permanent. Yet they are so senselessly bigotted to this particular spot, that when you would persuade them to settle in any place, they will not understand you, no more than if you discoursed to them in Latin or Greek.[41]

Well before the middle of the nineteenth century the settlers knew that in addition to occupying and exploiting their home territories Aborigines had deep emotional ties to their country. They were 'a most bigotted race of people to the ground on which they were born'.[42] Aborigines meeting Europeans identified themselves by reference to their country. The surgeon appointed to the first settlement at Albany noted that every Aborigine they met 'would immediately announce to us his tribal name and country'.[43] The pioneer West Australian settler G.F. Moore described the behaviour of his Aboriginal companion Coondebung while travelling with him in 1836 beyond the fringes of white settlement. 'We were', Moore wrote, 'now passing through his country, over his native soil, and he bounded along with a buoyant look and an elastic step as if glorifying in his vigour and exulting in his independence'.[44]

By the 1830s settlers were arguing that the Aborigines had a deep attachment to their land, that they were patriots who were impelled to defend their country against the invading Europeans. The West Australian pioneer Robert Lyon argued this point in a highly rhetorical speech to a meeting of settlers at Guilford in June 1833:

> Think not then that the aboriginal inhabitants of Australia,— offspring of the same great parent with yourselves, and partakers of all the kindred feelings of a common humanity, can resign the mountains and the seas, the rivers and the lakes, and plains and the wilds of their uncradled infancy, and the habitations of their fathers for generations imme- morial, to a foreign foe, without the bitterness of grief. What though the grass be their couch, and the tree of the forest their only shelter: their blue mountains, and the country where they first beheld the sun, the moon and the starry heavens, are as dear to them as your native land with all its natural and artificial beauties, its gilded spires and magnifi- cent palaces, is to you.[45]

Thirteen years later the Darling Downs pioneer C.P. Hodgson wrote in similar vein: 'Who does not know', he asked,

> by kindred feelings, how dear a tie it is that binds the patriot to his native land? who does not know how rankling the

enmity is towards the oppressor of national privileges, and the unnatural possessors of our property? But, when force of arms alone gives right of occupation, and when nothing in return is offered as compensation, but victims falling immolated at the shrine of liberty, how much more galling is the venom and deadly the hate! Could we have beheld with feelings of love the tricolor of Napoleon floating on our ancient towers? could we have felt regard for the seducers of our children, the violators of our wives and the oppressors of our Country? No, but Britons would never allow a foreign foe to remain on her shores; is that so? yes, and yet the same little brave island can countenance the overthrow of the weak, and the adaptation of another one's property to its own conveniences.[46]

Settler understanding of Aboriginal law, government and custom developed more slowly than knowledge about land use and tenure. When he gave evidence to the parliamentary committee in 1785 Sir Joseph Banks was asked: 'Have you any Idea of the nature of the Government under which they lived?' He answered: 'None whatsoever, nor of their Language'.[47] Writing soon after the arrival of the First Fleet in New South Wales Tench remarked that 'their form of government . . . yet remains untold'.[48] But in a short time the senior officers of the colony had concluded that each tribe had a chief. Hunter believed that in the case of conflict with neighbouring groups the whole tribe could be 'soon assembled' and in such circumstances 'they put themselves under the direction of a chief'.[49]

Belief in chiefly government was re-enforced by writers during the first half of the nineteenth century. William Thomas, Protector of Aborigines at Port Phillip, explained that 'their government is patriarchal'. Each tribe had a chief who 'directs all its movements'.[50] Other observers believed that authority was wielded by groups of elders. The prominent Victorian settler William Westgarth believed that the 'general control and management' of tribal affairs appeared to be 'by mutual consent, in the hands of the adult male respectively of each tribe'.[51] James Dredge, a Port Phillip Protector of Aborigines, concluded that for 'all general purposes' control and management of tribal affairs was directed by the 'mutual consent of the adult male members'.[52] Edward Eyre noted that: 'In an assembly of the tribe, matters of importance are generally discussed and decided upon by the elder men, apart from others.'[53]

The German missionary G.C. Tiechelmann argued that the South Australian tribes he was familiar with could best be called 'republican' tribes. The elder males were the 'leaders of all their affairs' but that 'no chieftainship whatever is recognized'.[54]

Ethnographers continued to debate the question of Aboriginal government during the second half of the nineteenth century, with opinion swinging between those who believed that chiefs exercised absolute authority and others who thought power was much more widely dispersed. James Dawson argued that every tribe had its chief 'who is looked upon in the light of a father, and whose authority is supreme'.[55] R. Brough Smythe asserted that the tribes were governed 'by regular councils of old men'[56] while Edward Curr believed that such delegation of power to a chief or council belonged 'to a stage of progress which the Australian race' had not reached.[57] The problem was that while most observers believed that authority was exercised the mechanism was difficult to detect. John Matthew thought, on the one hand, that in the tribes he studied in Queensland there was 'no chieftain, no organized government', but that on the other he believed that 'The older men, and especially those of conspicuous courage and force of character, laid down the hereditary law and saw it enforced'.[58]

The difficulty was addressed by A.W. Howitt in his study of 1904, *The Native Tribes of South-East Australia*:

> When an Australian tribe is looked at from the standpoint of an ordinary observer, the conclusion that there is no recognised form of government seems to be justified. Apparently no person, or group of persons, has the right to command, under penalties for disobedience, or who is obeyed by the whole community. There seems to be no person to whom the whole community yields submission, who has peculiar privileges which are patent to observation,

30

or who is surrounded by more or less of savage pomp and ceremony. All that is seen by a general superficial view of an Australian tribe is, that there is a number of families who roam over certain tracts of country, in search of food, and that while they appear to show a considerable respect to the old men, all the males enjoy such liberty of action, that each may be considered to do what seems best to himself.

A more intimate acquaintance with such a tribe, however, shows that there must be some authority and restraint behind this seeming freedom, for it is found that there are well-understood customs, or tribal laws, which are binding on the individual, and which control him, as well as regulate his actions towards others.[59]

From quite early in the history of settlement European discussion of Aboriginal politics and authority become enmeshed with consideration of law and custom. The colonists knew nothing of either when they arrived in Australia. Tench commented in 1789:

It would be trespassing on the reader's indulgence were I to impose on him an account of any civil regulations, or ordinances, which may possibly exist among these people, I declare to him, that I know not of any . . . Whether any law exists among them for the punishment of offences committed against society . . . I will not positively affirm.[60]

An understanding of law and custom evolved slowly but by the 1840s explorers like George Grey, Edward Eyre and Paul de Strzelecki had published books which provided readers with the first serious assessment of the situation. The three writers were impressed not by the absence or weakness of customary laws but by their strength and durability. Strzelecki believed that 'traditionary' customs were as 'rigorously adhered to as amongst civilized nations'.[61] Eyre went further arguing that: 'Through custom's irresistible sway has been forged the chain that binds in iron fetters a people, who might otherwise be said to be without government or restraint.'[62]

Grey was even more impressed by the 'tenacity and undeviating strictness' of customary law which was, he believed, 'fixed in the minds of the people as sacred and unalterable'. Arguing from his experience among Aborigines

31

in Western Australia he rejected the proposition that the tribesman was 'endowed with freedom either of thought or action'. He was 'in reality subject to complex laws' which deprived him of 'all free agency of thought'.[63] Edward Curr arrived at a similar conclusion about what he called 'savage life', writing that:

> The Englishman, noticing in the savage the absence of the manacles which civilization imposes, fancies that none other exist, and that the savage is a free man. Persons who have looked below the surface, however, are aware that the Australian savage, though absolutely untrammelled in some respects, is nevertheless, on the whole, much less free in a number of important particulars than the Englishman or Frenchman.[64]

Curr speculated on what was the 'hidden power' which secured the 'scrupulous compliance with custom' and concluded that the 'constraining power in such cases' was not government, 'whether by chief or council but *education*'.[65] A.W. Howitt pursued a similar line of argument twenty years later, explaining that laws and customs were obeyed because 'the native has been told, from his earliest childhood, that their infraction will be followed by some supernatural personal punishment'.[66] Baldwin Spencer and F.J. Gillen's classic study of 1899, *The Native Tribes of Central Australia*, gave a similar prominence to the power of customary law. The local Aborigines were 'bound hand and foot by custom'. Conduct was governed by a moral code and 'any known breaches' of it were 'dealt with both surely and severely'.[67]

From the 1870s onwards Australian ethnographers were aware of the complex nature of kinship systems and of the elaborate rules governing marriage, child rearing and inheritance. A series of studies gathered relevant information from hundreds of informants from all over the continent.[68] In their book *Kamilaroi and Kurnai* of 1880, Fison and Howitt detected a system of laws about marriage and descent which, they believed, spanned the continent. It was, they wrote,

> an arrangement, extending across a continent, which divides many widely scattered tribes into intermarrying classes, and

gives a man of one class marital rights over women of another class in a tribe a thousand miles away, and speaking a language other than his own.[69]

Nineteenth-century ethnographers, explorers and missionaries slowly unravelled the laws and customs which governed the internal life of Aboriginal tribes. They also considered the 'external' relations of tribes and the extent to which they functioned like small, but independent nations. Edward Parker, a Protector of Aborigines at Port Phillip in the 1840s, explained to his readers that:

I found on my first investigations into the character and position of these people, that the country was occupied by a number of petty nations, easily distinguished from each other by their having a distinct dialect or language as well as by other peculiarities. Each occupied its own portion of country, and, so far as I could learn, never intruded into each other's territory except when engaged in hostilities, or invited by regularly appointed messengers.[70]

Parker's colleague James Dredge concluded similarly that Aboriginal Australia was 'divided into a number of petty states' which, whether large or small, weak or powerful were 'entirely distinct from each other' as related to 'the territory they inhabit and the control and management of their affairs'.[71] Ethnographers of the next generation followed closely the observations of Parker and Dredge, Edward Curr explaining that the whole of Australia was 'parcelled out' among the tribes 'probably many centuries back' and prior to the arrival of the Europeans 'each tribe held its territory, when necessary [by force of arms] against all intruders'.[72] A.W. Howitt told a meeting of the Royal Society of Victoria in 1889 that each tribe

as a whole occupies a certain defined tract of country, which forms its hunting and food grounds, and which it claims exclusively, not admitting the right of any other tribe or any other individuals to use it unless they happened to be within its boundaries . . . as visitors . . . The boundaries of this tribal country coincide with the boundaries of the social organization of the classes of the . . . community.[73]

The British settlers knew almost nothing about Aboriginal society when the First Fleet dropped anchor in Botany Bay. During the nineteenth century, explorers, missionaries and ethnographers, both amateur and professional, gathered a large amount of information and despite their own powerful prejudices about 'savagery', 'primitive people' and social evolution, provided an intelligible, if not always accurate, picture of the world of the indigenous Australians. Their writing presented the image of a society which had exercised sovereignty before the arrival of the European settlers—that had a system of laws and customs that were generally obeyed and that the tribes, or variously the sub-tribal groupings exercised authority independent of any outside power. In a book of synthesis *The Tribe, and Intertribal Relations in Australia*, published in 1910, which collected material from all the major works of the nineteenth century and early twentieth century, ethnographer Gerald Wheeler summed up what were seen to be the known facts about Aboriginal society. While discussing government he wrote:

> The loose structure and wandering habits of the Australian tribes, together with the absence of permanent settlements, lead most of the early observers to deny the existence of any form of government. But more careful observation has shown that though the forms are not very precise there undoubtedly exist the rudiments of a regular government over and above the mere authority belonging to the head of each family.
>
> It is clear that the individual Australian is under the authority of well-understood customs or laws throughout his life, by which his relations with his fellows and with his physical environment are effectively controlled.[74]

Aboriginal politics has engaged the attention of anthropologists over the last 30 years with opinion swinging between those who argue that traditional society was without politics and others who assert the opposite. The weight of the argument has shifted from the first position towards the second since the 1950s. Writing of the Yir-Yoront of north Queensland, R.L. Sharp argued in 1958 that:

There are roles, and rules for the roles, and a system of law with specified kin serving as public agents with authority to act in defined circumstances, and provision for changes in the roles and rules through public action or inaction. But all this is simply kinship. In the field of conduct, there is no distinguishable social organization for economics, for religion or for government.[75]

A few years later M.J. Meggitt arrived at similar conclusions as a result of his study of the Walbiri published as *Desert People* in 1962. There were, he asserted, no tribal leaders, headmen or chiefs; 'nor was there any controlling or ruling class of old or important men whose power extended through the society'.[76] In a wider analysis of forms of government in all parts of Aboriginal Australia Meggitt argued that politics was little more than kinship extended, 'nothing more than domestic or quasi-domestic affairs'.[77]

Meggitt did not suggest that the result was anarchy or lack of order. Social behaviour was guided by people's 'knowledge and acceptance of established norms'. He explained that:

The absence of individuals or groups in Walbiri society with permanent and clearly-defined legislative and judicial functions does not mean that social interaction is chaotic. There are explicit social rules, which, by and large, everybody obeys; and the people freely characterize each other's behaviour insofar as it conforms to the rules or deviates from them.[78]

But even while authority was diffused internally Meggitt clearly believed the Walbiri maintained a form of external sovereignty. They regarded themselves as 'one people' who shared a common culture, occupied 'a continuous territory with definite boundaries', were 'not responsible to other Aborigines for their behaviour', and they 'claimed the right to defend themselves from injury from non-Walbiri'.[79]

There has been a significant reaction against the views of Meggitt and Sharp in recent years with numerous studies which have identified forms of politics, the exercise of social, religious and political power and the strategies adopted by powerful leaders to develop and enhance their authority.

Writing of Cape York Peter Sutton and Bruce Rigsby argued, in 1982, that: 'the evidence relating to land tenure from the Cape York Peninsula . . . shows that Aboriginal people do indeed "have" politics, and that having politics for them crucially involves control of land and resources.'[80]

In his penetrating assessment of politics in Pintupi life, Fred Myers explained the co-existence of egalitarianism and authority in a society where older men 'look after' those without ritual knowledge. 'The power and authority of older men', he argued,

> is seen as necessary to make everyone conform to the cosmic plan; essentially their ability to 'look after' the juniors, the legitimacy of their decisions is guaranteed by their proximity to the Law.
>
> Although this authority is not usually viewed as personal gain seeking or aggrandizement, the Law which they pass on as value is still the instrument of their power. Through it, men come to exert power and authority without accusation of being non-egalitarian or egotistical: they only mediate the Law. Thus is hierarchy achieved in an egalitarian society and thus is social consensus maintained for important social regulations. The social order and the prevailing power relations are secured through presenting the political order as the social organization of esoteric knowledge, presenting the power and domination of males as a result and mainstay of the cosmic order.[81]

The conclusion of Justice Burton in *R. v Murrell* in 1836, that the Aborigines had no law, no politics and no sovereignty, was clearly inaccurate but did not diverge far from what was generally known and understood about traditional society by the colonists at the time. The important ethnographic observations of explorers Grey, Eyre, Strzelecki and Leichhardt and by the missionaries and protectors Parker, Dredge and Teichelmann were not published until the mid-1840s. The same cannot be said about Lord Watson's 1889 judgement that in 1788 Australia had neither settled inhabitants, settled law, land tenure or even many people. His remarks were incidental to the actual case being considered—they were what the lawyers called *obiter dicta*—and may not have been based on any understanding or knowledge of Aboriginal society. While the remarks may have been good in law they were totally out of touch with what was widely known at the time both in Australia and in Britain.

So at the end of the nineteenth century the gap between the law and contemporary understanding of Aboriginal society was very wide. It narrowed in the twentieth century, significantly so in the 1971 case *Milerrpum v Nabalco* in the Supreme Court of the Northern Territory. While Justice Blackburn failed to recognise Aboriginal native title of the Yirrkala people he accepted that their society had both law and politics. He heard from those opposing the Yirrkala arguments that reflected the dismissive views of Aboriginal society which had circulated in the courts since the early nineteenth century. Council for the mining company Nabalco argued that 'in the aboriginal world there was nothing recognizable as law at all'.[82] The Solicitor-General of the Territory asserted that before any system of law could be recognised there 'must be not only definable community' to which it applied, but also 'some recognized sovereignty giving the law a capacity to be enforced'.[83] He contended that Aboriginal customs were religious in their nature rather than judicial. They could not be considered to be law at all in any recognisable sense.

Blackburn rejected the line of argument. Defining law as 'a system of rules of conduct which is felt as obligatory upon them by the members of a definable group of people', he concluded that the Yirrkala had such a system of law. The anthropological evidence presented to his court showed, he observed,

> a subtle and elaborate system highly adapted to the country in which the people led their lives, which provided a stable order of society and was remarkably free from the vagaries of personal whim or influence. If ever a system could be called 'a government of laws, and not of men', it is that shown in the evidence before me.[84]

Perhaps for the first time since European settlement, an Australian court had taken Aboriginal society seriously.

The implications of Blackburn's assessment are still with us, for if traditional Aboriginal society did, indeed, have a 'government of laws' it must also have exercised sovereignty over its territory. If that was so we are brought back to the question of how such sovereignty was lost short of conquest and cession and how, without them it was extinguished. To pursue the issue it is necessary to turn to international law because, as Justice Jacobs said 'in *Coe v the Commonwealth*, such questions are 'not matters of domestic laws but of the "law of nations"'.[85]

3

WERE ABORIGINAL TRIBES SOVEREIGNS?

COULD THE ABORIGINAL TRIBES be considered to have had sovereignty under the 'law of nations'? Much would have depended on when the question was asked and what international law was current at the time. Opinions on the matter have varied considerably over the last 250 years. In his classic 1928 study *The Acquisition and Government of Backward Territory in International Law*, M.F. Lindley concluded that the writers who had taken up the question could be grouped into three more or less definite classes:

1. Those who regard backward races as possessing a title to the sovereignty over the territory they inhabit which is good as against more highly civilized peoples
2. Those who admit such a title in the natives, but only with restrictions or under conditions
3. Those who do not consider that the natives possess rights of such a nature as to be a bar to the assumption of sovereignty over them by more highly civilized people.[1]

Lindley believed that the weight of opinion favoured the jurists in the first group. 'Comparing these three schools of thought', he wrote:

> we see that, extending over some three and a half centuries, there had been a persistent preponderance of juristic opinion

in favour of the proposition that lands in the possession of any backward peoples who are politically organized ought not be regarded as belonging to no one.[2]

The question of whether the Aboriginal tribes had sovereignty according to international law can most conveniently be considered in relation to the situation as it was in the early nineteenth century, in the early twentieth century and how it is today.

The matter was taken up by Justice Burton in *R. v Murrell* in 1836. He determined that the Aborigines 'had no sovereignty' because they 'had not attained at the first settlement to such a position in point of numbers and civilization, and to such a form of Government and laws, as to be entitled to be recognized as so many sovereign states governed by their laws of their own'.[3]

Burton considered the question in his case notes as well as in the published judgement. They allow a closer examination of his reasoning. 'Yet I deny', he argued:

that these tribes are entitled to be considered as so many Sovereigns or Independent tribes in as much as that depends not only upon their independence of any foreign control but having also attained to such a situation in point of numbers and civilization as a nation and to such a settled form of government and such settled laws that civilized Nations may and are bound to know and respect them.[4]

Burton's view was both controversial and contested. Exactly the opposite conclusion about Aboriginal sovereignty was arrived at by a Grand Jury in South Australia in 1847. Having considered whether two local tribesmen should stand trial for killing fellow Aborigines they expressed grave reservations about the matter in a letter to the Governor. Among other questions they indicated that they believed that the Aboriginal nations had exercised sovereignty before the coming of the Europeans and that this view would find support among jurists of the time. They explained that

the Grand Jury apprehends that from the occupation of this country by the Colonists, all the Native tribes, as distinct communities, however small, would have been held by all

jurists, to be in a situation to make laws and to adopt usages
for their own protection and Government.

Which view—that of the Grand Jury or that of Justice
Burton—had the strongest support in the law of nations?[5]

Did Burton's conclusions flow logically from the law of
nations as it was understood in 1836? Or had the jurisprudence
of New South Wales been corrupted by the needs and
prejudices of colonial society? To pursue this question it is
necessary to consider how sovereignty was perceived, how it
related to the control of territory, how big a tribe or nation
had to be and, what cultural, social and political characteristics
were required for sovereignty to exist.

In his *Elements of International Law*, published in 1836, the
year of Justice Burton's *R. v Murrell* judgement, Henry Wheaton declared: 'A sovereign state is generally defined to be any
nation of people, whatever may be the form of its constitution,
which governs itself independently of foreign powers.'[6]

The critical importance of independence had been stressed
by earlier writers. Every nation which governs itself, Vattel
wrote, 'under whatever form, and which does not depend on
any other Nation, is a sovereign state'.[7] A century earlier S.
Rachel argued in *De Jure Naturae* that:

> one state has no authority over another, nor one free people
> over another; nor is one of them under liability to another
> of them, and much less are several free people and States
> subordinate to some one power—but each of them has its
> own independence and self rule.[8]

Independence clearly depended on the ability to exclude others
from the sovereign territory. In his *A Methodical System of
Universal Law* of 1743, J.G. Heineccius observed that 'dominion consists solely in the faculty of excluding others from the
use of a thing'.[9]

Justice Burton conceded that the Aboriginal tribes had
been independent in 1788. They were, he said, 'entitled to
be regarded as a free and independent people'.[10] But having
passed the test of independence they failed on every other
one—numbers, civilisation, strength, government and laws,
and actual possession of territory. Was this a fair judgement?

Were Aboriginal tribes too small 'as to be entitled to be recognized as so many sovereign states'?[11] There is no ready answer to this question. The international jurists did consider the issue but provided no precise figure as to the size required for the exercise of sovereign authority. One of the earliest assessments of the necessary size of a state was made by Samuel Pufendorf in 1688, who thought it all depended on the comparative size of contiguous states. The 'just size of a state', he declared, 'should be measured by the strength of its neighbours'.[12] Eighteenth-century writers were more specific about numbers and 'strength' of states. Vattel argued that nations should be regarded as though they were 'so many free persons' living in a state of nature and who were by nature equal holding 'the same obligations and the same rights'. Strength or weakness counted for nothing. 'A dwarf is as much a man as a giant is', he observed, 'a small Republic no less a sovereign State than the most powerful kingdom'.[13] Vattel's mentor Christian Wolff pursued a similar line of argument in his *The Law of Nations*:

> It is not the number of men coming together into a state that makes a nation, but the bond by which the individuals are united, and this is nothing else than the obligation by which they are bound to one another. The society which exists in the greater number of men united together, is the same as that which exists in the smaller number. Therefore just as the tallest man is no more a man than the dwarf, so also a nation, however small, is no less a nation than the greatest nation. Therefore, since the moral equality of men has no relation to the size of their bodies, the moral equality of nations also has no relation to the number of men of which they are composed.[14]

John Austin, the eminent nineteenth-century British jurist, turned his attention to the same question in his *Lectures of Jurisprudence*:

> In order that an independent society may form a society political, it must not fall short of a *number* which may be called considerable. The lowest possible number which will satisfy that vague condition cannot be fixed precisely. But,

looking at many of the communities which are considered and treated as independent political societies, we must infer that an independent society may form a society political, although the numbers of its members exceed not a few thousand, or exceed not a few hundred.[15]

The small Australian tribes were perhaps in the lower fringes of what in European law could be considered sovereign nations. But that in itself was not enough to disqualify their claim to sovereignty. Were there cultural handicaps of the sort referred to by Justice Burton in his judgement in *R. v Murrell* that 'their practices are only such as are consistent with a state of the greatest darkness and irrational superstition'?[16]

Up until the early seventeenth century European jurists still divided the world between Christians and infidels, who were considered to have few legal rights at all. In Calvin's case in 1607 Lord Coke declared that all infidels were in law 'perpetual enemies' because the law presumed that they will not be converted and 'between them, as with the devil, whose subjects they be, and the Christian, there is perpetual hostility'.[17] Such views were already being superseded, however, when Coke delivered his judgement. The Spanish jurist Franciscus de Victoria declared in 1532 that the Indians of the New World had 'true dominion in both public and private matters, just like Christians . . .'. Even if it was admitted that they were 'as inept and stupid as is alleged' dominion could not 'be denied to them'.[18] A year after Calvin's case the founder of European international law Hugo Grotius discussed the question of the rights of 'infidels' in his *The Freedom of the Seas*. 'Surely it is a heresy', he urged:

> to believe that infidels are not masters of their own property; consequently, to take from them their possessions on account of their religious beliefs is no less theft and robbery than it would be in the case of Christians.
>
> Nor are the East Indians stupid and unthinking; on the contrary they are intelligent and shrewd so that the pretext for subduing them on the ground of their character could not be sustained. Such a pretext on its very face is an injustice. Plutarch said long ago that the civilizing of barbarians had been made the pretext for aggression, which is

to say that a greedy longing for the property of another often hides itself behind such a pretext. And now that well known pretext of forcing nations into a higher state of civilization against their will . . . is considered by all theologians . . . to be unjust and unholy. They [heathens and infidels] are not to be deprived of sovereignty over their possessions because of their unbelief, since sovereignty is a matter of positive law, and unbelief a matter of divine law . . . In fact I know of no law against such unbelievers as regards their temporal possessions. Against them no King, no Emperor, not even the Roman Church, can declare war for the purpose of occupying their lands, or of subjecting them to temporal sway.[19]

Grotius's ideas are critical to the legal and moral arguments associated with the British annexation of Australia and the implicit assumption that 'civilized' societies could legitimately extend their sway over 'savage' and 'barbarous' peoples. The question was taken up again in the eighteenth century by Christian Wolff who argued that:

Since a learned and cultivated nation ought to do whatever it can to make a barbarous and uncultivated nation learned and more cultivated, but since, if any nation wishes to promote the perfection of another it cannot compel it to allow that to be done; if some barbarous and uncultivated nation is unwilling to accept aid offered to it by another in removing its barbarism and rendering its manners more cultivated, it cannot be compelled to accept such aid, consequently it cannot be compelled by force to develop its mind by the training which destroys barbarism and without which cultivated manners cannot exist.

Barbarism and uncultivated manners give you no right against a nation . . . Therefore a war is unjust which is begun on this pretext.[20]

A substantial argument used by Anglo-Australian jurists against the Aborigines was that they lacked government and laws and that the tribes were, therefore, not entitled 'to be recognized as so many sovereign states' governed by laws of their own and as such 'entitled to retain them even after conquest itself until changed by the conquered'.[21]

It is a critical question and one familiar to the international jurists of the eighteenth and nineteenth centuries. In 1836 Henry Wheaton outlined the way in which a state is distinguished from an 'unsettled horde of wandering savages not yet formed into civil society'. A state, he explained, was a 'political society' and he quoted Cicero with approval to the effect that a state was 'a body political, or society of men united together for the purpose of promoting their mutual safety and advantage by their combined strength'.[22] Eighteenth-century jurists produced similar definitions, Vattel explaining that a nation or a state is: 'a political body, a society of men who have united together and combined their forces in order to procure their mutual welfare and security'.[23]

Wolff clearly distinguished between a nation and a group of unrelated families. A nation, he explained,

> denotes a number of men who have united into a civil society. For groups of men dwelling together in certain limits but without civil sovereignty are not nations, except through carelessness of speech they may be wrongly so called. Certain separate families dwelling in the same land are to be distinguished from nations, nor can those things be applied to them which we have proved concerning the rights and duties of nations.[24]

So, were Aboriginal tribes 'unsettled hordes' or civil societies according to European thinking in the late eighteenth century and early nineteenth century? Wheaton argued that the legal idea of a state necessarily implied 'that of habitual obedience of its members to those persons in whom the superiority is vested'.[25] Authority and obedience were seen as the critical measure of political society. Bentham believed the difference between the state of nature and political society lay 'in the *habit* of obedience'.[26] Obedience, however, was not to be seen as the response to what Blackstone called 'a transient sudden order from a superior, to or concerning a particular person' but something that was 'permanent, uniform and universal'. Unless there was some authority 'whose commands and decisions all the members are bound to obey' the community in question 'would still remain as in a state of nature, without any judge on earth to define their several rights, and redress their several wrongs'.[27]

Austin also believed that the fundamental difference between political and natural society was whether 'the generality of its members be in the *habit* of obedience'. In a natural society obedience was 'rendered by so few of the members, or general obedience [was] infrequent and broken'. In a political society, on the other hand, the bulk of the population were in 'a habit of obedience or submission to a determinate and common superior: let that common superior be a certain individual person or aggregate of individual persons'.[28] Austin directed his attention specifically to the 'case of tribes such as those who live by hunting or fishing in the woods or on the coasts of New Holland; and those tribes of Indians who range the unsettled parts of the North American continent'. He believed such groups were not independent political societies because 'the bond which connects the *congeries* of families of which they consist is too slight to say that they render habitual obedience to any certain superior, although they may on occasions unite in obedience to a leader for warlike purposes'.

Austin conceded however, that if tribal groups met the conditions of obedience to an established set of laws or customs they must be considered to be 'a congeries of independent political communities . . . *however small'*. They were 'strictly speaking, a congeries of groups having all the marks of independent political societies except size'.[29]

Perhaps an even more potent argument used to deny Aboriginal sovereignty was that they had not actually become the possessors of territory and therefore failed to meet one of the crucial tests, what Wheaton termed 'a fixed abode, and definite territory belonging to the people by whom it is occupied'.[30] In his case notes for *R. v Murrell* Justice Burton reasoned that the Aborigines 'at the time of the first settlement had not appropriated the territory' and therefore did not have the right 'to exclude others of the common family of mankind' from doing so in their stead. Their land use was such that they had never acquired 'the rights of domain and empire'. The British were therefore the first possessors of New South Wales; 'a tract of country before unappropriated by anyone' had been 'taken into actual possession by the King of England'.[31]

Could nomadic hunter-gatherers have sovereignty under European late eighteenth-century law? The critical issue was whether they were in actual possession of the land. If they were, sovereignty followed as a natural consequence. The one was the corollary of the other, Wolff explaining that a nation

> which inhabits a territory has not only ownership but also sovereignty over the lands and the things which are in it. In like manner, since the ownership of a nation is bound up with its sovereignty, ownership of a nation is occupied at the same time as the sovereignty.[32]

But did the Aborigines actually possess the land in ways recognisable by European law? They almost certainly did, particularly as there had never been anyone else with a prior or better claim. 'If possession be immemorial', Von Martens argued in 1788,

> if there exist no possession anterior to it; it is undoubtedly sufficient to set aside all the pretensions of others . . . founded upon the duration of this possession, it is the consequence of the natural impossibility of any other to prove a right better founded than that of possession.[33]

The international law of possession was based on the relevant Roman law, the principles of which were definitively outlined by Von Savigny in his classic study *Treatise on Possession* published in the early years of the nineteenth century. The major points were:

1. Possession, independent of all right, is the foundation of property. In any conflict over property the possessor has the benefit of the burden of proof being thrown on his adversary.
2. Possession is achieved by two crucial steps. The first is actual physical presence on the land, although it is not the 'mere act of treading with the feet which gives possession of the land, but the presence upon the spot which enables [the occupant], not merely to walk over every individual portion of it but to deal with it in any way he chooses

'. Personal presence is then the fundamental first
quiring possession; 'the only factum by which
sion of immovables is acquired'. And, crucially,
gny insisted that 'in order to acquire Possession
it is only necessary to be present on the land, without the
performance of any other act thereon'.

3. As well as being present the possessor must have the desire,
or the will to have the land as his own; the *animus possidendi*. Presence on the land must, therefore, 'be accompanied by a definite act of mind', consisting in the first
place 'in the fact of the possessor dealing with the subject
as his own property'.

4. Possession can only be lost when the land is physically
abandoned and a determination exists to give it up. Land
which is only visited occasionally—like alpine pastures for
instance—would not be considered abandoned because of
intermittent use. As Von Savigny argued: 'Where the use
is of such a nature that it only recurs at certain periods,
the omission to visit the land during the interval is not
evidence of any intention to give up possession'.[34]

Roman law recognised that landowners had rights over
pasture lands which were not permanently occupied and only
used on a seasonal basis. As long as the owner had the
intention to return to the land in question possession was
retained. The Roman jurist Ulpian explained that: 'we retain
possession of summer and winter pastures by intention . . .
the same implies in respect of any land which we depart from
without the intent thereby to give up possession'.[35]

To the extent that the question was discussed the seventeenth and eighteenth-century jurists appeared to consider that
hunting and fishing were sufficient to establish legitimate
possession. In his *Institutes of the Laws of England* of 1651
Cowell argued that:

Dominion or proprietary in things, by the laws of nature
and nations was first created by occupation and possession
of those things which did not belong to any person.
Occupation includes fishing, hunting, fowling, enclosing,

seising. The Law of Nations puts the property of things thus gotten into the person who hath possession, but ours does not.[36]

A hundred years later in his *A Methodical System of Universal Law*, J.G. Heineccius observed that: 'none therefore can deny that hunting, fishing, fowling, are species of occupancy, not only in desert places unpossessed, but likewise in territory already possessed.'[37]

Many of these themes were synthesised by Christian Wolff in *The Law of Nations*, the major work of international law in the middle years of the eighteenth century. He had no doubt that small nomadic bands had a form of tenure over their lands which he called a mixed community holding. The importance of the question demands that Wolff be quoted at length.

> If separate families dwell together in a certain territory and possess private lands, they have ownership in them, but the other places are the property of nobody or are still left in the primitive community holding. But if, indeed, those families have no settled abode but wander through uncultivated wilds, the lands which can be subject to their use are subject to a mixed community holding, the rest remaining in the primitive community holding.
>
> But if the families have no settled abode, but wander through the uncultivated welds, in that case, nevertheless, they are understood to have tacitly agreed that the lands in that territory in which they change their abode as they please, are held in common, subject to the use of individuals, and it is not to be doubted but that it is their intention that they should not be deprived of it by outsiders. Therefore they are supposed to have occupied that territory as far as concerns the lands subject to their use, and consequently to have jointly acquired the ownership of those lands, so that the use of them belong to all without distinction. Therefore those lands are subject to a mixed community holding.[38]

Despite the nomadic habits of the 'families' their tenure was secure against interlopers. Their wandering had economic purpose and could be taken to represent an appropriate use of the land despite the lack of permanent housing:

But if . . . separate families should be accustomed to wander about . . . particularly for the purpose of pasturing cattle or for some other purpose, the intention of wandering, which is governed by that intended use, gives sufficient evidence of the occupation of the lands subject to their use, although they have not established a permanent abode upon them. Therefore nothing is more natural than that the mixed community holding of separate families should be assumed in regard to them. Nay more, let us suppose that outside families wish to subject some of those lands to individual ownership, it is not to be doubted but that the separate families who wander here and there would resist, and so would adequately prove their intention of holding those lands in common for themselves to the exclusion of outsiders.[39]

Of major importance for the debate in Australia was Wolff's defence of the property rights of nomads who used different parts of their land alternatively. Land not in immediate use could not be considered ownerless. 'Ownership', he determined,

is not lost by non user. And if separate families wander through uncultivated places, they intend a use of the places only in alternation, a thing which is readily evident, if only you turn your attention to the reason which impels them to wander through uncultivated places.[40]

Equally relevant to the Australian case was the view that land which fell within the territory of a nation remained inviolate whether it was being used or not:

Since all lands and all things which are in territory occupied by a nation are subject to its ownership, if there are in any territory, where a nation inhabits, desert and sterile, or uncultivated places, those belong to the nation, consequently no one can dispose of them except the nation or the ruler of the state.

Since desert and sterile, or uncultivated places are the property of the nation which inhabits the territory, no one, either foreign or native, can occupy those places and make them subject to his ownership.

Ownership of things was introduced and is desired for the sake of their use; but whether the owner wishes or does not wish to enjoy the use, is left to his will, and for this reason another is not allowed to take away his property or to use the same. But what no one calls in question among private individuals must be allowed among nations also. The force of ownership with a nation is the same as with a private individual.[41]

The argument that nations of people like the Aborigines could be dispossessed because they didn't make proper use of their land received no support from Wolff at all. He observed that:

For although on account of ignorance or for some other reason a nation should make no use of a certain thing, or not care for that use for the present, never the less the use which things might have belongs likewise to that nation, and because it occupies the territory for the purpose of permanent use, it is assumed to have intended that use also which perchance those things might have for the future. Besides, it is certain that no one loses his ownership in his property for the reason that he handles it carelessly and does not make every use of it which it can have.[42]

He took the argument further and rejected the idea that more 'advanced' nations had the moral and legal right to take land from people who were not maximising its use. In doing so he struck at a central justification for the British annexation of Australia arguing that:

no right is created for you in regard to that which belongs to another, because he does not use and enjoy his own property as much as he could, however much it would have helped you, if he had used it and enjoyed it in another way . . .
    And how, I ask, can you show that for the sake of your advantage or that of another nation families may be made subject to your sovereignty without their consent, when from that which is useful to you no right arises? Indeed, if these reasons were to prevail, it would even be allowable to subject barbarous and uncultivated nations to your

sovereignty, in order that they might experience what is better for them.[43]

Clearly Wolff's work directly contradicts many of the ideas and assumptions which underpinned the legal basis for the British annexation of Australia and the justification for it provided by the colonial courts. Australian judges may not have been aware of Wolff's writing but they were certainly familiar with the work of his student Emmerich de Vattel. Indeed, Justice Burton's case notes for *R. v Murrell* make it clear that he was totally dependent on Vattel whose book may have been the only work of international law available to him. In a very real sense Burton's decision was only as soundly based as were Vattel's original arguments. A further difficulty with using Vattel so heavily is that his work is full of inconsistencies and contradictions. A nineteenth-century British international jurist observed in 1849 that Vattel was: 'more frequently cited than any other writer because he is more accessible, and because his doctrines are so loosely expressed that it is easy to find in his book detached passages in favour of either side of the question.'[44]

Vattel's book contains passages which concur with Wolff and others which don't, some which give strength to Justice Burton's views but others which undermine them. This can be seen most clearly in relation to the rights of nomadic hunters and gatherers and pastoralists.

Vattel follows Wolff closely when dealing with general principles, arguing that:

> When a country is occupied by wandering families, like those of pastoral tribes, which move from place to place according to their needs, it is possessed by them in common. They hold it to the exclusion of other peoples, and they cannot be justly deprived of lands of which they are making use.[45]

And in a similar passage he observed:

> Still, no other Nation has the right to restrict their possessions, unless it is in absolute need of land; for, after all, they are in possession of the country, they make use of it after

52

their own fashion, they obtain from it what is needed for their manner of life, as to which no one can dictate to them. [46]

But when it came to discussion of colonisation in the New World Vattel dramatically changed direction. In a much quoted passage he established the right of colonisation:

> There is another celebrated question, to which the discovery of the new world has principally given rise. It is asked if a nation may lawfully take possession of a part of vast country, in which there are found none but erratic nations, incapable, by the smallness of their numbers to people the whole? . . . Their removing their habitations through these immense regions, cannot be taken for a true and legal possession; and the people of Europe, too closely pent up, finding land of which these nations are in no particular want, and of which they make no actual and constant use, may lawfully possess it, and establish colonies there.[47]

But in establishing a right to colonisation Vattel does not provide the support for the British annexation of New South Wales to anywhere near the extent that Australian jurists, politicians and publicists have in the past supposed. He was referring to a right to establish colonies in a part of a given territory. The Indians were to be confined not dispossessed; they were not to want for land as a result of colonisation. What is more, Vattel nowhere suggests that the Indians were to lose their sovereignty over their lands left to them. The exaggerated British claim to the whole of the Australian continent had no support at all in Vattel's writing. Indeed he could have been referring to the settlement of Australia, still 30 years in the future, when he wrote:

> But it is questioned whether a Nation can thus appropriate, by mere act of taking possession, lands which it does not really occupy, and which are more extensive than it can inhabit or cultivate. It is not difficult to decide that such a claim would be absolutely contrary to the natural law.[48]

The use of force to dispossess the Aborigines was of even more dubious status in international law. 'I do not offer conquest', Vattel argued, 'or the desire to usurp the property of another as one of the purposes of offensive war; such a purpose, lacking even a semblance of right, is not the object of formal war, but of brigandage'.[49]

And in another passage he wrote,

> Whoever agrees that robbery is a crime, and that we are not allowed to seize by force the goods of another, will acknowledge, without other proof, that no nation has a right to chase another people from the country they inhabit, in order to settle in themselves. Will the conductors of nations despise a rule that constitutes all their safety in civil society? Let this sacred rule be entirely forgotten, and the peasant will quit his thatched cottage to invade the palaces of the great, or the delightful possessions of the rich.[50]

Contemporary commentators frequently argue that any assessment of the British annexation must be made according to the law as it was at the time and not as it became subsequently. They do so on the assumption that international law of the late eighteenth century and early nineteenth century strongly favoured the position of colonising powers as against indigenous people. But this is clearly not the case. Judgements like that of Justice Burton in *R. v Murrell* were not informed by a broad survey of what international law was at the time but of a partial and tendentious reading of a few passages in Vattel's *The Law of Nations*. What he did was to turn to those passages which supported attitudes towards the Aborigines which had developed within colonial society and twisted international law to a shape which justified what had already been done. The impetus came not from the courts and studies of far-away Europe but from the blood-stained frontiers of settlement. The law became a weapon wielded by the conquerors.

Had the law been applied with more impartiality it would have been possible to accord to the Aborigines both land ownership and sovereignty. The individual tribes, although very small, occupied discrete territories, which they defended against interlopers. They had existed for a long time and they were civil societies in which law was normally obeyed and transgression was punished. They had sovereignty according to the law of the time and performed what later writers assumed to be the fundamental roles of government, which Salmond in his classical study *Jurisprudence* defined as war and the administration of justice—defence against external enemies on the one hand and on the other, the 'maintenance of peaceable and orderly relations within the community itself'. This, Salmond argued, 'is the irreducible minimum of governmental action. Every society which performs these two functions is a political society or state, and none is such which performs them not'.[51]

However, international law became less sympathetic to non-European and tribal peoples as the nineteenth century unfolded and by the early twentieth century accorded them few rights and little standing. Lord Watson's view expressed in *Cooper v Stuart* in 1889, that Australia had been a *terra nullius* without sovereignty or property ownership, may have been informed by ignorance of contemporary ethnography but it was fully in accord with international law at the time which has evolved to serve the interests of the European powers at the high noon of imperialism and white racism.

International law itself came to be seen as applying only to 'civilized' states, T.J. Lawrence arguing in 1895 that it was a 'technical system of rules for determining the actions of states' and was, as a consequence, 'concerned with civilized communities alone'.[52] Nomadic people who were 'not permanently settled upon a portion of the earth's surface' could not be considered to have sovereignty. Lawrence argued: 'Even if we suppose a nomadic tribe to have attained the requisite degree of civilization its lack of territorial organization would be amply sufficient to exclude it from the pale of international law.'[53]

Territory inhabited by 'native tribes' could be occupied by Europeans without reference to the 'tribes' because they were unable to provide a government 'suited to white men'.[54] J. Westlake argued in his *International Law*:

> That civilized states should assume sovereignty over new but not uninhabited countries, on a system which they arrange among themselves without reference to the natives,

can only be justified by the necessity of a government where whites and natives meet, and of the inability of the latter to supply a government adequate to the white man's needs or to their own protection.[55]

The doctrine of *terra nullius* was enhanced so that it was applied much more widely than to uninhabited lands alone and included territory which had 'not previously been regarded as part of the dominions of any civilized power'.[56] Lawrence argued that:

Occupation as a means of acquiring sovereignty and dominion applies only to such territories as are no part of the possessions of any civilized state. It is not necessary that they should be uninhabited. Tracts roamed over by savage tribes have been again and again appropriated, and even the attainment by the original inhabitants of some slight degree of civilization and political coherence has not sufficed to bar the acquisition of their territory by occupancy. All territory not in the possession of states who are members of the family of nations are subject of International Law and must be considered as technically *res nullius* and therefore open to occupation. The rights of the natives are moral not legal. International morality, not international law demands that they be treated with consideration.[57]

However there were jurists who swam against the tide defending the rights of nomadic and tribal people. Pasquale Fioré argued, in 1868, that territory occupied by 'savages' could not be considered as *terra nullius*, because the right of ownership did not depend 'upon the level of the owner's civilization or culture'. He explained further:

Certainly if a savage population is not using a portion of their land, then a nation could occupy the empty land, create establishments and enjoy the land's profits. This foreign nation would become the owner of the establishments and of the occupied land, but it would never own the entire nation.[58]

In his 1889 study *L'occupation des Territoires Sans Maître* Charles Salomon called prevailing doctrine into question suggesting that:

nothing proves to be more difficult than defining the object of occupation, especially if one were to disregard the simple idea that territorium nullius is land which is not under any sovereignty. One must be careful when stating that the colour of skin or the state of an undeveloped civilization does not prevent savages from exercising certain sovereign rights. These rights may be rudimentary however they are sufficient enough to oppose all violent occupation of their country.[59]

There has been a strong reaction against the mainstream international jurists of the late nineteenth and early twentieth centuries and the pendulum has swung to a position much more favourable to indigenous people. The movement was foreshadowed by Lindley in *The Acquisition and Government of Backward Territory in International Law*. He addressed the question of whether inhabited land could be acquired by occupation as though it was *terra nullius* in the manner of the British annexation of Australia or whether it could only result from conquest or cession. He concluded that as long as the people in question have some form of government their territory could not be said to be without sovereignty. Such sovereignty

> as is exercised there may be of a crude and rudimentary kind, but, so long as there is some kind of authoritative control of a political nature which has not been assumed for some merely temporary purpose, such as a war, so long as the people are under some permanent form of government, the territory should not, it would seem, be said to be unoccupied.[60]

Lindley believed the critical question was whether a community was in practice a political society, whether a given society 'does in fact discharge functions which are of a political nature'. He argued that the most distinctive function of a political society was to:

> affect the members of the community . . . in such ways as to make their general conduct conform to certain standards in their mutual arrangements . . . so long as the standards are habitually conformed to, the reason for conformity

would appear to be of secondary importance. If, for example, the members of a community do indeed so conform, merely by force of custom or from fear of supernatural consequences, the society should never the less be regarded as a political one.[61]

An area could not be considered *terra nullius* if it was inhabited by a political society, by

> a numerous society . . . permanently united by the habitual conformity of the bulk of its members to recognized standards in their relations *inter se*; if laws set or imposed by the general opinion of the community are habitually observed or their breach punished, even though no one person, or no determinate body of persons short of the whole community, is charged with their enforcement.[62]

These questions were considered by the International Court of Justice in the Western Sahara Case of 1975 when it was asked to consider if the region in question was a *terra nullius* at the time of Spanish annexation in 1884 due to the fact that it was inhabited by nomadic tribes. The court provided 'posthumous rehabilitation of the classic authors of international law'[63] and sidestepped the late nineteenth-century theorists who had refused to accord status in international law to non-European societies. The effect of the court's deliberation was to determine that occupation as a method of obtaining title to territory was only open as regards 'uninhabited territories or territories inhabited only by a number of individuals not constituting a social or political aggregation'.[64]

Both Justice Brennan and Justice Toohey referred to the International Court's Western Sahara judgement in the Mabo case. Toohey recognised that the court had strongly supported the proposition that lands in regular occupation could not be *terra nullius*, which was a theory 'unacceptable in law as well as in fact'.[65] Justice Brennan argued appropos the judgement that:

> If the international law notion that inhabited land may be classified as *terra nullius* no longer commands general support, the doctrines of the common law which depend on the notion that native peoples may be 'so low in the scale of

social organization' that it is 'idle to impute to such people some shadow of the rights known to our law' (65) can hardly be retained. If it were permissible in past centuries to keep the common law in step with international law, it is imperative in today's world that the common law should neither be nor be seen to be frozen in an age of racial discrimination.

The fiction by which the rights and interests of indigenous inhabitants in land were treated as non-existent was justified by a policy which has no place in contemporary law in this country.[66]

These comments bring us back to the problem with which we began. If Australia was not a *terra nullius* in respect of property rights how could it have been in terms of sovereignty? As Lindley observed in 1928: 'It is difficult to see why, if the natives are to be regarded as capable of possessing and transferring property, they should not also be considered competent to hold and transfer the sovereignty which they actually exercise.'[67]

So if the Aborigines and Torres Strait Islanders did exercise sovereignty in Australia before the arrival of the British what happened to it? Was it like land lost in a piecemeal fashion over many years? Does it survive in some form? To approach these questions it is necessary to consider the ways in which the British Crown is supposed to have gained sovereignty in 1788, 1824, 1829 and 1879.

4

CUSTOMARY LAW

WHEN THE BRITISH ARRIVED in Australia in 1788 they knew nothing about Aboriginal customs or law. Marine captain Watkin Tench in 1789 wrote:

> Whether any law exists among them for the punishment of offences committed against society . . . I will not positively affirm . . . It would be trespassing on the reader's indulgence were I to impose on him an account of any civil regulations, or ordinances, which may possibly exist among this people. I declare to him, that I know not of any.[1]

The instructions given to Governor Phillip provided little guidance as to the status of Aboriginal law. He was encouraged to 'open an intercourse' with the local tribes, to 'conciliate their affections' and to endeavour to live in 'amity and kindness' with them. Settlers who committed offences against the Aborigines were to be 'brought to punishment according to the degree of the offence'.[2] The legal situation of the Aborigines was more clearly defined by David Collins when he established the settlement at Hobart in 1804, issuing an official statement that 'the Aborigines of this Country are as much under the Protection of the Laws of Great Britain', as were the settlers themselves. Indeed they were 'in the King's Peace' which would 'afford their Persons and Property the Protection of British laws'.[3] But questions remained: did

Aboriginal custom have any status 'in the King's Peace'? Could British law be used in cases involving offences committed within the Aboriginal community?

The problem concerned Governor Macquarie and in an attempt to curb internecine Aboriginal conflict in and near Sydney he issued a proclamation in June 1816 which included the provision:

> That the Practice, hitherto observed amongst the Native Tribes, of assembling in large Bodies or Parties armed, and of fighting and attacking each other on the Plea of inflicting Punishments on Transgressors of their own Customs and Manners at or near Sydney, and other principal Towns and Settlements in the Colony, shall be henceforth wholly abolished, as a barbarous Custom repugnant to the British Laws, and strongly militating against the Civilization of the Natives, which is an Object of the highest Importance to effect, if possible. Any Armed Body of Natives, therefore, who shall assemble for the foregoing purposes, either at Sydney or any of the other Settlements of this Colony after the said Fourth Day of June next, shall be considered as Disturbers of the Public Peace and shall be apprehended and punished in a summary Manner accordingly.[4]

Macquarie concluded with the demand that the Aborigines discontinue their 'barbarous Custom' not only 'at or near the British settlements but also in their own wild and remote Places of Resort'.[5]

It was an ambit claim which the colonial government had no way of enforcing, as the New South Wales Supreme Court recognised in 1829. An Aborigine living around Sydney was killed by members of another tribe one of whom, known to the Europeans as Bob Barrett, was arrested and gaoled. The Attorney-General sought the opinion of the Bench about Barrett's amenability to English law. Chief Justice Forbes declared that it had never been the practice 'in his Colony to interfere in the quarrels of the aboriginal natives'. Nor had it been the policy of any government

> to interfere with the savage tribes, whose countries we have taken possession. In occupying a foreign country, the laws

that are imported have reference only to the subjects of the parent state; I am not aware that those laws were ever applied to the transactions taking place between the original natives themselves.[6]

This policy of non-interference and of legal pluralism was up-ended in the same court seven years later. The issue was similar. In December 1835 two Aborigines, Jack Congo Murrell and George Bummary, were charged at Windsor with the murder of two countrymen Bill Tabenguy and Pat Cleary in retribution for an earlier murder of a kinsman. Murrell appeared before the Supreme Court Bench in February 1836. Defence counsel Sydney Stephen argued that the Aborigines had manners and customs of their own and as the country had been neither conquered nor ceded they were not bound by the colonist's laws. It was a plea decisively rejected by Justice Burton in a judgement supported by his two fellow judges.

Among many issues canvassed in Burton's judgement and supporting case notes was his assessment of the nature of Aboriginal law based in large part on a submission by missionary Lancelot Threlkeld. The missionary was aware that the Aborigines in the lower Hunter Valley had a system of law and methods of punishment for violations of it. It was a custom, he noted, 'in all cases of murder or supposed murder or other crimes' that the accused person 'should stand punishment according to their own rules'.[7] Death was not always the result of these trials. The old men and women consulted together 'with the opposite party and settle the mode of satisfaction'.[8] But Threlkeld was convinced that the Aborigines should be brought under the sway of British law explaining to the judges that, 'Although they do punish crime in a certain sense, yet it would be mercy perhaps to them, were they placed under the *protection* as well as the powers of the British laws'.

Burton followed closely along the lines of Threlkeld's submission. Their practices were, he argued, 'only such as are consistent with a state of the greatest darkness and irrational superstition'. Although they had some ideas of justice their customs were founded entirely upon principles of the most 'indiscriminating notions of revenge'.[9] They could not, therefore, be considered to be the ancient laws of the country that should survive 'until conquest or cession and a change of laws by the King'. They were to be regarded 'only in the light of lewd practices' which deserved as little respect as the 'laws of the Wild Irish'.[10] The Aborigines, therefore, could not be left to exercise their own laws and customs; the law of the colonist should be imposed on them in all situations. 'It were', Burton argued, 'a mild and merciful conquest thus to subdue them'.[11]

In South Australia Burton's colleague Justice Charles Cooper took a very different view of Aboriginal law and of crime within the indigenous community. In a letter to the Governor in 1847 he argued that it was a question 'of a very serious kind' as to whether it was 'a *proper* exercise of jurisdiction to interfere in matters of crime committed by Natives against other Natives'. Of even greater interest was Cooper's reference to a visit he made to New South Wales in 1840 where he discussed the question with Chief Justice Sir James Dowling and was informed that

> the Supreme Court never interfered in a case between Natives; and this information is consistent with the accounts given in books from the first settlements of New South Wales to the present time. It is consistent also with the conduct observed towards the Natives.[12]

Cooper's account of Dowling's conversation is very interesting. Had Dowling simply forgotten the case of *R. v Murrell* of four years before? He had concurred with Burton's judgement. Had he changed his mind by the time he spoke to the South Australian visitor? Was legal doctrine far less fixed at the time than subsequent commentators have supposed?

Members of a Grand Jury which sat in Adelaide during 1847 were deeply troubled when requested to send to trial two Aborigines for murders committed within the indigenous community. They had two main concerns. They wanted a definition of the limits within which British law could legitimately 'interfere between the Aboriginal natives in their own social relations', since the Grand Jury cannot but feel that if murder be an offence to be recognized, other infractions of the law, as adultery, or even polygamy—may become equally cognizable by our Courts and a whole train of anomalous proceedings, repugnant to every feeling of right and justice would be presented for the adjudication of the courts.

The Jurors' second concern was with the whole question of interference in matters that were within the province of Aboriginal custom. The decision to send the two men to trial had 'done violence' to their 'natural feeling of equity and justice'. They believed that the Europeans should 'in the first instance' confine their interference to the 'mutual protection of both races in their intercourse with each other' and that it was unacceptable to 'meddle with laws, or usages having the force of law . . . in their conduct towards their own race'.[13]

Counsel defending Aborigines in trials during the 1830s and 1840s argued that they should not be treated simply as British subjects and that account should be taken of their traditional laws and customs. In January 1842 the Aboriginal Wi-war was brought before the Quarter Sessions in Perth charged with the murder of his compatriot Dy-ung. He was defended by the barrister E.W. Landor who insisted that the court was not competent to try the case because,

this territory, being acknowledged by occupancy and not by conquest, the aboriginal inhabitants could not be subject to our laws for offences committed amongst themselves without their previous assent to and acceptance of those laws. That if this territory were acquired by conquest it would still be necessary to shew our laws had been expressly imposed upon the natives, and were thenceforth to be received by them in lieu of their own. That if they be subject to our laws, they must be subject to the whole machinery of the law, and ought to be punished for minor offences committed among themselves, such as slander, perjury, theft, indecent exposure of the person, &c. That the natives had laws of their own, and punishments for particular crimes, and, therefore, the prisoner had most probably been punished or acquitted for the same offence, by the only laws he was acquainted with, or bound to obey, and that it is contrary to all justice that he should be tried and punished again. That there is no Act of Parliament which provides that the aborigines shall, as among themselves be answerable to our laws; and that, as we choose to claim our title by occupancy, no local proclamation is of sufficient authority to make them so amenable for if the Governor has not arbitrary power to impose penal laws, by proclamation, upon us, who are really British subjects, *a fortiori*, he cannot possess that power over strangers. If they were already British subjects, there was no need of a proclamation, if they were not British subjects no proclamation could impose penal laws upon them.[14]

Landor's plea was rejected by the Chairman of the Bench W.H. Mackie who argued that 'as jurisdiction is clearly an inseparable incident of sovereignty' it followed that the 'British Nation, having taken possession, and assumed the sovereignty of a territory, the law of that nation must be paramount co-extensively with that territorial sovereignty'.[15]

Wi-war was arraigned, the trial proceeded and he was found guilty by the jury. But Landor's arguments caused further controversy. The editor of *The Inquirer* took up the question a week after the trial. In a long and thoughtful editorial he wrote:

It is certain that, on the in-coming of a people into a new country whether by treaty or by conquest, some difference has generally been made between them and the original inhabitants in the way the laws are administered; this difference obtained, no doubt, principally in civil cases, but the authorization of such a distinction even to the most limited extent, shews, we think that persons are not as a matter of course, expected to be governed by laws to which they are strangers. In most countries the law as obeyed is what may be called a territorial law, *i.e.* a rule of conduct observed by all the persons residing within one country under one government; but we read that this has not been always the case even among civilized nations, for under some governments the law is not territorial but *personal*— witness the state of the law that prevailed in France and the north of Italy after the conquest of these countries by the barbarians, where the right of being judged by their own laws was left to the Roman provincials—witness it in British India at this moment, where the law is not obeyed by all the subjects of one state but by all the members of one tribe or religion, and is attached to the person, or hereditary. Under the British rule in India the Mahommedians and Hindoos are guided by their respective civil laws, *the law of the defendant* is always taken as the guide. This distinction is *said* to be limited almost entirely to the Civil Law; if this were true it might be too much to argue from thence that persons of the same sect or tribe subject to the same laws, might murder each other under the sanction of some personal law authorising it, in opposition to the territorial law of the government under which they lived; although the very fact of any distinction at all being made, recognises the principle that some difference in the judicial system is necessary, and it is hard to say to what extent. But in real truth the destruction *is not* limited merely to the exercise of the Civil Law, but extends also to the criminal. Under the British rule in India it is notorious that many customs are in practice among the various tribes and sects in conformity with their own personal law, which the British law would look upon as criminal in the highest degree, and which are yet allowed to remain unpunished—for instance the immolation of widows on the funeral pile of their deceased husbands—the sacrifice of human beings to their beastly idols—the exposure of children to certain death on the Ganges—all these abominable practices are punishable by our own criminal law, which in India however is not put in force against them. Endeavours have indeed been made to root out these heathenisms, but not by the intervention of the British criminal law.

We shall not be supposed as in any way sanctioning these frightful customs, but we cite them in order to show that there are offences committed under the British rule, against which the British law in some places is inoperative; these offences are such as are committed by the original inhabitants, *inter se* (in conformity with their own laws and customs,) of a country taken possession of by strangers, to which class of offences that of the convict Wi-war belongs. So far then his punishment by us would seem to be unauthorised, and against precedent; but we do not see why we are compelled to follow the practice of the Indian government, or of any other government, in the exercise of a mistaken leniency. Assuming that Wi-war put Dy-ung to death in accordance with the personal law of his tribe, which is a matter not proved, it by no means follows that the British territorial law ought not to step in to punish the offender. We shall not lose ourselves in a maze of argument as to possession by treaty, conquest or occupancy especially of so savage a country as Australia, for after all, wherever a civilised people go, they carry their rights along with them, and the first is their power to protect themselves. This power must be exerted when necessary, and that it is necessary for, nay that it is the positive duty of, the new-comers to curb the savage inclinations of the original inhabitants, and to endeavour to lead them into the ways of civilization, is not to be doubted. In our own case, our safety in the country, which be taken as the first consideration, depends upon it, and although the exercise of our new laws may bear harshly at first on the aborigines, we have only the choice of an administration of them, bringing them by degrees under their influence, *or* of leaving them to themselves to live and die in their savage ignorance, which assuredly we should not be justified in doing. Our occupation of the country may or may not have been in accordance with the law of nations—which, by the way, can scarcely have reference to a people having no laws at all—but having occupied it, we are bound to protect ourselves in it, and not only ourselves, but to extend protection to such of the aborigines as are suffering from the brutality of their own tribe; and by so doing prove to them the advantage of living under settled laws, and serve the great end for which we are all of us here, viz., the clearing of a path for the admission of truth amongst them.[16]

Landor continued to debate the moral and legal issues surrounding the settlement of Australia. In his book *The Bushman* he reconsidered the trial of Wi-war arguing that:

if our laws had been imposed upon this people as a conquered nation, or if they had annexed themselves and their country to our rule and empire by anything like a treaty, all these proceedings would be right and proper. But as it is, we are two nations occupying the same land, and we have no more right to try them by our laws for offences committed *inter se*, than they have to seize and spear an Englishman, according to their law . . .

Look at the question in another point of view. Is jurisdiction a necessary incident of sovereignty? Do a people become subject to our laws by the very act of planting the British standard on the top of a hill? If so, they have been subject to them from the days of Captain Cook; and the despatches of Her Majesty's Secretaries of State, declaring that the natives should be considered amenable to our laws for all offences which they might commit among themselves, were very useless compositions. We claim the sovereignty, yet we disclaim having obtained it by conquest; we acknowledge that it was not by treaty; we should be very sorry to allow that it was by fraud; and how, in the name of wonder, then, can we defend our claim? Secretaries of State have discovered the means, and tell us that Her Majesty's claim to possession and sovereignty is 'based on a right of occupancy.' Jurisdiction, however, is not the necessary incident of territorial sovereignty, unless that sovereignty were acquired by conquest or treaty. We question, indeed, whether it is the necessary consequence even of conquest—the laws of the conqueror must first be expressly imposed. The old Saxon laws prevailed among the people of England after the Conquest, until the Norman forms were expressly introduced . . .

The most convenient and the most sensible proceeding, on the part of our rulers at home, would be to consider this country in the light of a recent conquest.[17]

Sydney Stephen, defence counsel in *R. v Murrell* advanced argument very similar to Landor's. Australia, he insisted, was not

originally desert, or peopled from the mother country, having had a population far more numerous than those that have since arrived from the mother country. Neither can it be called a conquered country, as Great Britain was never at war with the natives, nor a ceded country either; it, in fact, comes within neither of these, but was a country having a population which had manners and customs of their own, and we have come to reside among them; therefore in point of strictness and analogy to our law, we are bound to obey their laws, not they to obey ours. The reason why subjects of Great Britain are bound by the laws of their own country, is that they are protected by them; the natives are not protected by those laws, they are not admitted as witnesses in Courts of Justice, they cannot claim any civil rights, they cannot obtain recovery of, or compensation for, those lands which have been torn from them, and which they have probably held for centuries. They are not therefore bound by laws which afford them no protection.[18]

The comparable Port Phillip case of *R. v Bonjon* in 1841 brought forth a similar defence from Redmond Barry who observed that:

no treaty, no agreement had been entered into by the aborigines with the British authorities; such being the case, and being an independent people, they could not possibly be made subject to the British laws on cases *inter alia*; it would be, perhaps, thought necessary to show a jurisdiction among the aborigines in controversion of the claims of British adjudication; evidence could be produced to show that there exists a jurisdiction among the aboriginal tribes, a feeling of revenge is imprinted universally in the breast of the savage; such being the case, injuries would never escape without punishment of some kind or another.[19]

While Stephen's arguments were decisively rejected by the New South Wales Supreme Court, Barry's were taken up and incorporated in the judgement of Justice Willis. Calling on legal and constitutional developments from many parts of the Empire and from the United States Justice Willis asked pointedly whether 'any legislative enactment abolished the laws and customs of the aborigines, or declared that they should be governed by the law of the colony?'

It was not a case, he argued of 'foreigners in a country where the sovereign has entire sway' because in the Australian case 'the colonists, and not the aborigines, are the foreigners; the former are exotics, the latter indigenous; the latter the native sovereigns of the soil, the former uninvited intruders'.

Willis agitated the problem of how Australia was acquired if there was neither conquest nor cession:

Therefore, if this colony were acquired by occupying such lands as were uncultivated and unoccupied by the natives, and within the limits of the sovereignty asserted under the [i.e. Phillip's] commission, the aborigines would have remained unconquered and free, but dependent tribes, dependent on the colonists as their superiors for protection; their rights as a distinct people cannot, from their peculiar situation, be considered to have been tacitly surrendered.[20]

In his peroration Willis strayed even further away from Australian legal orthodoxy. 'I repeat', he said,

that I am not aware of any express enactment or treaty subjecting the aborigines of this colony to the English colonial law; and I have shown that the Aborigines cannot be considered as foreigners in a kingdom which is their own. From these premises . . . I am at present strongly led to infer that the aborigines must be considered and dealt with, until some further provision be made, as distinct, though dependent tribes governed among themselves by their own rude laws and customs.[21]

Willis concluded like Governor Arthur that treaties should be signed with the Aboriginal tribes writing that 'it appears that they are by no means devoid of capacity, that they have laws and usages of their own, that treaties should be made with them . . . '[22]

Willis's judgement caused consternation in official and legal circles in Sydney. Chief Justice Dowling dismissed it as being contrary to the decision of the Supreme Court in *R. v Murrell*. The views of the Governor were spelt out in greater detail. In a letter to the Chief Justice he gave his reasons for considering the Aborigines 'to be in all respects amenable to our laws'.

1. The sovereigns of Great Britain have, for more than half a century, assumed unqualified dominion over the parts of New Holland forming the territory of New South Wales, and have exercised unqualified dominion wherever their authority has been established.
2. It has been ordained by an Act of Parliament, 9 Geo. 4, c. 83, that within the colony of New South Wales, British law shall be established, without reference to any

other law, or laws, save such as may be made by the local legislature.

3. That in numerous official documents, issued under the immediate sanction of Her Majesty, the aborigines of this country are called Her Majesty's subjects, and declared to be entitled to the same protection as any other class of Her Majesty's subjects.

4. That upon British territory, no law save British law can prevail, except by virtue of some treaty or enactment; and no such treaty or enactment has ever been made, either with or in respect to the aborigines of New South Wales.

5. That even if the aborigines be looked upon as a conquered people, and it be even further admitted that a conquered people are entitled to preserve their own laws until a different law be proclaimed by the conqueror, still no argument in favour of a separate code of laws for the aborigines of New South Wales can be drawn therefrom; first, because the aborigines never have been in possession of any code of laws intelligible to a civilized people; and secondly, because their conquerors (if the sovereigns of Great Britain are so to be considered) have declared that British law shall prevail throughout the whole territory of New South Wales.

In conclusion, his Excellency directs me to state to your Honor, that although he thus contends that British law alone exists in the colony, he entirely admits that, in putting the law in force against the aborigines, the utmost degree of mercy and forbearance should be exercised.[23]

Chief Justice Dowling's dismissal of Willis's judgement in *R. v Bonjon* represented the decisive victory of the legal ideas embodied in *R. v Murrell*. They were not necessarily better intellectually or sounder in law but they were undoubtedly more convenient for colonial society and more suited to the interests and ideas current at the time. In point of fact, the intellectual underpinning of Justice Burton's 1836 judgement was decidedly shaky. He based his argument that the Aborigines were subject to British law on a series of paragraphs in Vattel's *Law of Nations* relating to the legal status of aliens resident in a foreign state, the most directly relevant of which read:

> But even in States which freely admit foreigners it is presumed that the sovereign only grants them access on the implied condition that they will be subject to the laws—I mean to the general laws established for the maintenance of good order and not operative only in the case of citizens or subjects. The public safety and the rights of the Nation and of the sovereign necessarily impose this condition, and foreigners impliedly submit to it as soon as they enter into the country, and can not presume to obtain admittance on any other footing. Sovereignty is the right to command throughout the whole country; and the laws are not limited to regulating the conduct of the citizens with one another, but they extend to all classes of persons in every part of the land.[24]

Burton, thus, up-ended the Willis view that the 'colonists, and not the aborigines are the foreigners'. His argument also begged the question of where the Aborigines had come from if they were legally equivalent to foreigners who had entered the society from outside unless, of course, he conceded that unsettled 'Aboriginal' Australia was in effect a foreign country. But this proposition, which made sense of colonial reality, could not be sustained while the overarching theory remained that British sovereignty reached to the farthest corners of the continent.

Ultimately all the arguments in the *R. v Murrell* judgement can be traced back to the starting point of *terra nullius* and to a few key passages in Vattel beginning with the proposition that 'all men have an equal right to things which have not yet come into possession of anyone'.[25] From there Burton followed Vattel as the argument ascended from the rights of individuals to those of nations. 'When a Nation takes possession of a country which belongs to no one', Vattel declared,

> it is considered as acquiring *sovereignty* over it as well as *ownership*; for being free and independent, it can not intend, when it settles a territory, to leave others the right to rule it, nor any other right which belongs to sovereignty. The

entire space over which a Nation extends its sovereignty form the sphere of its jurisdiction and is called its *domain*.[26]

By adopting *terra nullius* so completely in 1836 the New South Wales Supreme Court left little room for Aboriginal rights or interests beyond those bestowed by the colonial government. There could be no acceptance of the American concept of domestic dependent nations, as advocated by Justice Willis, because British sovereignty occupied the 'entire space'. Nor was there any scope to develop the more sophisticated and complex legal regimes which evolved in all parts of the Empire during the eighteenth and nineteenth centuries.

The New South Wales Supreme Court's decision in *R. v Murrell* cast a long shadow over Australian jurisprudence. The total disregard for Aboriginal law propelled the courts away from any concept of legal pluralism and helped undermine traditional authority all over the continent. Two Victorian cases of 1860 illustrated the application of the accepted legal doctrine. The case of *R. v Peter* was taken on appeal to the Supreme Court where it was argued by the defence that:

it was assumed that he [Peter] was a pure aboriginal of a still existing tribe, having a local residence apart from the white inhabitants of the colony. The point was whether Peter was amenable to British laws or amenable only to the assumed laws or customs and tribunals of his tribe.

But the Court would have none of it, holding that the 'Queen's writ runs throughout this Colony, and that British law is binding on all peoples within it'.[27]

Three months later a similar case was taken on appeal to the Supreme Court. An Aboriginal man known to the Europeans as Jimmy had been tried for killing his wife and found guilty of manslaughter. The question posed for the court was whether 'in the absence of evidence that either of these natives had become civilized, or had changed their habits or mode of life so as to be supposed voluntarily to have submitted themselves to British laws'.

The lawyer for the defence argued that it was possible for a sovereign authority to sanction pre-existing laws and 'to confine them in their operation to the race which was subject to them'. He pointed out that this had been done in both Ireland and the United States. But once again the court rejected any attempt to provide Australian jurisprudence with the flexibility available in other parts of the Empire, declaring that its jurisdiction was supreme throughout the colony 'and with regard to all persons within it'.[28]

Similar issues were discussed by the New South Wales Court in 1883. Cobby was convicted of manslaughter on the evidence of the woman he lived with. The legal question involved in the appeal was whether the woman's evidence could be received given her relationship with the defendant. The Chief Justice Sir James Martin concluded that the woman was not a wife 'such as one as is contemplated by the law, so as to prevent her giving evidence against her husband at a criminal trial'. To extend the law to the Aborigines

> or to take the statement of their customs from one of themselves, is to go too far. We may recognize a marriage in a civilized country, but we can hardly do the same in the case of the marriages of these aborigines, who have no laws of which we can take cognizance. We cannot recognize the customs of these aborigines so as to aid us in the determination as to whether the relationship exists of husband and wife.[29]

Burton may have thought the overriding of Aboriginal law was a mild and merciful conquest but it was a conquest none the less. It resulted far less from the inner dynamics of British law than from the ignorance and prejudices of the Australian colonists during the 1830s. The decision in R. v Murrell did not have behind it the momentum of a long tradition of the common law but rather the short history of the troubled relations between the indigenous Australians and the British invaders. In fact, the common law was far more complex, and far more flexible, than the Australian courts allowed. It had, after all, absorbed or accommodated a richly complex pattern of customary laws in England, Wales and Ireland, and from the sixteenth century onwards widely differing legal systems all over the world as British influence expanded across the globe.

In his eighteenth-century study of the history of the common law Sir Matthew Hale described the 'settling of the common law of England' in Ireland and Wales. 'Tis true', he explained, 'many ancient Irish customs continued in Ireland, and do continue there, even into this day'. In Wales there were 'very many laws and customs' which were 'utterly strange' to the laws of England.[30] By its very nature customary law was unwritten and of ancient lineage. The great seventeenth-century jurist Coke observed that custom 'is one of the maine triangles of the laws of England, those laws being divided into common law, statute law, and custome'.[31] The seventeenth-century jurist Sir John Davies observed in 1674 that:

> The common law of England is nothing else but the Common Custom of the Realm . . . It can be recorded and registered no-where but in the memory of the people. For a Custom taketh beginning and groweth to perfection . . . when a reasonable act once done is found to be good and beneficial to the people, and agreeable to their nature and disposition, then do they use it and practise it again and again, and so by often iteration time out of mind, it obtaineth the force of a Law. And this Customary Law is the most perfect and most excellent, and without comparison the best, to make and preserve a Commonwealth.[32]

Custom was by definition a local law—a *lex loci*—applying in a particular area as Chief Justice Tindal declared in *Tyson v Smith* in 1838. Custom, he said, is a usage 'which obtains the force of law, and is, the binding law, within a particular district or at a particular place'.[33] Even more to the point in relation to the Australian experience is that customary law is by definition contrary to the common law, that it is 'in some fundamental respect an *exception* from the ordinary laws of the land'.[34] Lord Kenyon remarked in *Horton v Beckman* that it was 'no objection to a custom that it is not comfortable to the common law of England'. It was of the 'very essence of a custom that it should vary from it'.[35]

The place of custom in the British Isles illustrates a flexibility of law which was never displayed in the way the Australian colonists responded to the indigenous societies with which they shared the continent. The same lesson can be learnt from the history of the adaption of British law in the overseas Empire. In his study of British Colonial Law, T.O. Elias noted that: 'Whenever English law was introduced into a colony the traditional British policy has been to give recognition to such aspects of customary law as are found to be well-established and not contrary to morality or justice.'[36]

In his *A History of English Law* William Holdsworth considered the legal effects of the Imperial expansion which included the elaboration of old, and the evolution of new rules of constitutional law and the 'introduction of leading English lawyers to new social and economic needs and problems, and in the East, to new systems of religion, philosophy and law'.[37]

These developments 'broadened the intellectual horizon of English lawyers'. No such broadening can be noticed in Australia in the first 150 years of settlement. It wasn't until 1971 that an Australian court determined that the Aborigines had a system of law worthy of study.

The relationship between the laws of Britain and those of the many societies subject to imperial domination was discussed by jurists throughout the history of the Empire. In the seventeenth century the main distinction was between Christian and non-Christian or 'pagan' societies as Coke outlined in *Calvin's Case* of 1609:

> There is a diversity between a conquest of a kingdom of a Christian King, and the conquest of a kingdom of an infidel; for if a King come to Christian kingdom by conquest . . . he may at his pleasure alter and change the laws of that kingdom: but until he doth make an alteration of those laws the ancient laws of that kingdom remain. But if a Christian King should conquer a kingdom of an infidel, and bring them under his subjection, then *ipso facto* the laws of the infidel are abrogated for they be not only against Christianity, but against the law of God and nature . . . [38]

Later in the century the blanket rejection of all 'infidel' laws was modified. In 1694, in the case of *Blankard v Galdy* Chief Justice Holt presented a much more realistic and subtle picture of the legal consequences of conquest. The laws of non-Christians, he remarked, 'do not entirely cease, but only such as are against the laws of God'. He continued:

> In case of an uninhabited country newly found out by English subjects, all laws in force in England, are in force there: but Jamaica being conquered, and not pleaded to be parcel of the kingdom of England, but part of the possessions and revenue of the Crown of England; the laws of England did not take place there, 'till declared so by the conqueror or his successors. The Isle of Man and Ireland are part of the possessions of the Crown of England; yet retain their antient laws: and it is impossible the laws of this nation, by meer conquest without more, should take place in a conquered country; because for a time, there must want officers, without which our laws cannot be executed. Jamaica was not governed by the laws of England after the conquest thereof, until new laws were made; for they had neither sheriff or counties, but were only an assembly of people which are not bound by our laws, unless particularly mentioned: and if our law did take place in a conquer'd country, yet they in Jamaica having power to make new laws, our general laws may be altered by theirs in particulars.[39]

The legal distinction between conquered and settled colonies was hammered out during the eighteenth century and received classic definition in William Blackstone's famous *The Commentaries on the Laws of England*. The rule relating to settled colonies was that:

> if an uninhabited country be discovered and planted by English subjects, all the English laws then in being, which are the birthright of every subject, are immediately there in force. But this must be understood with very many and very great restrictions. Such colonists carry with them only so much of the English law, as is applicable to their own situation and the condition of an infant colony.[40]

The complex reality of the Empire, however, meant that the clear distinction between settled and conquered colonies was largely an academic one. Most situations diverged from the ideal. Policy in India, for instance, shared characteristics of both settled and conquered colonies as Lord Lyndhurst pointed out in 1828 in the case of *Freeman v Fairlie*:

> The acquired territory was not newly discovered or uninhabited, but well peopled, and by a civilized race, governed by long established laws, to which they were much attached, and which it would have been highly inconvenient and dangerous immediately to change. On the other hand those laws were so interwoven with, and dependent on, their religious institutions, as Mahomedans and Pagans, that a great part of them cannot possibly be applied to the government of a Christian people . . . Some new course was to be taken in this peculiar case; and the course actually taken seems to have been, to treat the case, in a great measure, like that of a new discovered country for the government of the Company's servants, and other British or Christian settlers using the laws of the mother country, as far as they were capable of being applied for that purpose, and leaving the Mahomedan and Gentoo inhabitants to their own laws and customs.[41]

The legal pluralism, which evolved in India, became common in all parts of the Empire as the Privy Council noted in 1930. English law, the Bench observed, was modified in racially mixed communities arising from the necessity 'of preventing the injustice or oppression which would ensue if that law were applied to alien races unmodified'.[42] The general principles involved were outlined by E.W. Ridges in his *Constitutional Law of England* first published in 1906. 'Where, in any colony', he explained,

> whether settled, conquered, or ceded, there exists already a native population with laws and customs of their own, though from their nature inapplicable to Englishmen, these laws and customs are not generally entirely suppressed, but retained and respected as personal or tribal in character so far as is compatible with the dictates of humanity.[43]

The judicial tests applied to traditional law in the colonies were very similar to those used to assess the standing of customary law in Britain—the law had to be of long standing and not at variance with natural justice, equity and good conscience. 'What the law requires', the High Court of Madras laid down in 1866,

> before an alleged custom can receive the recognition of the Court, and so acquire legal force, is satisfactory proof of usage so long and invariably acted upon in practice as to show that it has by common consent been submitted to as the established governing rule of the particular family, class or district or country.[44]

The problem of transplanting English law to the colonies was under consideration during the period which spanned the foundation and early years of Australian settlement. In 1774 Warren Hastings rejected proposals to replace Indian laws and customs arguing that:

> It would be a grievance to deprive the people of the protection of their own laws, but it would be a wanton tyranny to require their obedience to others of which they are wholly ignorant, and of which they have no possible means of acquiring knowledge.[45]

The British establishment of a colony at Penang in 1786 led to a very different legal outcome than the settlement at Sydney Cove two years later. The Royal Charter of Justice of 1807 paid attention to the 'several religions, manners and customs' of the resident inhabitants. The local application of English law was discussed in the 1869 case of *Choa Choon Neo v Spottiswoode*. Chief Justice Marshall explained that:

> In this Colony, so much of the laws of England as was in existence when it was imported here, and as is of general (and not merely local) policy, and adapted to the conditions and wants of the inhabitants is the law of the land: and further, that law is subject in its application to the various alien races established here, to such modifications as are necessary to prevent it from operating unjustly or oppressively on them.[46]

Similar principles were expressed in the *New Zealand Constitutional Act* of 1852 which contained the provisions:

- Within such districts (as may be declared) the laws, customs, and usages of the aboriginal inhabitants, so far as they are not repugnant to the general principles of humanity, shall for the present be maintained . . .
- The jurisdiction of the Courts and magistrates . . . shall extend over the said aboriginal districts, subject only to the duty . . . of taking notice of and giving effect to the laws, customs, and usages of such aboriginal inhabitants.[47]

The New Zealand government progressively drew back from the principles enunciated in the above clauses, however they were increasingly important in British Imperial policy as it developed in Asia, Africa and the Pacific. The Royal Charter of the British North Borneo Company of 1881, for instance, stipulated that: 'In the administration of justice by the Company to the people of Borneo . . . careful regard shall always be had to the customs and laws of the class or tribe or nation to which the parties respectively belong . . .'[48]

So widely accepted did these principles become that in the twentieth century the establishment and growth of 'a separate native law system alongside British established courts' was the 'outstanding feature' of judicial policy in all parts of the Empire. The indigenous legal system

> was charged with the development of customary law and institutions in the traditional mould, though under certain restrictions where 'barbarous custom' was forbidden. The two systems might be integrated or might run parallel, but it is generally true to say that throughout the colonial possessions native law was permitted to exist, usually by enabling statute or by charter, so long as it did not conflict radically with English law conceptions.[49]

In 1844 the Secretary of State for the Colonies Lord Stanley wrote to Governor Fitzroy of New South Wales explaining that he knew:

> of no theoretical or practical difficulty in the maintenance under the same Sovereign of various codes of law for the governance of different races of men. In British India, Ceylon, at the Cape of Good Hope, and in Canada, the

aboriginal and the European inhabitants live together on these terms.[50]

Stanley did not include Australia in his list. Ten years before the Supreme Court of New South Wales had determined that there was only one code of law in the colony, that Aboriginal customary law could only be regarded in 'the light of lewd practices' and had no place in the developing judicial system. But the principles espoused by Stanley had a long and vigorous life before them and were embraced throughout the British Empire during the second half of the nineteenth century and the first half of the twentieth century. Australian jurisprudence remained locked into the outlook and attitudes of colonial society in the 1830s. It missed out on the rich elaboration of law elsewhere in the Empire and the many variations in the melding of British and local law. This was so despite the fact that throughout the nineteenth and early twentieth centuries the Australian colonists were continually coming into contact with new Aboriginal tribes. The frontier moved but the attendant legal principles didn't. Aboriginal groups meeting with Europeans for the first time in the 1930s were brought within a legal system which still bore the stamp of the 1830s and the ethnographic ignorance of Justice Burton and missionary Threlkeld. There were very few voices in Australia between the wars who would have accepted the admonition of the Privy Council in 1930 of the need to modify English law in order to prevent the 'injustice or oppression' which resulted when 'laws were applied to alien races unmodified'.

The Australian community expressed growing interest in the Aboriginal 'question' during the 1920s and 1930s. Some of that attention was directed to the question of customary law and its relationship with the legal system. In 1933 the Aborigines Friends' Association argued that:

> In all cases of breaches of law in which Aborigines are concerned, full consideration should be given to tribal traditions and customs, in order that full justice may be done. It would be the duty of the field officers not only to be familiar with tribal language, laws, traditions and customs, but to explain to the Aboriginal so much of the white man's

law as he is expected to obey. Many cases could very well be dealt with in the locality in which they arise, whereby many complications and much expense and inconvenience would be avoided.[51]

Similar concerns were voiced in a petition of '60 jurors' from the Northern Territory to the local Supreme Court. They advocated the need for a tribal court,

functioning under milder laws of punishment than our present criminal system provides. It is known that if one Aboriginal unlawfully and violently injures another, his tribe will see to his proper punishment, irrespective of what the white man does to him. It is strongly urged that the whole question should be investigated and reported to the Government by men who have lived amongst the natives and have knowledge of their codes, and by men who have studied their laws and customs from a scientific point of view, and by men who are genuinely and sympathetically interested in the Aborigines. Such men are the likeliest to point out the best manner in which to achieve the desired result. Leaving the matter in the hands of those who have no knowledge of the Aboriginal would only result in a remedy worse than the disease.[52]

Responding to these and other similar representations the Commonwealth Government began to reform legal practices in the Northern Territory issuing a Crimes Ordinance which included the provision:

Where an Aboriginal native is convicted of murder, the Court shall not be obliged to pronounce sentence of death; but, in lieu thereof, may impose such penalty as, having regard to all the circumstances of the case, appears to the Court to be just and proper . . . For the purpose of determining the nature and extent of the penalty to be imposed where an Aboriginal native is convicted of murder, the Court shall receive and consider any evidence which may be tendered as to any relevant native law or custom and its application to the facts of the case.[53]

In 1936, Western Australia legislated to enable special Courts of Native Affairs to be established by proclamation for the trial of any offence committed by an Aborigine against a fellow Aborigine. *The Aborigines Act Amendment Act* provided that the court could, 'take into account in mitigation of punishment any tribal custom which may be set up and proved as the reason for commission of the offence'.

The Act also allowed the court to 'call to its assistance a headman of the tribe' to which the accused person belonged.[54]

The strong assimilationist current of official policy during the 1940s, 1950s and 1960s militated against any further consideration of recognition of customary law. But with the radical changes of the 1970s in both Aboriginal and mainstream politics the question returned to the agenda. In 1977 the then Federal Attorney-General R.J. Ellicott asked the Australian Law Reform Commission to investigate the question 'whether it would be desirable to apply either in whole or in part Aboriginal customary law to Aborigines, either generally or in particular areas or to those living in tribal conditions only'.[55]

When it finally reported nine years later the Commission had determined that customary law existed in many parts of Australia 'as a real force, influencing or controlling the acts and lives' of those Aborigines for whom it was part of the substance of daily life. The Commission believed there were good arguments for recognising customary law including—

- The need to acknowledge the relevance and validity of Aboriginal customary law for many Aborigines.
- Their desire for the recognition of their laws in appropriate ways.
- Their right, recognised in the Commonwealth Government's policy on Aboriginal affairs and in the Commission's Terms of Reference, to choose to live in accordance with their customs and traditions, which implies that the general law will not impose unnecessary restrictions or disabilities upon the exercise of that right.
- The injustice inherent in non-recognition in a number of situations.[56]

The Commission concentrated on areas of family and criminal law in its recommendations and prepared a draft bill 'to make provision for the recognition of Aboriginal customary law' in relation to marriage, legitimacy of children, inheritance, adoption as well as such aspects of the criminal law as evidence and sentencing.[57]

Government has been slow to react to the main thrust of the Commission's recommendations. Eight years after the publication of the report the Federal Minister for Aboriginal Affairs Robert Tickner issued a paper on Commonwealth implementation of the proposals and the difficulties that had been experienced in implementing them. In an address in August 1994 Tickner urged all Australian governments to adopt policies which would ensure that indigenous customary law 'shall be recognized and applied to the extent that it continues to be traditionally practiced by indigenous people provided that such application by the courts shall be reasonable and in accordance with Australia's international obligations'.[58]

Many commentators think that the recommendations of the Commission are far too modest. Justice Michael Kirby believes that even if they were implemented 'to the letter' the result would 'simply scratch the surface' in removing the major sources of injustice 'presented by the Australian legal system to the Aboriginal people of Australia'.[59] Others go much farther arguing that mainstream jurisprudence itself has to change and accommodate elements of Aboriginal law. In his recent essay, 'Towards an Australian Contract Law', M.P. Ellinghaus argued that:

> An integration of Aboriginal elements into our legal tradition, while of specific concern to lawyers, must be justified in wider terms. Our civilization cannot come to maturity without the complete integration of its indigenous component. We have adopted the kangaroo and the emu, the opossum, the frilled lizard, the echidna, the lyre bird and the platypus as civic emblems. In other words, we have declared our identity by reference to indigenous animals and plants. We have not yet made an analogous gesture towards the human natives of this continent. One reason for this is, of course, that such a gesture is immensely more difficult . . . [because] . . . it involves the recovery and assimilation of the intellectual achievement of the Aborigines . . . Our history of ideas includes that of more than forty millennia

of Aboriginal presence . . . We must recover and re-instate the Aboriginal past before we can be at ease on this continent.[60]

Ellinghaus quoted with approval the belief of novelist David Malouf that what Australia needed was 'a sense of continuity', a line passing through from the 'remotest past into the remotest time to come'. The law, he believed, had failed to come to terms with the Aboriginal past but it too would 'have to incorporate the Aboriginal tradition'. The fact that no 'explicit Aboriginal element' had been 'admitted past the periphery of our jurisprudence' showed only that lawyers were 'as usual lagging behind'.[61]

5

HOW DID AUSTRALIA
BECOME BRITISH?

HOW DID AUSTRALIA BECOME BRITISH? The short answer is by
the assertion of sovereignty on four occasions in 1788, 1824,
1829 and 1879. But how and why were the claims legally
effective? In themselves they didn't amount to much—small
parties standing around a flagpole, the reading of a
proclamation, a round or two of gunfire, a few ragged
cheers—and a continent passed into the hands of the British
Crown. They were little events with big consequences. What
legal alchemy effected the change?

Acquisition of territory has attracted an extensive literature
since the sixteenth century. The acquired sovereignty could
be either original or derivative, a nineteenth-century American
jurist explaining:

> The principle and rule to be deduced respecting title to
> unoccupied regions, or those in the possession of the
> aboriginal inhabitants . . . are that acquisition and title may
> be original or derivative; that original title includes discov-
> ery, use and settlement which are ingredients of occupation
> and will constitute a valid title, but that derivative title
> comes of conquest, treaty and transfer.[1]

The legal doctrine relating to Australia has always been
that Britain acquired an original title, that because there was
no existing sovereignty the British Crown was the first

sovereign. Acquisition was, therefore, by means of discovery and occupation. Both propositions need careful examination before an assessment can be made as to whether the basic premise—that of original title—needs to be reconsidered.

Theology shaped the early European claims to territory in the New World. In 1493 the Pope divided the world between Spain and Portugal. European adventurers sallied forth confident of their right to conquer infidels. But when the other maritime powers joined Spain and Portugal in the race for colonial possessions a new way was found to balance their conflicting claims. The American jurist Joseph Story provided a classic account of the adoption of the idea of title by discovery. 'That title', he wrote in 1833,

> was founded on right of discovery, a right which was held among the European nations a just and sufficient foundation on which to rest their respective claims to the American continent. Whatever controversies existed among them (and they were numerous) respecting the extent of their own acquisitions abroad, they appealed to this as the ultimate fact, by which their various and conflicting claims were to be adjusted. It may not be easy upon general reasoning to establish the doctrine that priority of discovery confers any exclusive right to territory. It was probably adopted by the European nations as a convenient and flexible rule by which to regulate their respective claims. For it was obvious, that in the mutual contests for dominion in newly discovered lands, there would soon arise violent and sanguinary struggles for exclusive possession, unless some common principle should be recognized by all maritime nations for the benefit of all. None more readily suggested itself than the one now under consideration; and as it was a principle of peace and repose, of perfect equality of benefit in proportion to the actual or supposed expenditures and hazards attendant upon such enterprises, it received a universal acquiescence, if not a ready approbation. It became the basis of European polity, and regulated the exercise of the rights of sovereignty and settlement in all the cisatlantic Plantations.[2]

The British claim to eastern Australia consummated by Cook's assertion of sovereignty at Possession Island in 1770 was fully in accord with current European doctrine. But the claim by itself did not mean all that much; it was directed at competing European powers and not at the indigenous people. Chief Justice John Marshall of the American Supreme Court explained in 1832 that claims of discovery 'asserted a title against Europeans only and were considered as blank pages so far as the rights of the natives were concerned'.[3] M.F. Lindley summed up the accepted view of the issue in *The Acquisition and Government of Backward Territory in International Law*. Discovery, he explained,

> was adapted to regulate the competition between European Powers themselves, and it had no bearing upon the relations between those Powers and the natives. What the discoverer's State gained was the right, as against other European powers, to take steps which were appropriate to the acquisition of the territory in question. What those steps were would depend on whether there was already a native population in possession of the territory.[4]

Discovery gave what was termed an inchoate title which could only be developed further by actual occupation. This had been established well before 1788, Hugo Grotius remarking that an act of discovery was sufficient to give a clear title to sovereignty 'only when it is accompanied by actual possession'.[5] The individual or nation, J.G. Heineccius observed in 1743, who only 'seized a thing with his eyes, but does not take hold of it, cannot be said to occupy'.[6] The settlement of 1788 was, then, more significant than the discovery of eighteen years before. It converted an inchoate title into an actual one. But how good was the claim to the whole of eastern Australia?

Had the British really taken hold of New South Wales? They had, after all, not even seized most of it 'with their eyes'. They were only in occupation of a tiny part of the land in question. For a generation most settlers were within a day's ride of Sydney. The area which could be legitimately claimed following the planting of a colony on coastline unclaimed by other Europeans was, of necessity, clearly defined in the work of international lawyers. The area claimed could only stretch inland as far as the crest of the watershed of rivers flowing into the ocean on the line of coast actually occupied. The length of coastline which could be legitimately annexed was harder to define. In his 1889 *A Treatise on International Law*, W.E. Hall addressed the question of what area was affected by an act of occupation.

> What then in this case is involved in the occupation of a given portion of shore? It may be regarded as settled usage that the interior limit shall not extend further than the crest of the watershed; but the lateral frontiers are less certain. It has been generally admitted that occupation of the coast carries with it a right to the whole territory drained by the rivers which empty their waters within its line; but the admission of this right is perhaps accompanied by the tacit reservation that the extent of coast must bear some reasonable proportion to the territory which is claimed in virtue of possession, but it can hardly be conceded, that the whole of a large river basin is so attendant upon the land in the immediate neighbourhood of its outlet that property in it is acquired by merely holding a fort or settlement at the mouth of the river without also holding lands to any distance on either side.[7]

Australian claims to the territory effectively occupied have often been exaggerated. In the case of *Williams v Attorney-General of New South Wales* in 1913, Justice Isaacs declared that it was an 'unquestionable position' that as soon as Governor Phillip received his commission from George III on 12 October 1786 'the whole of lands of Australia were already in law the property of the King of England'.[8] This was too much for the leading authority on British Commonwealth law Sir Kenneth Roberts-Wray who declared:

> This . . . is indeed startling and, indeed, incredible. The first settlement in Australia was founded in 1788; but even if it had been in 1786, could a foothold in a small area on the east side of a sub-continent 2000 miles wide be sufficient in English law (as it certainly would not in international law) to confer sovereignty but also title to the soil throughout the hinterland of nearly three million square miles.[9]

Clearly the British claim to the whole of New South Wales was weak in international law, a point illustrated by the reaction to possible threats of rival colonies which sparked the extension of settlement in outlying areas of the continent. The British claim survived less because of its intrinsic strength, or as a result of a rapid spread of settlement, and more because no European power was in a position, or had the inclination, to challenge it.

Discovery was less significant in justifying the annexation than occupation which was a concept with a considerable history even in 1788 and needs careful examination. It developed from the Roman legal principle of *occupatio* which became the foundation of 'all modern International Law on the subject . . . of the acquisition of sovereign rights in newly discovered countries'.[10] But the problem of applying occupation to the settlement of Australia is that it specifically related to land that had either never belonged to anyone or had been abandoned. 'The notion of occupation', Wolff explained, 'assumes that a thing capable of occupation belongs to nobody . . . nor can ignorance give a right to that which otherwise you would have no right'.[11] The traditional legal view is that Australia became British by occupation on the day (or days) that annexation took place while the Aborigines in thousands of years of living in the continent had never acquired sovereignty over it. In all that time they had not become the legal occupiers.

From a legal point of view occupation worked best if the land in question was actually uninhabited. The principles involved were first enunciated in English courts by Justice Holt in the case of *Blankard v Galdy* in 1693 when he referred the 'case of an uninhabited country newly found out by English subjects' where English laws were immediately in force.[12] In the case *Dutton v Howell* in the same year the courts discussed the legal status of Barbados which was 'a plantation or new Settlement of Englishmen . . . in an uninhabited Country'. As a consequence the common law 'must and doth oblige there'.[13] Similar principles were outlined in a memo of the Privy Council in 1722 which distinguished the legal situation of conquered countries and 'a new and uninhabited country' which was to be governed by the laws of England.[14] The same emphasis on uninhabited territory can be found in the legal texts of the early nineteenth century. In his *A Treatise on the Law of the Prerogative of the Crown* of 1820, J. Chitty clearly distinguished those colonies which had been obtained by conquest or treaty from those which resulted from 'our taking possession of, and peopling them, when we found them uninhabited'.[15] Clark's *A Summary of Colonial Law* of 1834 declared that colonies were 'acquired, 1, by conquest; 2, by cession under treaty; or 3, by occupancy, viz. where an uninhabited country is discovered by British subjects, and is upon such discovery adopted or recognized by the crown as part of its possessions'.[16]

A jurist with greater influence on Australia was William Blackstone whose *Commentaries on the Laws of England*, first published in 1765 and republished many times over the following decades, dealt with the establishment of overseas colonies and the transfer of English law. He drew a clear distinction between colonies won by conquest or treaty and those where 'lands are claimed by right of occupancy only, by finding them desert and uncultivated, and peopling them from the mother countries'.[17] It is unclear whether Blackstone was referring to 'uninhabited' territory or not. Given the general understanding about the occupation of uninhabited land it is probable that he was. But the ambiguity allowed later commentators to argue that only cultivated land was in actual possession and that Australia was a *terra nullius* despite the presence of indigenous people.

Continental jurists writing in the first half of the nineteenth century took the view that only uninhabited land could be considered as *terra nullius*. In 1831 J.L. Klueber argued that for occupation to be legitimate the chosen territory 'must be susceptible to an exclusive proprietorship, and the object must belong to no-one else . . .'. Consequently no nation 'regardless of its qualities can rob another of its property, not even from savages or nomads'.[18] Thirteen years later the German scholar A.W. Heffter observed that occupation only applied to those countries without a sovereign. He explained that:

It notably applies to uninhabited countries and islands but no power on earth has the right to impose its laws on nomads or savages. Nations could try to create commercial ties with these savage populations, stay with them and even negotiate a voluntary cession of a portion of land, destined to be colonised. Nature does not forbid nations to extend their empires across the earth, but it does not permit one single nation to establish dominion wherever it pleases.[19]

A more common method of dealing with the legal problems of settling in an already populated country was to ignore the presence of the indigenous people altogether. The British Government's senior legal officers advised the Colonial Secretary Lord Bathurst in 1819 that New South Wales had not been acquired by conquest or cession but by taking possession of 'a desert and uninhabited' territory.[20] The legal adviser to the Colonial Office repeated the advice in 1822.[21] In a judgement in 1849 the Chief Justice of New South Wales referred to the Australian colonies as 'newly discovered and unpeopled territories'.[22] Mr Justice Holroyd of the Victorian Supreme Court observed in 1885 that 'from the first' Australia was occupied 'as if it were an uninhabited and desert country'.[23] In 1889 the Privy Council determined that in 1788 Australia had been 'practically unoccupied'.[24] The phrase 'practically unoccupied' was of critical importance in allowing a territory with *some* people to be treated as though it were uninhabited.

While it was possible in law, and from the remote splendour of the Privy Council in 1889, to ground British sovereignty on the proposition of peaceful settlement of a practically uninhabited land, it was less easy in the colonies. Two other ways of justification found favour at the antipodes—the belief that the Aborigines did not use the land in such a way as to possess their home territories and the related argument that they had neither law nor government. All in all, it was argued, they brought their dispossession on themselves. They were neither productive enough nor did they have sufficient organisation to allow for negotiations or treaties.

The legal position of the Aborigines solidified in the 1830s at a time when the colonists were still extremely ignorant

92

about traditional society, culture and economy. Having set in that mould the relevant jurisprudence retained its shape until well into the twentieth century. When referring to Australia in the 1830s Lindley remarked that 'as the facts presented themselves at the time, there appeared to be no political society to be dealt with' and whatever ethnographic information subsequently became available, 'occupation was the appropriate method of acquisition at the time'.[25] But the facts did not 'present themselves'. The settlers chose those pieces of information—and misinformation—which best suited their interests then acted accordingly. The British seaman Captain J.C. Stokes who visited Australia in the 1840s concluded that when dealing with the Aborigines the colonists

> started with an erroneous theory, which they found to tally with their interests, and to relieve them from the burden of benevolence and charity. That the Aborigines were not men, but brutes, was their avowed opinion; and what cruelties flowed from such a doctrine.[26]

Modern jurisprudence still carries a colonial residue. In his standard work *International Law*, D.P. O'Connell declared in 1970 that Australia was treated as *terra nullius* 'since the Australian aborigines were held incapable of intelligent transactions with respect to land'.[27] The distinguished Australian jurist Elizabeth Evatt observed in 1968 that:

> Australia is in fact one of the rare examples of a large tract of inhabited territory acquired peaceably by occupation without any consent being sought from the native population. There is a practical explanation for this, for although a State might prefer to obtain some form of consent where there is an organized community with a recognized chief, this was impossible in Australia, inhabited by scattered unorganized tribes.[28]

Ten years later Professor J.R. Andrews adopted and further embellished Evatt's argument. The practical explanation for the failure to consult the Aborigines was the 'scattered, disorganised and extremely backward and inhibited nature of Aboriginal society'.[29] In his *The Creation of States in International Law* James Crawford added to the chorus of jurists who refer to the exceptional nature of Australian settlement and of Aboriginal society. Referring to those few cases which actually were *terra nullius* he wrote:

> Put negatively, this involves the proposition that only 'an unsettled horde of wandering savages not yet formed into civil society' [the quotation is from Wheaton, 1836], or more neutrally, only nomadic tribesmen lacking all regular political organization, could be regarded as not legal occupants of their territory. In the light of modern anthropological knowledge it can be seen that unoccupied territories as so defined are few indeed: only Australia and the South Island of New Zealand were treated as falling within that category, apart from scattered islands or totally uninhabited tracts.[30]

While discussing international law and native sovereignty Lindley considered the law in relation to acquisition of territory:

> If the territory is uninhabited or is inhabited only by a number of individuals who do not form a political society, then the acquisition may be made by way of occupation. If the inhabitants exhibit collective political activity, which, although of a crude and rudimentary form, possess the elements of permanence, the acquisition can only be made by way of Cession or Conquest or Prescription.[31]

From the middle of the nineteenth century anyone in Australia, or for that matter anyone in the English-speaking world, could have discovered from existing literature that Aboriginal society possessed the elements of permanence and exhibited collective political activity of 'a crude and rudimentary form'. But the law failed to turn that corner and sped on in a straight line with its freight of ignorance and racial prejudice and carried it deep into the twentieth century with many contemporary jurists going along for the ride.

If Lindley is right then Australia could not have been legitimately acquired by occupation but must have been added to the British Empire by cession, conquest or prescription. The British title must, therefore, be a derivative and not an original one. Did the British consummate their title to Australia by conquest? Were they at war with the Aborigines?

Colonists have characteristically preferred to see themselves as settlers rather than conquerors. In 1573 the Spanish authorities issued an ordinance to the effect that the word 'conquest' should no longer be employed in relation to the South American Indians, that 'pacification' was the appropriate term to use.[32] Australian colonists displayed similar habits of mind. In 1890 the Governor of Queensland Sir Charles Lilley remarked that he regretted the apathy displayed towards the Aborigines 'on the part of their brothers—he could not say conquerors'.[33] An earlier Governor, George Bowen, writing at a time of intense frontier conflict, referred to the 'triumph of peaceful progress . . . victories without injustice or bloodshed, conquests not over man, but over nature'.[34] Bowen was certainly not the first to write in this way; one of the earliest histories of New South Wales, published in 1816, expressed the belief that Australian colonisation was especially peaceful.

> For here there are no scenes . . . of desolating war and bloodshed to contemplate, no peaceable inhabitants driven from their smiling dwellings, and deprived of the comforts of life, by means of the destroying invader. Our settlers have not established themselves by the sword, nor willingly done injury to the naked miserable stragglers, who were found on these barren shores.[35]

Australia still strongly resists the idea that the British invaded the country. The reasons are legal, moral, political; the emotions are powerful as recent controversy has made abundantly clear. The courts have determined that the idea of peaceful settlement is a central—indeed skeletal—feature of the legal system, Justice Gibbs asserting in *Coe v the Commonwealth* that: 'It is fundamental to our legal system that the Australian colonies became British possessions by settlement and not by conquest.'[36]

Overshadowing contemporary judicial decisions is the declaration by Lord Watson in *Cooper v Stuart* in 1889 that:

> There is a great difference between the case of a Colony acquired by conquest or cession, in which there is an

established system of law, and that of a Colony which consisted of a tract of territory practically unoccupied . . . at the time when it was peacefully annexed to the British dominion.[37]

Debate about the historiography of colonisation—whether it was a case of settlement or invasion—has run on for years, sporadically intensifying and breaking into the mainstream media. During 1994 controversy over a Queensland social science curriculum drew in a state premier, leading federal politicians and media commentators. Queensland Premier Wayne Goss remarked that: 'I think that just about all Australians would not regard what happened in 1788 as an invasion. There is a world of difference between the arrival of the First Fleet and what most people understood as an invasion.'[38]

Summing up the controversy the editor of *The Weekend Australian* observed: 'It is a fascinating question of our times: were the First Fleeters . . . invaders or settlers?' After considering both sides of the argument he concluded:

Nobody doubts that killings and violence occurred as a result of the interaction between Europeans and Aborigines in Australia. Nobody doubts the full extent of the injustice done to the Aboriginal people must be recognized. But teaching our school children that the modern origins of this nation began in an invasion, pure and simple, will only compound our difficulties. Most Australians do not accept and will never accept the denial of the legitimacy of their civilization which the term invasion implies.[39]

Australians, it seems, need to cling to the idea of peaceful occupation both for the security of the legal system and the legitimacy of their civilization. But the evidence is recalcitrant and points obstinately in the opposite direction.

Frontier conflict was ubiquitous. It began within a few weeks of the first settlement at Sydney Cove and continued until the 1930s or 1940s. Nobody who had lived in frontier districts or knew about what went on there had any doubt about the matter. Metropolitan newspapers were full of horror stories for many decades. Writing in 1880 the ethnographers

A.W. Howitt and Lorimer Fison summed up the experience of a century of conflict:

> It may be stated broadly that the advance of settlement has, upon the frontier at least, been marked by a line of blood. The actual conflict of the two races has varied in intensity and in duration, as the various native tribes have themselves in mental and physical character . . . But the tide of settlement has advanced along an ever widening line, breaking the tribes with its first waves and overwhelming their wrecks with its flood.[40]

Howitt and Fison's colleague Edward Curr drew similar conclusions about the nature of frontier conflict:

> In the first place the meeting of the Aboriginal tribes of Australia and the White pioneer, results as a rule in war, which lasts from six months to ten years, according to the nature of the country, the amount of settlement which takes place in a neighbourhood, and the proclivities of the individuals concerned. When several squatters settle in proximity, and the country they occupy is easy of access and without fastnesses to which the Blacks can retreat, the period of warfare is usually short and the bloodshed not excessive. On the other hand, in districts which are not easily traversed on horseback, in which the Whites are few in number and food is procurable by the Blacks in fastnesses, the term is usually prolonged and the slaughter more considerable . . .
>
> Hence the meeting of the White and Black races in Australia, considered generally, results in war. Nor is it to be wondered at. The White man looks on the possession of the lands by the Blacks as no proper occupation, and practically and avowedly declines to allow them the common rights of human beings. On the other hand, the tribe which has held its land from time immemorial and always maintained, according to native policy, the unauthorized digging up of one root on its soil to be a *casus belli*, sudddenly finds not only that strangers of another race brought with them a multitude of animals, which devour wholesale the roots and vegetables which constitute their principal food, and drive off the game they formerly hunted.[41]

Modern historical research has fully borne out the nine-teenth-century assessments of Curr, Howitt and Fison. Local, regional and colonial-wide studies have all come up with similar results and have uncovered countless stories of violence and death. No part of the continent seems to have been immune from frontier skirmishing; at least 20 000 Aborigines died along the 'line of blood'.

During the controversy of 1994 critics of revisionist history argued that the attempt to replace the term 'settlement' with 'invasion' was an example of bending the past to conform to contemporary political agendas. The conservative lobbyist Gerard Henderson argued: 'History is about what happened in the past. It should not be used as a weapon in contemporary political debates.'[42]

In the past however, many colonists thought they were invaders. 'We are at war with them', a correspondent to a Launceston newspaper wrote in 1831, 'they look upon us as enemies—as invaders—as oppressors and persecutors—they resist our invasion'.[43] 'We ought to feel', another Tasmanian correspondent wrote, 'that we have invaded a domain from which our invasion has expelled those who were born, bred, and providentially supplied in it'.[44] Yet another calling himself 'Border Settler' wrote to the *Tasmanian* in 1827 describing the Aborigines as 'a race of people whose crime is that of repelling the invaders of their country'.[45] But it was not just anonymous letter writers who believed that the colonists were, in fact, invaders. The Governors of the Van Diemen's Company issued formal instructions to their Superintendent Edward Curr that it was incumbent upon each and every servant of the company to treat [the Aborigines] as fellow creatures, 'to make allowance for their ignorance and remember that we are the invaders spreading ourselves over a country which they first possessed, that we are gradually and constantly encroaching upon their hunting grounds'.[46]

Such sentiments were not peculiar to Tasmania or the 1820s. It was absurd, a New South Wales settler argued in 1839, to see the Aborigines 'in the light of occasional rioters' because they were 'enemies arrayed in arms and waging war against Europeans as their invaders'.[47] A visitor to the colonies in the 1840s argued that it 'must not be forgotten . . . that their country is occupied by force'.[48] In a letter to Governor Bourke in 1837 the Quaker missionary James Backhouse wrote:

> It is scarcely to be supposed that in the present day any person of reflection will be found who will attempt to justify the measures adopted by the British, in taking possession of the territory of this people, who had committed no offence against our nation; but who, being without strength to repel invaders had their lands usurped, without an attempt at purchase by treaty, or any other offer of reasonable compensation.[49]

The editor of the *Moreton Bay Courier* wrote in 1848:

> If we hold this country by the right of conquest, and if that right gives us a just claim to its continual possession we must be empowered to enforce our claim by the strong arm when necessary. One law *must* apply to all conquered nations.[50]

'We are invading this country', the editor of the *Northern Territory Times* remarked in 1875, 'and they have a perfect right to . . . do their best to obstruct our passage through it'.[51] The Government Resident in Darwin concurred. 'Entry into their country is an act of invasion', he observed, and 'they will halt at no opportunity of attacking the white invaders'.[52]

It wasn't just anxious settlers who talked of warfare. For the first 50 years of settlement the legal status of the Aborigines was uncertain. Although technically British subjects they were frequently treated as outlaws who could be shot down without any legal complications. Martial law was declared for short periods in New South Wales in 1816 and 1824 and operated in Tasmania for five years between 1828 and 1833. The Tasmanian Solicitor General outlined the legal consequences of martial law which was 'to place the aborigines, within the prescribed limits on the footing of open enemies of the King, in a state of actual warfare against him'.[53] British policy in the 1820s worked on the assumption that the Aborigines had the same legal status as foreign enemies. The Secretary of State for the Colonies Lord Bathurst instructed the governors of both New South Wales and Tasmania that when confronted with Aboriginal resistance they were to:

> understand it to be your duty, when such disturbances cannot be prevented or allayed by less vigorous measures to oppose force by force, and to repel such Aggressions in the same manner, as if they proceeded from subjects of an accredited state.[54]

It was not just a case of many colonists shaping their ideas from their own experience; they were also often aware of the official ideology that Australia was an occupied rather than a conquered territory and rejected it outright. One of the most articulate critics of legal orthodoxy was the pioneer Western Australian lawyer E.W. Landor, who wrote in 1847:

> Nothing could be more anomalous and perplexing than the position of the Aborigines as British subjects. Our brave and conscientious Britons, whilst taking possession of their territory, have been most careful and anxious to make it universally known, that Australia is not a conquered country; and successive Secretaries of State, who write to their governors in a tone like that in which men of sour tempers address their maladroit domestics, have repeatedly commanded that it must never be forgotten 'that our possession of this territory *is based on a right of occupancy*'.
>
> A 'right of occupancy!' Amiable sophistry! Why not say boldly at once, the right of power? We have seized upon the country, and shot down the inhabitants, until the survivors have found it expedient to submit to our rule. We have acted exactly as Julius Caesar did when he took possession of Britain. But Caesar was not so hypocritical as to pretend any moral *right* to possession. On what grounds can we possibly claim a *right* to the occupancy of the land? We are told, because civilized people are justified in extending themselves over uncivilized countries. According to this doctrine, were there a nation in the world superior to ourselves in the arts of life, and of a different religious faith, it would be equally entitled (had it the physical power) to the possession of Old England under the 'right of occupancy'; for the sole purpose of our moral and social

improvement, and to make us participants in the supposed truths of a new creed.

We have a right to our Australian possessions; but it is the right of Conquest, and we hold them with the grasp of Power. Unless we proceed on this foundation, our conduct towards the native population can be considered only as a monstrous absurdity. However Secretaries of State may choose to phrase the matter, we can have no other *right* of occupancy. We resolve to found a colony in a country, the inhabitants of which are not strong enough to prevent our so doing, though they evince their repugnance by a thousand acts of hostility.

We build houses and cultivate the soil, and for our own protection we find it necessary to declare the native population subject to our laws.

This would be an easy and simple matter were it the case of conquerors dictating to the conquered; but our Secretaries of State, exhibiting an interesting display of conscientiousness and timidity, shrink from the responsibility of having sanctioned a conquest over a nation of miserable savages, protected by the oracles at Exeter Hall, and reject with sharp cries of anger the scurrilous imputation. Instead, therefore, of being in possession by right of arms, we modestly appropriate the land to ourselves, whilst making the most civil assurances that we take not this liberty as conquerors, but merely in order to gratify a praiseworthy desire of occupying the country. We then declare ourselves seized in fee by right of occupancy. But now comes the difficulty. What right have we to impose laws upon people whom we profess not to have conquered, and who have never annexed themselves of their country to the British Empire by any written or even verbal treaty.[55]

Many colonists believed that the British had invaded Australia, but was that objectively the case? Recent opponents of the proposition compare events in Australia with better known invasions—the Norman invasion of 1066, the German invasion of Poland and the Soviet Union in the Second World War—and conclude that the British incursions of 1788 were not at all comparable. The editor of *The Weekend Australian* argued that in 1066 there was 'a genuine invasion':

That was when one king set out with the force of arms to invade another country, fight and kill its king and occupy its territory. That classic account of an invasion is quite different from the story of the arrival of Europeans on this continent.[56]

But by adopting this line of argument opponents of the invasion thesis are doing the very thing they accuse their opponents of doing—applying standards of the present and of the distant past—to the specific events of 1788.[57]

Another argument mounted against the invasion thesis is that Govenor Phillip was instructed 'to treat the indigenous inhabitants well',[58] with 'amity and kindness' to use the official words. There is no doubt that Phillip had good intentions. While still in England he wrote that it would be 'a great point gained' if the settlers could proceed 'in this business without having any dispute with the natives'.[59] But it is surely not enough to take official expressions of benevolence at their face value, they were standard phrases which had been used by European nations for generations before 1788. Phillip II of Spain, for instance, issued an ordinance to the effect that colonisation 'must be made with all peace and charity we desire. We do not wish to give occasion or pretext for force or injury to the Natives'.[60]

Three hundred years of accumulated experience of European colonisation should have suggested that the indigenous people would resist incursion and expropriation. It didn't take exceptional prescience to assume the whole endeavour would end as Francis Bacon expected, that the 'displanting' of people would end in 'an extirpation'. The likely outcome of the expedition to Botany Bay was foreshadowed by a correspondent writing in London's *Morning Herald* in September 1786. 'The voyages of our late Navigators', he recalled,

are full of shocking instances of murder, and show us how improbable it is that any plantation can be made upon the lately discovered islands of the continent, without a cruel disregard for the lives of the natives . . . [B]ecause they are justly and naturally jealous of such invasion [the natives] must be destroyed by the armed force which is sent out with the convicts, to support the occupancy of lands not their own.[61]

Gerard Henderson argued that 'on any analysis' the First Fleet was 'not an invasion force', it was 'too small by far, under-supplied and inadequately armed'.[62] But the force available was carefully calculated to effect the objective in mind. The British authorities were keenly aware of the need to provide sufficient military power for the establishment and security of the settlement. In an important meeting of the House of Commons Committee on Transportation in May 1786 Sir Joseph Banks was closely questioned about the capacity of the Aborigines to resist a European landing.

Committee:	Is the coast in General or the particular part you have mentioned much inhabited?
Banks:	There are very few Inhabitants.
Committee:	Are they of peaceable or hostile Disposition?
Banks:	Though they seemed inclined to Hostilities they did not appear at all to be feared. We never saw more than 30 or 40 together . . .
Committee:	Do you think that 500 men being put on shore there would meet with that Obstruction from the Natives which might prevent them settling there?
Banks:	Certainly not—from the experience I have had of the Natives of another part of the same coast I am inclined to believe that they would speedily abandon the country to the newcomers.
Committee:	Were the Natives armed and in what Manner?
Banks:	They were armed with spears headed with fish bones but none of them we saw in Botany Bay appeared at all formidable.[63]

In August 1789 Governor Phillip sent a despatch to London indicating that he had carefully calculated the size of the military force necessary to meet, and, if necessary crush any likely Aboriginal resistance. He explained that 500 troops would be sufficient. 'It will appear to your Lordship', he wrote, after what has been said of the natives, that a less force will be wanted for the security of the settlement than what I considered as necessary soon after my arrival in this country, although that was not considerable . . . I presume that a battalion of 500 men will be sufficient, which will admit of one hundred being detached for the security of Norfolk Island.[64]

So if Australia was invaded does this undermine the legitimacy of the Australian state? There is no clear answer to that question. In a recent article in the *Melbourne University Law Review*, G. Simpson argued that the High Court should resolve the problems associated with the belief that Australia was acquired by occupation and accept the reality of conquest. 'It was', he observed,

important to realize that the High Court can do this without challenging the basis of Australian sovereignty. Conquest was a legitimate method of acquisition at international law prior to 1945, and, according to the doctrine of intertemporal law the acquisition of Australia can be judged according to international law norms prevailing at the time.

Simpson believed that such a declaration would have positive advantages. It would:

allow the Court to declare Australia as conquered territory. This would be significant in respect of both native title and the recognition of Aboriginal customary law generally. Both the common law and international law regulating conquered territory from Blackstone to the present day, insist that the indigenous or sovereign laws in existence at the time of conquest shall remain in force until expressly extinguished by the Crown.[65]

In 1983 the Senate Standing Committee on Constitutional and Legal Affairs investigated the issue surrounding the British acquisition of sovereignty while considering the question of a treaty with the Aborigines. The Committee argued that while the acquisition might appear repugnant to contemporary morality, it stood beyond challenge as a result of the principle of inter-temporal law—that it, that it was legal at the time. Bolstering the legitimacy of the claim, the Committee found, was the rule of prescription which, it explained, arose in circumstances where no clear title to sovereignty can be shown by way of occupation, conquest or cession, but the territory in question has remained under the continuous and undisputed sovereignty of the claimant for so long that the position has became part of the established international order of nations. The conclusion to be drawn from the application of this rule to the Commonwealth's position, is that if there were any defect in Australia's title, the rule of prescription would apply to overturn the defect and to vest sovereign title in the Commonwealth Government.[66]

Does the rule of prescription give Australia a fallback position which protects the status quo regardless of what happened in the past? The situation is not as simple as the Senate Committee suggested. Prescription is founded on two principles: 'display of authority by the one party, acquiescence in that display by the other'.[67] The nineteenth-century jurist Richard Phillimore argued that internationally prescription must be 'founded upon a presumption of voluntary abandonment of dereliction for former owners'. A forcible and unjust seizure of a country, 'which the inhabitants, overpowered for the moment by the superiority of physical force, ineffectually resist' is a possession which 'lacking an originally just title, requires the aid of time to ensure its original defect'. With the passage of time the usurper could point to 'continued occupation, absence of interruption, aided no doubt generally, both morally and legally speaking, by the employment of labour and capital upon the possession'.

Phillimore observed that in every legal system there was a period when *de facto* became *de jure* ownership, when possession became property. 'The nature of man, the reason of the thing, the very existence of society, demand that such should be the case'. But the issue could not be finally settled if a former owner continued to agitate the issue. Any original defect in the title could only be resolved during a period of silence, 'or the passiveness, or the absence of any attempt to exercise proprietary rights, by the former possessor'.[68]

Vattel pursued a similar line of argument. He realised that there was a need to settle disputes over title. 'In view of the peace of nations', he remarked, 'the safety of States, and the welfare of the human race, it is not to be allowed that the property, sovereignty and other rights of nations should remain uncertain, and always furnishing cause for bloody wars'.

However, prescription depended on the occupation being both long continued and uncontested. Silence from a previous owner did not necessarily establish the required acquiescence provided he could

> set forth valid reason for his silence, such as the impossibility of speaking, a well founded fear *etc.*, because there is then no ground for the presumption that he abandoned his right. It is not his fault if a presumption has been formed to that effect, and he should not have to yield to it and can not be refused an opportunity of proving his title clearly. This method of defence against the claims of prescription has often been employed against princes who by their formidable power had for a long time reduced the weak victims of usurpation to silence.[69]

The Senate Committee did not, perhaps, fully appreciate that in Australia's circumstances prescription is a double-edged sword demanding both long exercise of authority and presumed acquiescence by prior owners. What is a sufficient display of authority and what is needed to counter claims of acquiescence are still matters of intense international debate. In the Australian context the continued assertion of sovereignty by government is clear enough. Less apparent, but still very real, is the Aboriginal resistance to that assertion of sovereignty. The 1983 Senate Committee heard evidence from central Australian Aborigines who argued that:

> Since 1788 our nation has been invaded by ever-increasing numbers of Europeans who, with superior weapons, have attempted to defeat our people and destroy our law and culture and seize, without compensation, our land. We have never conceded defeat and will continue to resist this on-going attempt to subjugate us. The crimes against our nation have been carefully hidden from those who now make up the constituency of the settler state . . . The Aboriginal people have never surrendered to the European

invasion and assert that sovereignty over all of Australia lies with them. The settler state has never recognized the prior ownership of this land belonging to the Aboriginal nation.[70]

The claim to Australia is still contested. The competing arguments are possibly irreconcilable, but the issues are not new. They were outlined in 1840 by the American jurist Twiss who observed that:

Title, then, by settlement, though originally imperfect, may be thus perfected by enjoyment during a reasonable lapse of time, the presumption of law from undisturbed possession being, that there is no prior owner, because there is no claimant—no better proprietary right, because there is no asserted right. The silence of other parties presumes their acquiescence: and their acquiescence presumes a defect of title on their part, or an abandonment of their title. A title once abandoned whether tacitly or expressly, cannot be resumed.[71]

6

LAW AND HISTORY

HOW WERE THE LEGAL PRINCIPLES under discussion worked out in the historical developments between the arrival of Captain Cook in Australian waters in 1770 and the early years of the twentieth century?

It is clear that in the eighteenth century the British considered that the normal procedure in establishing colonies was to negotiate with the indigenous people in question. Cook was instructed in 1768 to act accordingly: 'You are also with the Consent of the Natives to take possession of Convenient Situations in the Country . . . or, if you find the Country uninhabited take possession of it.'[1]

There was an obvious distinction between an uninhabited and a populated country. Cook's instructions for the voyage of the *Resolution* and *Discovery* in 1776 were similar:

You are also with the Consent of the Natives to take possession, in the name of the King of Great Britain, of convenient situations in such Countries as you may discover, that have not already been discovered or visited by any other European Power . . . But if you find the Countries so discovered are uninhabited, you are to take possession of them for His Majesty.[2]

The same principles were enunciated by members of the House of Commons Committee on Transportation in 1785 when they were considering the establishment of a penal colony in South-West Africa. They thought it 'highly probable that the Natives would, without Resistance, acquiesce in Ceding as much land as may be necessary, for a stipulated Rent'. They observed as well that the 'Portuguese and Dutch possessions on that Coast have been so acquired'.[3] The same principle was insisted upon by Britain in 1790 during a dispute with Spain over Nootka Sound in the north-west coast of North America. British negotiators demanded for their countrymen the right to form settlements 'with the consent of the natives of the country not previously occupied by any of the European nations'.[4] The British authorities returned to this principle in 1800, twelve years after the settlement of Sydney Cove. The Duke of Portland gave instructions to Lieutenant Grant before he embarked on a voyage on the *Lady Nelson* around the Australian coast which included the clause:

> He will take possession in His Majesty's name with the consent of the Inhabitants, if any, under a discharge of Musquetry and Artillery and to record the whole Proceedings at length both in his logbook and his Journal and if uninhabited to set up some proper description as first discoverer and Possessor.[5]

Why wasn't Phillip told to seek the 'consent of the Inhabitants' before he set sail for Botany Bay? The matter was raised in the crucial evidence given by Sir Joseph Banks to the 1785 House of Commons Committee on Transportation. The exchange included the following questions and answers:

> Do you apprehend, in Case it was resolved to send Convicts there, any District of the Country might be obtained by Cession or purchase?
> There was no probability while we were there of obtaining any thing either by Cession or purchase as there was nothing we could offer that they would take except provisions and those we wanted ourselves.
> Do you think that 500 men being put on Shore there would meet with that Obstruction from the Natives which might prevent their settling there?

Certainly not—from the Experience I have had of the Natives of another part of the same coast I am inclined to believe that they would speedily abandon the Country to the New Comers.[6]

It is impossible to be certain about how influential Bank's evidence was, although he was clearly seen as the most authoritative expert on Australia, but we can assess what he was saying from a legal aspect. The most critical points were that the country was 'practically' uninhabited and that the 'very few inhabitants' would leave the land chosen by the British for the colony which would become in a legal sense a *terra nullius* by abandonment.

Subsequent legal opinions suggested that the critical factor in the British decision to treat Australia as a *terra nullius* was its apparent lack of people, that it was as Banks wrote 'thinly inhabited even to admiration'.[7] This, after all, is precisely what the leading British legal authorities said in the generation after settlement. We can only assume they meant what they wrote in carefully drafted official advice to government. The Attorney and the Solicitor-General jointly advised the Colonial Secretary Lord Bathurst in 1819 that New South Wales had not been 'acquired by conquest or cession, but taken possession of by him as desert and uninhabited'.[8] The Colonial Office's own legal adviser James Stephen made the same observation three years later. The colony was 'acquired neither by conquest nor cession, but by the mere occupation of a desert or uninhabited land'.[9] The Privy Council's Lord Watson was drawing on an old tradition when he declared, in *Cooper v Stuart* in 1889, that New South Wales in 1788 had 'consisted of a tract of territory practically unoccupied, without settled inhabitants'.[10]

Subsequent accounts of British policy have suggested that there were other reasons for treating Australia as *terra nullius*. They usually relate to putative deficiencies of indigenous society. The country, one argument ran, was inhabited by 'scattered unorganized tribes' which had no recognised chiefs who could conduct negotiations with the Europeans.[11] An alternative interpretation was that the problem arose because the Aborigines were thought to be incapable of 'intelligent transactions with respect to land'.[12]

The difficulty with such assessments is that they were made after settlement had taken place and were repeated many times thereafter, gaining the status of received wisdom in the process. But in 1786 the British knew very little about Aboriginal society. Banks was asked by the Commons Committee in 1785: 'Have you any Idea of the nature of the Government under which they lived?'

He answered: 'None whatever, nor of their language.'[13]

Thus the officials who planned the First Fleet had no idea if there were chiefs in Australia with whom they could negotiate. Once the Fleet arrived the general assumption was that each tribe was led by a chief. This was the view of Phillip, Hunter and King as it was of the majority of early explorers, pioneer missionaries and ethnographers.

Given the fact that the members of Cook's expedition had no meaningful communication with the resident Aborigines they were in no position to judge whether they were capable of 'intelligent transactions with respect to land'. All that Banks had said was that the British had nothing to offer which the Aborigines valued. That was a different matter altogether.

A more general and historically sensitive explanation of British attitudes at the time is that contemporary European thinking suggested that peoples with simple technology of the sort observed in 1770 would be expected to lack political and social organisation. In British eyes the Aborigines

> had scarcely begun to develop social, political or religious organizations as the Europeans understood these. They had advanced so far from the absolute state of nature as to use language, and they discernibly lived in families. Of larger structures the [*Endeavour*] voyagers found no sign.

The Aborigines, historian Allan Frost explained, 'were simply too unEuropean' for the early explorers and settlers to comprehend.[14]

As an historical assessment there can be no substantial argument with this. It merely underscores the problem of advancing into the twenty-first century with a legal system whose foundations rest on the attitudes and values of men who were born before the middle of the eighteenth century.

When the British decided in 1800 to establish a settlement on or near Bass Strait they were given a second chance to define the legal status of the Aborigines. By then they knew much more about Australia.

Whatever view the British had of New South Wales in 1788, they did not consider Tasmania to be a *terra nullius* when they made the decision to colonise the island. The European expeditions which had visited the south-east coast from 1772 onwards reported that the island was well populated. By the time Collins arrived on the Derwent in 1804, the British had the benefit of considerable experience with the Aborigines. They had learnt that, while nomadic, the Aborigines confined their movements to specific territories which they regarded as their homelands. Collins himself had come to understand this while in New South Wales between 1788 and 1796. The various clans around Sydney Harbour were, he wrote, distinguished from each other 'by being found in particular residences'. 'Strange as it may appear', he observed, 'they have also their real estates'. 'Each family', he noted elsewhere, 'had a particular place of residence from which it derived its distinguishing name'.[15]

Collins had decided before he arrived in Tasmania that the legal position of the Aborigines had to be defined from the beginning of settlement. Soon after arriving on the Derwent he issued a General Order to the effect that the native inhabitants had been placed 'in the King's peace' so as to 'afford their Persons and Property the Protection of the British laws'.[16] Clearly the protection of property did not extend to the purchase of land in advance of settlement. But Tasmanian settlement was premised on the ideas of Vattel's *Law of Nations* which provided justification for the establishment of colonies in the New World while giving the strong message that the indigenous people were not to be dispossessed. The new settlers could establish themselves in part of the country but should confine themselves 'within just bounds'. The natives could be confined 'within narrower limits' but they were not to be 'reduced to want land'.[17]

What Vattel pointed to was a negotiated redistribution of land rather than a complete dispossession. This is indeed a thread which runs through the policies of Governor George Arthur during the 1820s. The language used in official correspondence recalls Vattel's own phrases. Secretary of State Huskisson wrote to Arthur in May 1828 approving Arthur's attempt to 'confine their limits' but warning that the 'restless character' of the Tasmanians would make it difficult to 'confine them to any particular limits within the Colony'.[18] Huskisson's successor, Sir George Murray, used similar language, accepting the policy of 'confining the haunts of the Natives to particular limits' but insisting that there should be 'no unnecessary harshness' used while confining the 'Coloured Inhabitants within the boundaries which you have fixed'.[19] The principles were clear enough, Arthur's problem was to apply them on the ground.

Early in 1828 he wrote to London explaining that he hoped to settle the Aborigines in some remote quarter of the island 'which should be strictly reserved for them'. The government would supply them with food and clothing 'on condition of [them] confining themselves peaceably to certain limits'.[20] He had begun to plan for this outcome a few months earlier. The Surveyor General and the Land Commissioners were requested to 'point out an eligible district' where the Aborigines could be settled and supplied with food.[21] The surveyors recommended the north-east coast 'as being the most advantageous situation'. They believed that the Aborigines themselves would prefer it to any other district 'on account of its being the best sheltered and warmest part of the island, and remote from the settled district'.[22] In his dispatches to London, Arthur explained that he intended to give up one district to the Aborigines, 'to allot and assign certain specified tracts of land, for their exclusive benefit, and continued occupation'. Application of the plan was to 'form a part of the intended negotiation' which he proposed to conduct with 'certain chiefs of aboriginal tribes'.[23] The contemporary historian and newspaper editor Henry Melville reported a conversation between Arthur and Black Tom, a 'civilized' Aborigine whom Arthur wished to employ 'as a negotiator'.

Tom asked the Governor what he intended to do with the Aborigines, to which Arthur replied, 'Make friends with them and tell them "I have given you all this part of the country" (pointing out a line on the map), to themselves, where no white man will go near them'.[24] Similar views were abroad in the community: the editor of the *Colonial Times* explained that the government had divided the colony 'into two parts', once side to belong 'to the English inhabitants, and the other, to the Aborigines'.[25] He argued that:

> The British inhabitants of Van Diemen's Land do not claim an exclusive property in the soil; the Government has taken care to fix certain boundaries, beyond which the Aborigines are perfectly secure, and furnishing an ample extent for all the purposes of that precarious subsistence to which they are accustomed.[26]

Fierce frontier conflict frustrated Arthur's attempt to arrange for a negotiated division of the Island. But even when he decided to impose a settlement by force the intention was to place the troublesome tribes on the two peninsulas—Tasman and Forrestier—in the south-east corner of the island. When the Aborigines were finally exiled in Bass Strait there was a clear understanding that Flinders Island was a new country provided by way of compensation for Tasmania. The agreement made between the Aborigines and George Augustus Robinson that resulted in them going to Flinders Island was, in effect, an unwritten treaty similar to written ones which were being negotiated at much the same time in North America.

Having lived through Tasmania's Black War Governor Arthur was keenly aware of the legal and political problems which arose from treating the country as a *terra nullius*. He believed that the way to avoid future conflict was to negotiate treaties with the Aborigines. His views are so pertinent to the questions at hand that they should be considered at length. In 1832 he became aware of plans to establish a new colony in southern Australia and wrote to the Colonial Office offering the fruits of his eight years' experience at the antipodes. It was, he explained, a fatal error in the first settlement of Van Diemens Land, that a treaty was not entered into with the natives, of which savages well comprehend the nature—had they received some compensation for the territory they surrendered—no matter how trifling—and had adequate laws been from *the very first*, introduced, and *enforced* for their protection, His Majesty's Government would have acquired a valuable possession, without the injurious consequences which have followed our occupation, and which must ever remain a stain upon the Colonization of Van Diemens Land.[27]

Arthur returned to the subject three years later in another letter to the Colonial Office. 'On the first occupation of the colony', he observed,

it was a great oversight that a treaty was not, at that time, made with the natives, and such compensation given to the chiefs as they would have deemed a fair equivalent for what they surrendered, a mere trifle would have satisfied them and that feeling of injustice, which I am persuaded they always have entertained would have had no existence.

His advice for the new colony was that:

Every effort, I submit, ought to be made, to come to an understanding with the Natives of Southern Australia before operations are commenced by the Emigrants, otherwise some cause of offence may unfortunately arise not less detrimental to the interests of the latter than subversive of that future goodwill, without which it will be impossible to prevent a long continued warfare in which the whites as well as the Aborigines gradually becoming more and more inflamed as their mutual injuries accumulate will destroy each other in detail.[28]

Contemporaries of Arthur advocated similar policies. The commandant of the military forces at the infant Swan River Colony Colonel F.C. Irwin argued in 1836 that all future dealings with the Aborigines should be governed by the treaties negotiated between the two parties.[29] In the same year the former Attorney-General of New South Wales Saxe-Bannister told a House of Commons Select Committee that: 'we ought forthwith to begin, at least, to reduce the laws and usages of the aborigines to language, print them and direct our courts of justice to respect those laws in proper cases'.[30]

Arthur's desire to see an 'enlarged plan of proceeding' which included purchase of land and negotiation of treaties was not incorporated into colonial policy nor was Bannister's idea of codifying Aboriginal law.[31] Such developments would undoubtedly have changed the character of Australian settlement and given a more secure juridical foundation to the colonial venture.

In South Australia, Governor Gawler referred directly to Vattel when seeking to explain the relationship between the settlers and the Aborigines. The Swiss jurist provided him with justification for settlement, Gawler quoting the passage which referred to hunters and gatherers and herdsmen who:

> usurp more extensive territories than with a reasonable share of labour they would have occasion for; and have, therefore, no reason to complain if other nations, more industrious and too closely confined, come to take possession of a part of their lands.

The establishment of colonies in North America was therefore 'extremely lawful' as long as the colonists confined themselves 'within just bounds'. Gawler believed that South Australian policies reflected the principles outlined by Vattel—the Aborigines had been 'confined' but they had been compensated. 'To the tribes whose territory has been occupied by settlers', he observed, 'the greatest liberality has been extended. Lands have been assigned to them for cultivation, clothing and subsistence have been furnished, and means have been taken to protect, instruct, and civilize them'.[32]

Before the Mabo judgement the traditional view was that when the British annexed the various parts of Australia in 1788, 1824, 1829 and 1879 the Crown became both the absolute sovereign and the beneficial owner of the land. In Mabo the High Court decided that the second part of that equation was wrong, that while the Crown gained the so-called radical title to the land, the indigenous people continued to maintain a legal interest in their ancestral territories which survived until it was formally extinguished. But the extension of sovereignty was not questioned—nor were the necessary implications of that development including the proposition that from the moment of annexation there was only one sovereign and one code of law in Australia.

How did this contention measure up with Australian reality? The greatest problem was that for much of the nineteenth century the colonial authorities controlled less than half the territory of the continent. When, in 1836, the Supreme Court of New South Wales declared that there was only one legal system in the colony the colonists were in occupation of less than half the land mass and almost certainly represented less than half the total population. While the claim of *external* sovereignty was not contested by any other country the assertion of complete *internal* sovereignty represented an ambition for the future rather than an objective achieved. Even in 1889, when Lord Watson re-affirmed the decision of 1836, there were many Aborigines who were yet to see the white people let alone accept their authority. The High Court conceded in Mabo that the Aborigines lost their land in a piecemeal fashion over a long period. Manifestly the same gradual process must have happened with the transfer of sovereignty. The hundreds of Aboriginal tribes that, in 1836, had no experience of Europeans continued to act as independent political communities—autonomous in their internal arrangements and free from outside control. There were far fewer independent tribes in 1889 and Aboriginal Australia had been considerably reduced in size but there were bands who remained beyond the reach of government until the 1960s.

The vast size and the nature of the Australian continent made nonsense of theories of sovereignty which emerged in the British Isles during the early modern period. At any time in the nineteenth century there were many sovereigns in Australia and many systems of law. The fiction of settlement by occupation allowed this reality to be overlooked, something which couldn't have occurred if it had been accepted that the British established themselves by cession or conquest. If colonial governments had sought to have Aboriginal communities cede sovereignty they would have been required to do the hard work of negotiation over a long time in all parts of Australia. Treaties or other formal agreements would mark the spread of British sovereignty and pin it down in time and space. Likewise with conquest—the defeat of Aboriginal tribes in battles fought over many decades would signal the moment when they individually lost their independence and were brought in under the reach of British sovereignty.

The air of unreality surrounding the prevailing legal and constitutional pretentions was apparent to clear-eyed settlers and more particularly those who spent time with the Aborigines. James Dredge, the Assistant Protector of Aborigines at Port Phillip, noted in 1845:

> Their present position now claims our attention, and here let it be observed that no change has taken place in the constitution of their national character, their civil relations one to another remain undisturbed; and although they have been taken under British power, and are declared subjects of the British Crown, it is entirely without their knowledge and concurrence—a matter which, it is verily believed, they have never yet been able to comprehend—no wonder they have failed to appreciate the privilege. Hence they adhere to, and consider themselves justified in, the use of their ancient customs *inter se*. [i.e. between themselves][33]

Dredge was writing about an area where European settlement had been established for a decade or more. The situation he described was typical of vast areas of the continent where pastoral occupation had occurred while Aboriginal society continued to function with little interference from the small resident European population. Typically the young men and women worked for the pastoralists for at least part of the year but the older people lived in camps where they had little contact with the white people. The two worlds existed side by side with only minimal interaction. Across the vast monsoonal areas of the north the wet season saw the 'station blacks' returning to their traditional lifestyle, often remaining out of contact with the Europeans for months on end. A similar pattern of movement into and away from the isolated European stations was apparent on many frontier missions.

The Aborigines continued to live in two worlds, subject to two laws, although in most outback districts the Europeans neither had the means nor the interest to impose their own legal system unless the Aborigines attacked white people or their property. In many areas of northern and central Australia Aboriginal law continues to run parallel with European law. A Pitjantjatjara man explained to representatives of the Australian Law Reform Commission in 1981 that there were two laws: the first was the 'law that belongs to here, to the land, to Australia, that is the law that was here first'.

The other law, 'the law from Canberra and Sydney from the courts, came over from England and it came here second, it came here a long time after the law here was strong'.[34]

Australian reality constantly tugged at imported theory. Even senior officials were sceptical of the doctrine of an all embracing sovereignty 'asserted without reserve'.[35] While considering how to define the limits of the new colony in South Australia in 1835 James Stephen wrote to his Minister Lord Glenelg:

> H.M. [His Majesty] is to fix the boundaries of the Province. How this is to be done in a Terra incognito I cannot imagine, nor how it can be done at all with any due regard to the rights of the present Proprietors of the Soil or rulers of the country.[36]

While the memo was an internal one not meant to be seen outside the Colonial Office it does reflect the private view of the most distinguished colonial official of the time. Clearly Stephen believed that in those areas of Australia which for the Europeans were unvisited *terra incognito* the Aborigines continued to be both owners and sovereigns, both 'proprietors' and 'rulers of the country'.

Some members of the colonial judiciary—notably Justice Cooper in South Australia and Justice Willis at Port Phillip—were sceptical of official doctrine. Cooper drew a distinction between Aborigines living in the 'settled' areas and those outside them. He believed that the law could be applied only to the 'native population as have in some degree acquiesced in our dominion' those who 'were in friendly intercourse with

119

the settlers—had partaken of their hospitality—and had acquired familiar English names'.

In the settled districts the British had 'assumed a dominion . . . in which the native prisoners appeared to have acquiesced'.

The position of Aborigines beyond the frontiers of settlement was quite different. He explained that they:

> must be considered as much strangers as Governor Hindmarsh and the first settlers were to the whole native population when they raised the British standard on their landing at Glenelg. And as I apprehend, no one would think of trying, according to the forms of English law, any of the native population who might have attacked the British settlement the day after its establishment, so I conceive that, by the same reasoning, it would be impossible to try, according to these forms, people who are now almost as much strangers to us as the whole native population were to the first settlers—a people, towards a political union with whom, no approach has been made.

He made his remarks with regard to the people of the Coorong who the Europeans knew as the Milmenrura tribe who were, he wrote,

> a wild and savage tribe whose country, although within the limits of South Australia, has never been occupied by settlers—people who have never submitted themselves to our dominion, and between whom and the settlers there has been no social intercourse. It is a maxim of the English law, that no person is subject to be tried by it who does not owe some obedience to it . . . I do not know how it can be said that the Milmenrura tribe owe any obedience whatever to the English law.[37]

While dealing with the same subject Governor Gawler pushed Cooper's proposition further, concluding that Aborigines in the remote parts of the colony had to be considered as independent societies which had to be dealt with by applying the law of nations. While addressing his Executive Council in September 1840 he sought to define the 'precise position in which the natives of this Province stand, in relation to the Government'. He argued that:

> The doctrine that they are to be held and dealt with as British subjects, and, under no circumstances, to be tried or punished, except according to the ordinary forms of our law cannot be received without modification. It may be true, in its full extent, as regards those tribes with whom we have constant and peaceable intercourse—for whose subsistence we provide—who acquiesce in, and acknowledge a friendly relation with us—and who are making advance towards civilization. To our intercourse with these, the ordinary forms of our Constitution and laws may be beneficially and effectually applied. The extension to them of the full rights of British subjects may be practicable, and attended with no evil result. But it would be assuming too much to hold that the same maxims and principles must be applied without modification to distant tribes inhabiting a territory beyond the limits of our settlements with whom we have never communicated under friendly circumstances, whose language is equally unknown to us as ours is to them, and who betray in all their intercourse with Europeans, the most savage and brutal hostility—who have never acknowledged subjection to any power, and who, indeed, seem incapable of being subjected to authority or deterred from atrocious crimes, except by military force. Nor can it be doubted that circumstances may occur, in which, for the safety of the colonists, and for the prevention of plunder and bloodshed, it may be necessary to view such tribes, however savage and barbarous their manners, as a *separate state or nation*, not acknowledging, but acting independently of, and in opposition to, British interests and authority.[38]

Thinking about sovereignty in Australia was influenced by two powerful ideas—the doctrine of *terra nullius* which suggested that the British became the first sovereign in a hitherto legal desert 'without settled inhabitants or settled law' and the view of sovereignty deeply rooted in the common law which was, as Blackstone argued, that in every polity there must be one 'supreme, irresistible, absolute, uncontrolled authority'.[39] But the application of these ideas in the antipodes created problems which are still unresolved. The common law view of sovereignty did not match that which derived from Roman jurisprudence and flowed from there into international law. The distinguished nineteenth-century jurist Sir Henry Maine drew a clear distinction between the British concept of the 'indivisibility of sovereignty' and the one derived from international law which held that the powers of sovereigns were 'a bundle or collection of powers' which could, and often were 'separated one from another'.[40]

Maine pointed to the many developments in European Empires which illustrated the point, an issue taken up by the English scholar W.E. Hall in his 1894 book *A Treatise on the Foreign Powers and Jurisdiction of the British Crown*. Hall drew attention to the disparity between contemporary legal theory and the practical realities of Imperial administration. While jurists spoke of indivisible sovereignty, constitutional arrangements indicated that it could 'scarcely any longer be seriously argued that the sovereign powers of a state are incapable of being divided between different persons or bodies of persons'. Evidence to the contrary was 'always plentiful' but the 'eyes of English lawyers declined to rest upon it'. Hall referred particularly to such 'complex colonial arrangements' as protectorates and spheres of influence where the division of sovereignty was manifest and various. 'If once it be granted', he argued,

> that sovereign powers are divisible, there can be no reason why the British Crown in the exercise of its prerogative rights, should not acquire a portion of the territorial sovereignty of a state or tribal community for the purpose of establishing a protectorate, in the same way as it can undoubtedly acquire the whole of such sovereignty by cession or conquest for the purpose of annexing territory to the Empire . . . In protectorates the exclusion of foreign states is the primary object; external sovereignty is therefore appropriated together with so much of the internal sovereignty as is needed to be its complement.[41]

In situations where British sovereignty was even more tenuous a sphere of influence could be established. It was a term which, when Hall was writing, still had 'no very definite meaning' attached to it but indicated

> the regions which geographically are adjacent to or politically group themselves naturally with, possessions or protectorates, but which have not actually been so reduced into control that the minimum of the powers which are implied in a protectorate can be exercised with tolerable regularity. It represents an understanding which enables a state to reserve to itself a right of excluding other European powers from territories that are of importance to it politically as affording means of expansion to its existing dominions or protectorates . . .[42]

Hall's outline of the complexity of 'colonial arrangements' is directly relevant to Australia and allows the development of a conceptual framework which brings legal theory far closer to colonial conditions than the assertion that Britain exercised complete sovereignty over the continent from the moment the various regions were formally annexed in 1788, 1824, 1829 and 1879.

Britain certainly claimed and exercised external sovereignty over the Australian colonies from the beginnings of settlement and no other power challenged that assertion, however, when it came to internal sovereignty the story was far more complex. At the beginning the colonial authorities exercised effective sovereignty over a tiny area which was under their direct control. Around the fringes of settlement sovereignty was exercised only occasionally and unevenly but vast expanses of the continent were, as James Stephen noted, *terra incognito* where the Aborigines were totally independent and sovereign but their territory could be thought of as coming within the British sphere of influence. The three bands of territory—which in effect were colonial possession, protectorate, sphere of influence—were unstable and as settlement expanded the first encroached on the second and the second on the third. The process has continued for most of white Australia's history and many would argue that it is still not complete.

Hall noted the fluid and changing circumstances which were common on the frontiers of the Empire. A sphere of influence was not 'in its nature a permanent relation between the European country and the native tribes'. It was a 'temporary phrase' which would inevitably give way to a situation where native chiefs would be subjected to 'steady influence and pressure'.[43]

While arrangements in various parts of the Empire provide interesting parallels and contrasts with the situation in Australia, it is necessary to look to North America for developments which are even more directly relevant to the legal theory of colonisation. The American courts were forced from the earliest times to consider the nature and justice of European claims to the New World, the rights of Indians and the troubled relations between them and the immigrants. The United States Supreme Court thoroughly sifted these questions in the first decades of the nineteenth century beginning with the issue of the rights which followed from European 'discovery'. In the famous case of *Worcester v Georgia* Chief Justice Marshall began with the proposition that before the arrival of the Europeans America had been 'inhabited by a distinct people' who were independent of each other and from the rest of the world, 'having institutions of their own and governing themselves by their own laws'. In a passage which cut to the core of the matter Marshall declared:

> It is difficult to comprehend the proposition that the inhabitants of either quarter of the globe could have rightful original claims of dominion over the inhabitants of the other, or over the land they occupied; or that discovery of either by the other should give the discoverer rights in the country discovered which annulled the pre-existing rights of the ancient possessors.

The court was realistic about the gap between the claims made by pioneer settlers and the charters they brought from Europe and the situation on the ground. It was an 'extravagant and absurd idea that feeble settlements made on the sea coast' acquired legitimate power to 'govern the people, or occupy the lands from sea to sea'. All that the settlers acquired was 'the exclusive right of purchasing such lands as the natives were willing to sell'.

Exploration and discovery conveyed far less to the European nations than has generally been thought to be the case in Australia. Marshall concluded that they were no more than a means by which the Europeans were able to determine their 'respective rights between themselves'. He declared that:

> This principle, acknowledged by all Europeans, because it was the interest of all to acknowledge it, gave to the nation making the discovery, as its inevitable consequence, the sole right of acquiring the soil and of making settlements on it. It was an exclusive principle which shut out the right of competition among those who had agreed to it; not one which could annul the previous rights of those who had not agreed to it. It regulated the right given by discovery among the European discoverers, but could not affect the rights of those already in possession, either as aboriginal occupants, or as occupants by virtue of a discovery made before the memory of man. It gave the exclusive right to purchase, but did not found that right on a denial of the possessors to sell.[44]

America was not considered to be a *terra nullius*, a legal vacuum. The Indians had both rights of possession over their land and sovereign rights to run their own affairs. The Royal Proclamation of 1763 declared that

> It is just and reasonable, and essential to Our Interest and the Security of Our Colonies, that the several nations or Tribes of Indians, with whom We are connected, and who live under Our Protection, should not be molested or disturbed in the Possession of such Parts of Our Dominions and Territories as, not having been ceded to, or purchased by Us, are reserved to them, or any of them, as their Hunting Grounds . . .[45]

While the Crown claimed sovereignty the native title of the Indians was respected. In *Johnson v McIntosh* in 1823 Chief Justice Marshall observed that they were 'admitted to be the rightful occupants of the soil, with a legal as well as just claim to retain possession of it'. It had, he concluded, 'never been contended that the Indian title amounted to nothing'. In fact, their right of possession had 'never been questioned'.[46]

In American law there was never any distinction between land under cultivation and territory used for hunting and gathering. Possession was not determined by the method of land use or the economic activities performed in a particular area. It was, Marshall declared, 'a matter of no concern' to the United States whether the whole territory was 'devoted to hunting grounds' or whether an 'occasional village, and an occasional cornfield interrupted, and gave some variety to the scene'.[47] Three years later he was even more emphatic, explaining in *Mitchell v the U.S.* that:

> Indian possession or occupation was considered with reference to their habits and modes of life; their hunting grounds were as much in their actual possession as the cleared fields of the whites; and their rights to its exclusive enjoyment in their own way or for their own purposes were as much respected, until they abandoned them, made a cession to the government, or an authorized sale to individuals.[48]

But it was not just rights of possession which the Indians held as a result of their prior possession. They also retained limited rights of sovereignty which survived from the era prior to the arrival of the Europeans. The Supreme Court determined in 1832 that the Indian communities were nations in the sense of being peoples who were 'distinct from others', which had been considered as 'distinct, independent political communities'.[49] They were not foreign nations but 'domestic dependent nations' in Marshall's famous phrase.[50] As such the Indian nations had political rights as well as native title, Justice McLean observing in *Worcester v Georgia* that 'all rights which belong to self-government have been recognized as vested in them'.[51] These assessments of the 1830s were confirmed in many subsequent judgements. In the 1885 case of *U.S. v Kagama* the Supreme Court determined that the Indians

> were, and always have been, regarded as having a semi-independent position when they preserved their tribal relations; not as States, not as nations, not as possessed of the full attributes of sovereignty, but as a separate people, with the power of regulating their internal and social

relations, and thus far not brought under the laws of the Union or of the State within whose limits they resided.[52]

A consequence of the status of being domestic dependent nations was that the British and United States governments accepted both that the Indians had systems of law and that they should be free to apply them without hindrance in their own communities. The relevant decisions in the Canadian and United States courts are of particular interest given that Australia at much the same time moved in quite a different direction. When dealing with the status of the Oneida-Iroquois in the New York Supreme Court in 1823 Chancellor Kent remarked:

> Do our laws even at this day, allow these Indians to participate equally with us in our civil and political privileges? . . . Do we interfere with the disposition, or descent, or tenure of their property, as between themselves? Do we prove their wills, or grant letters of administration upon their intestate's estates? Do our Sunday laws, our school laws, our poor laws, our laws concerning infants and apprentices, or concerning idiots, lunatics, or habitual drunkards, apply to them? . . . Are they subject to our laws of marriage and divorce, and would we sustain a criminal prosecution for bigamy, if they should change their wives or husbands, at their own pleasure, and according to their own customs, and contract new matrimonial alliances? I apprehend, that every one of these questions must be answered in the negative . . . They have always been, and are still considered by our laws as independent tribes, governed by their own usages and chiefs, but placed under our protection, and subject to our coercion, so far as the public safety required it, and no further.[53]

The question of whether Indian marriages could be upheld by American courts was discussed in the Alabama Supreme Court in 1845. The critical point was whether the laws of the Choctaw Indians had been superseded by any European law or whether they had become invalid merely by the fact that they lived within the territorial boundaries of the United States. Justice Goldthwaite observed that it was difficult to ascertain the precise period of time when one nation, or tribe, is swallowed up by another, or ceases to exist; but until then, there can not be said to be a merger. It is only by positive enactments, even in the case of conquered and subdued nations, that their laws are changed by the conqueror. The mere acquisition, whether by treaty or war, produces no such effect. It may therefore be considered, that the usages and customs of the Choctaw tribe continued as their law, and governed their people, at the time when this marriage was had. The consequence is, that if valid by those customs, it is so recognized by our law.[54]

A legal situation similar to that of *R. v Murrell* in the New South Wales Supreme Court came before the US Supreme Court in the 1883 case *Ex Parte Crow Dog* when it was decided that the murder of one Indian by another on a reservation was not within the jurisdiction of the courts. The court determined that to decide otherwise would be to extend,

over aliens and strangers; over the members of a community separated by race, by tradition, by the instincts of a free though savage live, from the authority and power which seeks to impose upon them the restraints of an external and unknown code, and to subject them to the responsibilities of civil conduct, according to rules and penalties of which they could have no previous warning; which judges them by a standard made by others and not for them, which takes no account of the conditions which should except them from its exactions, and makes no allowance for their inability to understand it. It tries them, not by their peers, nor by the customs of their people, nor the law of their land, but by superiors of a different race, according to the law of a social state of which they have an imperfect conception, and which is opposed to the traditions of their history, to the habits of their lives, to the strongest prejudices of their savage nature; one which measures the red man's revenge by the maxims of the white man's morality.[55]

The legal situation which arose on the frontiers of settlement when a small European population, both British and French, was living among numerically superior Indian tribes was discussed in the Quebec Superior Court in 1867 in the case of *Connolly v Woolrich*. Justice Monk concluded that the colonists carried their own law with them into the wilderness to the extent that it could be applied on the frontier. But that did not mean that Indian law ceased to exist. 'Will it be contended', he asked rhetorically,

> that the territorial rights, political organization such as it was, or the laws and usages of the Indian tribes, were abrogated—that they ceased to exist when these two European nations began to trade with the aboriginal occupants? In my opinion, it is beyond controversy that they did not—that so far from being abolished, they were left in full force, and were not even modified in the slightest degree in regard to the civil rights of the natives.[56]

The legal and constitutional situation of the Indians in North America did not protect them from loss of land and severe discrimination during the late nineteenth and twentieth centuries. In 1885 the legal independence of communities was sharply reigned in with the passage in Congress of the *Seven Major Crimes Act* which ensured that serious crimes committed on Indian reservations would be tried in federal courts. Eighty years later Congress passed the *Indian Civil Rights Act*, the object of which was to 'protect the individual members from arbitrary tribal action' by providing a range of protective measures.[57] But the doctrine of Indian sovereignty is still affirmed by the courts. Speaking of the *Indian Civil Rights Act* the Supreme Court observed that it was 'not intended that historical sovereignty of a tribe be abolished'. The clear inference was that: 'Congress left to Indian Tribal Courts jurisdiction over all crimes not taken by the federal government itself therefore Indian tribal Courts have inherent jurisdiction over all matters not taken over by the federal government.'[58]

The constitutional position of Indian nations was redefined recently in a case which re-affirmed their freedom from state taxes and regulations. 'It must always be remembered', the Supreme Court declared, 'that the various Indian tribes were once independent and sovereign nations, and that their claim to sovereignty long predates that of our own Government'.[59]

129

The very difference of United States legal and constitutional history, however, limits its direct relevance to contemporary Australia. Of greater interest are debates in Canada over the question of whether the Indians and Inuit, the first nations, have an inherent right of self-government.

Many of the issues under discussion to this point were canvassed recently in the case of *Delgamuukw v British Columbia* which was heard on appeal before the British Columbia Court of Appeal in 1993.[60] Of particular relevance to Australian jurists is the dissenting judgement of Justice Lambert who referred frequently to the Mabo case. Observing that the High Court had recognised the traditional land title of the Meriam people, Lambert concluded that his Australian colleagues had in the process affirmed what in Canada is known as the doctrine of continuity—the view that indigenous rights were grounded in the social, legal and political traditions which predated the arrival of the Europeans in North America. But Lambert believed that the Mabo judgement embodied implications which carried the question far beyond the matter of property rights. The decision, he believed, made a 'major contribution to an understanding of the Doctrine of Continuity and to other aspects of aboriginal title and aboriginal rights of self-government'.[61]

Given the relevance of this interpretation for Australian jurisprudence it is necessary to follow Lambert's line of argument with some care. He began with questions which are central to issues already canvassed above. The Indian nations concerned, the Gitskan and Wet'suuweten, had traditionally organised their social system in accordance with their own customs, traditions and practices which had produced 'an orderly society capable of managing its own affairs'.[62] The date when British sovereignty was asserted over Gitskan land was not easy to define precisely. It did not occur, Lambert argued, when Europeans landed on the coast and established small settlements there because sovereignty involved both 'a measure of settled occupation and a measure of administrative control'.[63] Even when sovereignty was extended into the interior there was no instant and comprehensive extinguishment of Indian law and custom in the manner suggested by Australian jurists. Lambert's reasoning pointed in quite a different direction. Indigenous local laws were not replaced but were incorporated into the common law and while the British had acquired the power to abrogate or alter them such an outcome could not be casually assumed. An overriding change in the situation of the indigenous people 'would only occur if it were brought about by a clear and plain intention to do so'.[64] The rule adopted by the High Court in relation to the extinguishment of native title—that the Crown must display a clear and plain intention to so act—has been extended in Canadian courts to include a far wider range of issues including the continuing right to self-government. The prominent Canadian legal scholar Brian Slattery argued that the Indian nations 'continue to hold a residue of the sovereignty they once possessed'.[65] In a similar vein Justice Lambert concluded that:

> Aboriginal rights, including aboriginal title, aboriginal hunting, fishing, gathering rights and rights of self government and self regulation, have their origin in aboriginal society and continue to exist after the assumption of sovereignty by virtue of the Doctrine of Continuity unless inconsistent with sovereignty or unless specifically extinguished.[66]

The legal doctrine in question runs parallel with the views of Canadian First Nation leaders who believe that their rights to internal sovereignty have never been lost. The Indian leader J. Mathias, while speaking on behalf of the Assembly of First Nations, informed a meeting of federal and provincial leaders in Ottawa in 1986 that:

> when we express the notions of sovereignty or sovereign title to our lands we emphasize that, prior to 1763, at 1763 and up to today, the chain of sovereign existence of our peoples has been unbroken; it continues now, comes to us from the past and it will continue in the future. The intervention of settlement in this country these past three or four centuries has not broken that sovereign existence of our people. Our point of departure lies in our basic understanding that we have no other way to relate to Canada except as sovereign people.[67]

Speaking on behalf of the Metis National Council, Clem Chartier told a similar gathering in 1983 that aboriginal title included the right to collective ownership of land, water and resources as well as 'a right to self-government, a right to govern yourselves with your own institutions'.[68] What the right might realistically include was outlined by the legal scholar Patrick Macklem who believed that a working definition of native self-government included,

> the need for a territorial base on native land, some forms of administrative and political structures and institutions for the airing of native voices and political decision making, the transfer of jurisdictional responsibilities from Parliament to native people, the ability of native people to organize their societies and pass laws governing their lives free from federal or provincial interference, and access to sufficient fiscal resources to meet these responsibilities.[69]

First Nation leaders and legal scholars have contributed to the recently completed Royal Commission on Aboriginal People which has called for a new understanding of constitutional law. Central to this new understanding is the recognition that Aboriginal peoples 'have the inherent right of self-government within Canada'.[70] But of more interest to Australians are the reasons which brought the Royal Commission to this position. The right is seen as being

> *inherent* in its source, in the sense that it finds its origins within Aboriginal communities, as a residue of the powers they originally held as autonomous nations. It does not stem from constitutional grant, that is, it is not a *derivative* right. The distinction between an inherent and a derivative right is not a mere matter of symbolism. It speaks to the basic issue of how Canada emerged and what it stands for. According to the 'derivative' viewpoint, Aboriginal peoples have no rights of government other than those that the written Constitution creates or that the federal and provincial governments choose to delegate. By contrast under the 'inherent' doctrine, Aboriginal peoples are the bearers of ancient and enduring powers of government that they carried with them into Confederation and retain today. Under the first theory, Aboriginal governments are new-

comers on the constitutional scene, mere neophytes among governments in Canada. Under the second doctrine, Aboriginal governments provide the Constitution with its deepest and most resilient roots in the Canadian soil.[71]

But the conceptual re-arrangement in Canadian jurisprudence reaches even deeper, disturbing the long standing legal doctrine regarding the acquisition of territory. The distinction between conquest and cession on the one hand and occupation on the other, which Australian courts have carefully preserved, has been blurred. Justice Lambert concluded that in all three cases of acquisition—by conquest, cession and occupation—the same rules applied in relation to the pre-existing indigenous law. Local custom, he asserted, was held to remain in force in the absence of acts to the contrary because the same rule applied 'regardless of whether the territory [was] deemed to have been acquired by conquest, cession, peaceful settlement, or in some other way'.[72]

There is, then, a wide gulf between Australian and Canadian jurists in relation to this question of the acquisition of territory. In Canada *terra nullius* has been overturned in relation to both property and sovereignty. In Australia it has been jettisoned in respect to the first but clung to in relation to the second. Brian Slattery recently discussed the theoretical basis for the survival of native customary law in Canada, including the inherent right to self-government. He explained that:

> when the Crown gained sovereignty over American territory, colonial law dictated that the local customs of the native people would presumptively continue in force and be recognizable in the courts, except insofar as they were unconscionable or incompatible with the Crown's assertion of sovereignty. In this respect, the rule resembles that applied in conquered or ceded colonies, where the local law is held to remain in force in the absence of acts to the contrary.[73]

In the Canadian discussions of the doctrine of continuity the fundamental inconsistency running though the Mabo judgement has been exposed. In their article 'Aboriginal Rights and Canadian Sovereignty'[74] Macklem and Asch work on the assumption that the indigenous people exercised sovereign powers before the arrival of the Europeans and that the belief that they lost them as a result of settlement 'ultimately rests on unacceptable notions about the inherent superiority of European nations' and does violence to such fundamental principles of the modern world as the assumed equality of peoples and their basic right to self-determination. They draw on principles enunciated in Mabo and turn them to new and unexpected ends. They find particularly pertinent the argument of Justice Brennan that legal doctrine must be judged by contemporary standards and that if

> founded on unjust discrimination demands reconsideration. It is contrary both to international standards and to the fundamental values of our common law to support a discriminatory rule which, because of the supposed position on the scale of social organization of the indigenous inhabitants of a settled colony, denies them a right to occupy their traditional lands.[75]

If it is unjust to deny a continuing right to occupy land, the Canadian scholars argue, why is it not equally unjust to deny indigenous people the right to preserve their inherent right to self-government? In a comparative article on Canada and Australia Macklem took the argument further:

> In Mabo, Brennan J. offers a passionate and persuasive critique of the injustice of the principles that the Crown became the absolute beneficial owner of all land at the moment of the assertion of Crown sovereignty. In his view, '[j]udged by any civilized standard, such a law is unjust.' Equally unjust, however, and for the same reasons as those offered by Brennan J., is the principle that the Crown acquires sovereignty over territory inhabited by an indigenous population by the mere act of settlement. The principle that the 'discovery' of lands inhabited by an indigenous population vests sovereignty in the 'discovering' nation is based on the proposition that indigenous people are insufficiently civilized or Christian to merit being viewed as competing sovereign powers. Fortified by the illusion of superiority, European powers claimed that the act of settlement in itself divests indigenous peoples of any and all sovereign authority over their land and their people.

Indigenous people became subject to the sovereign authority of the settling nation, despite the fact that they had ruled themselves (and presumably newcomers to their worlds) according to their own laws for centuries.

Just as it is unjust to deny the validity of Aboriginal rights with respect to land based on the fallacy of European superiority, it is also unjust to deny the validity of Aboriginal rights of governance on the same fallacy. Aboriginal rights of governance ought to be recognized as surviving the assertion of Crown sovereignty according to the same principle of justice governing the survival of Aboriginal rights with respect to land.[76]

7

SELF-GOVERNMENT, AUTONOMY AND TREATIES

IN AUSTRALIA THERE HAS BEEN little discussion in the courts about Aboriginal government but contending views jostle in the political arena. It must be said at the outset that a great many people reject the idea that any special constitutional provisions should be made for indigenous communities. So the focus must be on those who agree that the question is an important one but differ as to the means and ends to be pursued. Even amongst those who advocate some form of special political status for Aborigines and Torres Strait Islanders opinion arches across a broad reach of territory. Indigenous and non-indigenous advocates can both be found widely dispersed according to their stance but for ease of analysis they will be considered separately.

Most Aboriginal and Islander spokespeople reject the assimilationist idea that all Australians must have the same rights and loyalties while still accepting the protection provided by domestic statutes and locally ratified international treaties. They equally eschew the status of being just one more ethnic group in multicultural Australia with rights to cultural maintenance. Lois O'Donoghue, Chairperson of the Aboriginal and Torres Strait Islander Commission (ATSIC), takes the view that her organisation, the 'centre-piece of the government's policy of greater self-management and self-determination' has led to real empowerment for indigenous Australians which has been reflected in decision making, in funding, in a better knowledge and understanding of the bureaucratic system and the machinery of government, the power to negotiate, increasing acceptance by state and local government, greater recognition of ATSIC both by Aboriginal and Torres Strait Islander people and by the broader community, development of communications and a national and regional network which facilitates priority and decision making.[1]

While speaking on the reform of the constitution O'Donoghue called for formal recognition of the 'special status and cultural identity of indigenous people' and their recognition as the 'original occupiers and owners of this land'. Such recognition would 'set the record straight for all Australians' which for Aborigines and Islanders would 'clear the way for us to participate fully and equitably in the development of this nation, a nation that can be expected to address our needs and aspirations as first Australians'.[2]

The Aboriginal and Torres Strait Islander Social Justice Commissioner Michael Dodson travels in the same direction as O'Donoghue but goes much farther toward asserting a separate national identity. While addressing a 1993 conference on citizenship he declared in his opening sentence that indigenous Australians had two citizenships, 'one in relation to our indigenous nations, and one in relation to the Australian nation'. He continued:

For Aboriginal and Torres Strait Islander people, it is not just a matter of 'seeking to include us', or working out how to arrange the pieces on the board to construct 'the most desirable' Australian nation. We question the Board itself, and the basic rules of the game. If we are going to enjoy our rights, and more than that to survive as distinct peoples and cultures, creative new concepts and structures will have to be set in place.

We assert, and will continue to assert, that there are indigenous political and legal systems which must be recognised as having a place, whether that place be within the basic structures underlying so-called mainstream society, or parallel to that society. But the fact is that the foundations of the Australian nation exclude and fail to recognise those pre-existing social and political orders.[3]

In developing his argument Dodson moved along paths examined in some detail above, asserting that the general assumption that Aborigines and Islanders had 'at some time willingly, albeit implicitly', accepted the Australian state and the power to govern them did 'not apply to indigenous peoples'.[4] Turning from the past to the future Dodson powerfully argued the case for self-determination. In his 1993 report as Social Justice Commissioner he acknowledged that the 'crucial importance of self-determination' to Aboriginal and Torres Strait Islander people was little appreciated by non-indigenous Australians but that 'correctly understood, every issue concerning the historical and present status, entitlements, treatment and aspirations of Aboriginal and Torres Strait Islander peoples is implicit in the concept of self-determination'.[5]

Dodson rested his claim on the grounds that indigenous Australians had always possessed distinct identities and could, consequently, freely determine their political status and pursue their economic, social and cultural development.

Just as Dodson's views overlap with O'Donoghue's they also correspond with those of Michael Mansell, spokesperson for the Australian Provisional Government. There is a continuum from O'Donoghue's desire for special status within one nation, to Dodson's quest for national autonomy within the one state and on to Mansell's call for separate statehood and de-facto secession. Our people, Mansell argued,

> must be allowed to go beyond struggling for better conditions. The right to control ourselves on our own land without interference from others is a basic human right. To be and act as a nation of people independent of whites ought not to be a controversial issue but an entitlement. To impose our own laws in our own communities; to raise our own finances from our own portions of the continent; to have our own Olympic team and our own diplomats and passports is our right as a nation of people. Those rights are or should be the aim of our movement.[6]

The Provisional Government's model includes the objectives of creating

> a nation exercising total jurisdiction over its communities to the exclusion of all others. A nation whose land base is at least all so called crown lands. A nation easily raising its own economy which, based on Government figures would approximate $4 billion in royalties and lease payments alone.[7]

While the destination is clearly determined the way to reach it is poorly articulated and appears to be a combination of withdrawal from Australian Government authority inside the country and pressure solicited from the international community. Land-owning Aborigines would reject 'any authority purporting to exercise any rights over them, unless in the interim it is with the consent of the people'.[8] The process was further defined as proceeding from a political unification of land-owning communities which would form the 'developing Aboriginal Nations territory'. The strategy would be:

> to rally all Aboriginal people around a particular community which is seeking to reclaim certain areas of land. Following passive resistance by Aboriginal people to police efforts to remove them from those lands, control would eventually be conceded by the white authorities as being re-invested in the Aboriginal communities.[9]

Internationally the Aboriginal movement would seek to focus attention on Australia and to organise trade sanctions.

While the plans of the Aboriginal Provisional Government lack detail and substance there are many other groups, committees and organisations which are preparing blueprints for new political and constitutional arrangements.

The most creative thinking to date on the question of the constitutional relations between Aborigines and Islanders and the state can be found in a discussion paper titled *Towards Self-Government* produced after extensive discussions throughout Queensland by a five-member Aboriginal and Islander Review Committee established by the State Government.

The Committee's case for reform is similar to arguments in favour of 'inherent jurisdiction' advanced by the Canadian Indians and Inuit. The Committee advocates legislation which would enshrine the principle that 'there be a recognition of the pre-existing rights of Aboriginal and Torres Strait Island people to self-government'. This proposal arose from deeply held beliefs expressed repeatedly to the Committee, which reported:

> Aboriginal and Torres Strait Islander communities consulted by the committee had no doubt about the survival of their rights. The committee was often asked why the Queensland and commonwealth parliaments, and the Australian High Court, must be the ultimate adjudicators of Aboriginal and Torres Strait Islanders rights. The question is important because it highlights a fundamental issue relevant to Aboriginal and Torres Strait Islander self-government. Whatever the legal situation, Aboriginal and Torres Strait Island people do not regard any powers to govern which they exercise as being 'derivative', or originating from any mainstream government.

The proposed legislation would enable Aboriginal and Islander communities to opt, by referendum, to progressively assume responsibility for a wide range of matters including education, health, justice, social welfare, economic development, conservation, and cultural and language policy. Self-government would apply to existing communities which now have land rights and already have elected community councils. Details would be developed by each community in consultation with constitutional advisers. Therefore there could be significant variations between communities. What is being proposed is a comprehensive restructuring of the political system to give Aboriginal and Islander communities all the powers of existing local authorities, many of the powers of state administrations and some of those of the Federal Government.[10]

While the committee focussed on the details of community government they were, however, inevitably drawn towards the question of sovereignty, remarking that:

An obvious issue associated with self-government is sovereignty. Are the powers associated with independent nationhood, i.e. sovereignty, necessary? Aboriginal and Torres Strait Islander people have in recent times claimed sovereignty. If such a claim were recognised, the question of whether Aboriginal and Torres Strait Islander communities would in practise choose independence, instead of say arrangements with the Federal Government, regional autonomy, or local government is another question which is as yet unresolved by many Aboriginal and Torres Strait Islander communities. The Committe has chosen not to pre-empt Aboriginal and Torres Strait Islander community resolution of this practical question. The upper level of autonomy therefore is not determined in this discussion paper. It is an open question which inevitably hinges on community priorities, and also judicial rulings as to Aboriginal and Torres Strait Islander rights, the policies of Governments and fiscal realities.[11]

More recently the organisers of the Northern Territory Aboriginal Constitutional Convention put together a long document which is probably the most detailed and sophisticated case for self-government available to date. Given its importance it needs to be quoted at length. It was presented in the form of a series of questions and answers:

1. What is Aboriginal self-government?

    A process of redrawing the ancestral domain through the right of Aboriginal self-government. This is a fundamental human right of indigenous people.

    The inherent right of Aboriginal people to govern themselves is not beyond the capacity of the Federal Government to recognise and demarcate. It is simply creating a 'fairer' division of power and sovereignty. Particularly, in all areas Aboriginal people regard as important, over their members and over the lands and resources for which they have recognised jurisdiction.

    This can take the form of a government body/bodies in a given territory with jurisdiction and financial means to determine and manage governmental programs of importance, e.g. cultural, social, health, education and employment.

2. What are some of the important principles in the development of Aboriginal self-government?

   (a) Aboriginal people must design the principles;
   (b) Aboriginal people cannot rely on anyone except themselves;
   (c) Principles must concentrate on what happens in everyday life e.g. work, health, children, etc.;
   (d) Powers that cannot be violated by external governments;
   (e) Must reflect traditional ways;
   (f) Land Rights and self-government must mirror each other;
   (g) Must be able to control the future of the land;
   (h) Must be able to sort out the current forms with the traditional forms of government;
   (i) Equality and sharing amongst Aboriginal people;
   (j) Every aspect of self-government to be tied to our economic future;
   (k) The division of power starts at clan/land trust level.

In the long term negotiations of our fundamental human rights—which are as much issues for the Australian government as they are ours—the negotiating positions should be:

   (a) The United Nations draft declaration on the rights of indigenous peoples to be the starting point for Constitutional reconciliation, with:
       Constitutional entrenchment of the inherent right of Aboriginal peoples to self-government;
       Constitutional recognition of Aboriginal peoples as distinct societies;
   (b) Guaranteed representation by and for NT Aboriginal people in all Federal processes on the development of a Republic/Constitutional Reforms.

3. What are some of the important functions of self-government that need to be defined?

   (a) cultural preservation—the maintenance of traditional lifestyle, language and culture;
   (b) cultural adaptation—assisting a culture and community to change so that it and the individuals within

it can interact effectively with the economy and lifestyle of non-Aboriginal society;

(c) service delivery—the economic and effective provision to the community, in a form adapted to and suitable to its needs and circumstances, of services such as health, welfare, education, justice;

(d) economic development—the active involvement of the self-governing unit in projects and activities which improve the well-being of individuals and the community;

(e) resources and environmental management—Aboriginal control over the resources of their land base;

(f) land and enforcement—the relationship with the land and the judicial system.

The right to Aboriginal self-government evolves from original government, or indigenous self-determination.

4. What does Aboriginal self-government mean?

- Greater Aboriginal self-determination and autonomy;
- Owning the design of decision-making structures that are appropriate to the local situation, needs, and culture;
- Control and authority over internal affairs;
- Setting own priorities and determine policy, program design;
- Selectively taking on the delivery of services e.g. education, child welfare, social services, health, policing and justice, land and resource planning and environment protection.

5. What Aboriginal self-government does *not* mean?

- Full independence or sovereignty for Aboriginal people;
- The creation of a sovereign entity outside the boundaries of the Australian nation state.

6. What Aboriginal self-government should mean?

No single approach or model will meet the needs or aspirations of all Aboriginal people;

Each community should—

- determine for itself the form of government;
- process for establishing it;
- priorities and level of service.

Grants that contribute to economic development, e.g.—

- the fiscal arrangements should be compatible with the economic circumstances of the recipient community;
- funding for progress where the Federal Government is the agent of the national interest, e.g. health, job creation—grants conditional by agreement;
- priorities purely local in nature e.g. recreation, road maintenance supported by unconditional funding.

Having dealt with the purpose and function of Aboriginal government the anonymous authors of the document turned their attention to the question of how self-government could be negotiated.

(a) In the Mabo decision the High Court recognised Native Title under Common law. This could include Aboriginal political rights under that title—the right of self-government.

(b) The right to self-govern could be achieved through contracts, or treaty agreements of inter-governmental agreement—memorandum of understanding with the Federal government.

Aboriginal self-government could be created under sections of the Constitution which empowers the Federal Government to create:

self-government territories or states (without the requirement of a national referendum s. 121).

This would require a Declaration of Political Intent between the Federal/State governments and Aboriginal people which provides principles on which to base negotiations. It should include a target date for various agreements, and identification of sectors in which agreements are to be negotiated. However, specific self-government agreements have to be negotiated regionally.

Negotiation should be bilateral—Aboriginal people and Federal Government.

Implementation bilateral—Aboriginal people and Federal Government.

(c) Secured through constitutional entrenchment. The inherent right to self-government must be circumscribed—That is recognised co-existence with the Federal and State/Territory government as equal. Three equal levels of government. None is subordinate. It should be sovereign in its own sphere. Laws within the Aboriginal self-governing structure are not subordinate to Federal/State laws. No Constitutional reform should take place without the consent of Aboriginal people.

The concept of 'inherent right' stems from the simple fact that Aboriginal people already have a sophisticated system of government centuries before the arrival of Europeans. This right has never been relinquished. The traditions and practices of self-government in Aboriginal communities have never died. Aboriginal government derives from our history with our lands from time immemorial.

Recognition of the inherent right of Aboriginal self-government will provide a new framework and perspective between Aboriginal and non-Aboriginal people in the future. It will shift from 'asking' or 'demanding' to exercising rights already possessed. It requires a political commitment on the part of the Federal/State governments.

(d) The right to self-govern could be a part of a negotiated modern treaty between Aboriginal people and the people of Australia. The treaty could be the foundation of the new Republic of Australia in 2001. Under the treaty Aboriginal governments should be an independent and higher source of authority than the Federal Constitution.[12]

Indigenous communities have displayed growing interest in what are now known as regional agreements and see them as a way to negotiate with government and industry about a wide range of issues including land title and management, resource exploitation, environmental controls and delivery of services. Such agreements are particularly attractive to large and sophisticated organisations like the major land councils which feel confident in their ability to deal on equal terms

145

with white authorities. It seems likely that many of the advances in Aboriginal influence and authority will come as a result of a slow accretion of power at the local level. Sovereignty will return to indigenous society more quickly from the bottom up than from the top down. Regional organisations will grow in authority long before change arrives from the centre via legislation, litigation or constitutional change. A new level of government will emerge in the federal system whether the Constitution knows of it or not. What we will see is what Dr H.C. Coombs has termed 'bottom up federalism'.[13] Change may well come most quickly for those in the Torres Strait whose leaders have committed themselves to achieving regional autonomy by the end of the decade and the sort of free association with Australia that the Cook Islands enjoy with New Zealand. Getano Lui, the chairperson of the Torres Strait Regional Authority, is motivated by what he believes is 'an inherent god given right to self-government which comes from within'.[14] But the Islanders have approached the task with systematic care, commissioning consultants' reports on the economic and political viability of an autonomous region and sending delegates to the South Pacific and Norfolk Island to study possible models for a new relationship with the Australian state. In his 1993 Boyer Lecture, Lui explained the objectives the Islanders were pursuing:

> We need to be able to make decisions about social, cultural, economic, and environmental matters in our region, but not just the right to attend advisory meetings which may, or may not, pass our ideas up the line. We need a clear, legally enforceable regime of land and sea rights. We need real control of staff and office budgets, not the appearance of control as through ATSIC. We need the means and facilities to secure and develop our culture.[15]

Lui believed that if properly handled the drive towards autonomy could be an important success story for Australia 'and a proof to the Asia-Pacific region, and to European sceptics, that modern Australia has turned its back on the racist policies of the past'.[16]

The vigorous debate inside indigenous Australia about political and constitutional change has attracted little informed interest in the wider community. The Mabo decision and subsequent controversy has eclipsed other issues and property is much more tangible than sovereignty as a matter of concern. The small amount of research that has been done into community attitudes suggests that proposals for autonomy or for Aboriginal sovereignty meet with little understanding and less approval. A fair measure of support for such matters as land rights and cultural protection falls away dramatically when it comes to the question of self-government and autonomy.[17] But a number of non-indigenous academics and commentators have made important contributions to the unfolding debate about the future relations between Aborigines and the state.

In a recent book Dr H.C. Coombs has argued powerfully for autonomy which, experience has convinced him, Aborigines 'see as vital to their own personal existence'.[18] He does not think the pattern of self-government could be determined in advance but should emerge slowly from local meetings all over the country. 'What Aboriginal people want in this respect', he argued, 'must come out of regional meetings where, alone at that stage, they are in reasonable charge of what is happening'. The objective at the end of the period of negotiations, which could well take some years, would be:

> to reach an agreement about possible options for self deter-mination that would be put formally to the Aboriginal population. Such options could include agreed divisions of responsibility and powers between Aboriginal Australians and the Commonwealth on a regional basis, similar to those negotiated between the Commonwealth and the Northern Territory, the Australian Capital Territory and other terri-tories including Cocos Islands where diverse cultural groups exist.[19]

Following the completion of these long, bottom-up, negoti-ations Australia would have a mandate for an internationally recognised Act of Self-determination.

Professor Russell Mathews, Emeritus Professor of Econom-ics at the Australian National University, published a paper

Towards Aboriginal Self-Government in July 1993 which was a useful complement to Coombs's work in that it began with an outline of principles and objectives rather than with the process by which negotiations could be conducted. Coombs wrote with a view from regional Australia and from below, Mathews from the centre and from above. He listed what he considered were the principles and objectives of Aboriginal self-government. They were that:

Negotiations should commence with representative bodies such as ATSIC and the land councils to develop broad principles and objectives of self-government as a basis for detailed negotiations with particular groups. Those principles and objectives should cover such issues as the following:

- Recognition of the right of Aborigines to some form of self-government within the existing structure of Australian government.
- As with land claims, recognition that the Aboriginal right of self-government stems from their prior occupation of Australia and from a desire on the part of the non-Aboriginal population to redress past repression, injustice and deprivation. The special powers proposed for Aborigines must not be seen as providing a precedent for special treatment for other ethnic groups in Australia's multicultural population, since they chose freely to accept existing forms of government.
- Recognition that any self-governing territory will remain an integral part of the Australian federation and will not practise racial segregation.
- The extent to which the geographical area of Aboriginal land is to determine the legislative competence of the self-governing entities, and whether some form of Aboriginal citizenship . . . is to be adopted to extend the range of their powers outside their boundaries. Any Aboriginal citizenship should be consistent with continuing Australian citizenship for Aborigines and what that implies for the rights and responsibilities of Australians generally—both Aboriginal and non-Aboriginal.
- The basis on which responsibility for land tenure, land management and resource management is to be handed over to the self-governing entities, and the manner in

which resource revenues are to be collected and distributed.

- The respective rules of self-governing entities and other governments in promoting economic development and providing opportunities for employment growth and social progress.
- The constitutional and legal status of self-governing entities and their relationship to existing governments.
- The form and structure of institutional arrangements for legislative and executive government, for public administration and the public accounts, and for the administration of justice in the self-governing entities.
- The relationship between the powers of self-governing entities and the civil and economic rights of residents of their territories, both Aboriginal and non-Aboriginal.
- The range of legislative powers in the self-governing entities with respect to spending, taxing, borrowing, regulation of business and consumer activities, and administration of programs and services, including powers of delegation and of adoption of laws of existing governments.
- The financial relationship between the self-governing entities and existing governments, including the adjustments necessary when powers are transferred from the latter.
- The manner in which a financial settlement is to be achieved, including an undertaking by the Commonwealth to apply principles of fiscal equalisation to funding arrangements for the self-governing entities, with the objective of enabling them to provide comparable standards of services if they impose comparable levels of taxation.
- Transitional arrangements and a timetable to establish electoral procedures; put in place the institutions of government; provide the necessary training in the skills of government, administration and finance; develop procedures for the handing over of powers, programs and services, public sector assets and obligations of existing governments; and establish co-ordinating machinery where other governments will continue to deliver services or act in other ways on behalf of the new self-governing entities.

- Recognition that the system of self-government that is adopted must be compatible with the existing framework of government in Australia, which is based on principles of parliamentary democracy, responsible government, financial accountability, a federal structure with exclusive Commonwealth powers, and a judicial system one element of which is the common law.
- Recognition also that, without prejudice to the foregoing, the self-governing entities may wish to develop their own forms of government and systems of law, based on traditional approaches, provided that in doing so they respect the rights of both Aboriginal and non-Aboriginal persons and institutions as interpreted elsewhere in Australia.[20]

Although both Coombs and Mathews believe that change can be best secured through the normal political process it was inevitable that indigenous issues would become entangled with contemporaneous moves to reform the Federal Constitution. Many suggestions have been made as to how the Constitution could provide greater recognition to, and enhanced rights for, indigenous Australians. One of the more obvious changes advocated is for a new preamble: the Council for Reconciliation recommending that 'an appropriate new preamble' to the Constitution be prepared for submission to referendum 'to acknowledge the prior occupation, and continuing dispossession of Aboriginal and Torres Strait Islander peoples'.[21] ATSIC went one better actually suggesting the wording:

Whereas the territory of Australia has been long occupied by Aboriginal peoples and Torres Strait Islanders whose ancestors inhabited Australia and maintained traditional titles to the land for thousands of years before British settlement;

And whereas many Aboriginal peoples and Torres Strait Islanders suffered dispossession and dispersal upon exclusion from their traditional lands by the authority of the Crown;

And whereas Aboriginal peoples and Torres Strait Islanders, whose traditional laws, customs and ways of life have evolved over thousands of years, have a distinct cultural status as indigenous peoples;

> And whereas the people of Australia now include Aboriginal people, Torres Strait Islanders, migrants and refugees from many nations, and their descendants seeking peace, freedom, equality and good government for all citizens under law;
>
> And whereas the people of Australia drawn from diverse cultures and races have agreed to live in one indissoluble federal Commonwealth under the Constitution established a century ago and approved with amendment by the will of the people of Australia.[22]

The Reconciliation Council considered the idea of providing for dedicated seats in the Federal Parliament based on an indigenous electoral roll. During consultations with Aboriginal and Islander communities they uncovered significant support for the inclusion of a specifically indigenous Bill of Rights in the Constitution which would deal with such issues as cultural and heritage protection, access and equity issues, and also enforceable rights to health, housing and education.[23] But discussion of specific constitutional reforms eventually leads to the vexed question of whether there should be a treaty or some other document establishing on a new footing the entire relationship between the indigenous people and the Australian state.

The idea of a treaty was first promoted by a group of prominent non-indigenous Australians who formed an Aboriginal Treaty Committee and launched the cause in a full-page advertisement in *The National Times* on 25 August 1979. The signatories called for a negotiated 'Treaty, Covenant or Convention' which they believed should provide for:

(i) the protection of Aboriginal identity, languages, law and culture;
(ii) the recognition and restoration of rights to land by applying, throughout Australia, the recommendations of the Woodward Commission [into land rights in the Northern Territory];
(iii) the conditions governing mining and exploitation of other natural resources on Aboriginal land;

(iv) compensation to Aboriginal Australians for the loss of and damage to traditional lands and to their traditional way of life;

(v) the right of Aboriginal Australians to control their own affairs and to establish their own associations for this purpose.[24]

The question was taken up by the Senate Standing Committee on Constitutional and Legal Affairs which issued a report, *Two Hundred Years Later*, in 1983. While rejecting the idea of a treaty, because of its connotations of an agreement between sovereign states, the Committee was in favour of a compact to be eventually inserted into the Constitution by referendum. Members favoured this course of action because they appreciated there were, as discussed above, real problems about the issue of Aboriginal sovereignty:

> It may be that a better and more honest appreciation of the facts relating to Aboriginal occupation at the time of settlement, and of the Eurocentric view taken by the occupying powers, could lead to the conclusion that sovereignty inhered in the Aboriginal peoples at that time. However, the Committee concludes that, as a legal proposition, sovereignty is not now vested in the Aboriginal peoples except insofar as they share in the common sovereignty of all peoples of the Commonwealth of Australia. In particular, they are not a sovereign entity under our present law so that they can enter into a treaty with the Commonwealth. Nevertheless, the Committee is of the view that if it is recognised that sovereignty did inhere in the Aboriginal people in a way not comprehended by those who applied the *terra-nullius* doctrine at the time of occupation and settlement, then certain consequences flow which are proper to be dealt with in a compact between the descendants of those Aboriginal peoples and other Australians.[25]

Little followed from the Committee's report but the question of a treaty did not go away. In June 1988 the Prime Minister Mr Hawke visited the Barunga Festival in the Northern Territory and, in response to a petition presented to him by Aboriginal leaders, gave a commitment to a series of proposals which included:

Firstly, that there shall be a treaty negotiated between the Aboriginal people and the Government on behalf of all the people of Australia.

Secondly, that many Aboriginal people should decide what it is you want to see in that treaty.

The third step is that I have agreed that we should provide you with assistance to establish those consultation processes. In particular, that there should be a committee of seven of your traditional owners who will have the responsibility for organising those consultations with a view to organising an Australia-wide convention, which will represent the culmination of your own negotiations.

Fourthly, that when you have conducted these processes of consultations that we as a Government should then be prepared to receive and to consider the results of your thinking and your consultation.

And fifthly, we agree that these processes should start before the end of this year, and that we would expect and hope and work for the conclusion of such a treaty before the end of the life of this Parliament.[26]

The Prime Minister's temporary enthusiasm for a negotiated agreement soon dissipated. Sporadic discussion of the question since had not advanced the cause to any appreciable extent although the Council for Aboriginal Reconciliation, established by legislation in 1991, has been charged with the task of determining whether any document of reconciliation would 'benefit the Australian community as a whole'.[27]

The implications of negotiating a treaty stretch well beyond the Australian community. Opponents of the idea argue that only nation states have international standing and are capable of entering into treaties. Supporters of the proposal point to the long tradition of treaty making in Canada and the USA and argue that the international community will take a close interest in local developments. The international jurist Garth Nettheim remarked in 1989 that:

any progress towards an Australian treaty (or treaties) will proceed not in a national vacuum but in the context of a rapidly developing set of international principles on the rights of indigenous peoples and an emerging international interest in the effectiveness and equity of such treaties.[28]

It is time, then, to consider the international principles which apply to the indigenous people of the world. Their significance for developments within Australia are little understood.

8

NATIONS AND STATES IN INTERNATIONAL LAW AND POLITICS

IN THE HIGH COURT CASE of *Coe v the Commonwealth*, discussed in chapter 1, Justice Jacobs observed that questions about the sovereignty of the Crown and the legal status of indigenous Australians were as much matters of international as of domestic law.[1] Indeed, international law flows into Australia through many channels and for their part Aborigines and Islanders have sought to pursue their objectives outward into the international community utilising the same conduits. There has always been an international dimension to the political relationship between Aborigines and the colonists and their Australian born descendants, although for a long time it was mainly confined to an imperial-colonial context within the overarching Empire.

During the 1830s and 1840s the Colonial Office attempted to provide some protection for the Aborigines against the worst excesses of the frontier and continued to do so in Western Australia up to and even after the granting of responsible government in 1890.[2] Aborigines and their humanitarian supporters frequently appealed to the British Government, to missionary and human rights organisations and beyond them to public opinion at 'Home'. As early as 1846 a group of Tasmanian Aborigines living on Flinders Island petitioned the Queen seeking redress for a cluster of grievances.[3] It was the first of many such petitions presented over the following 130 years. Colonists who were disturbed by the violence and brutality of the frontier appealed to Britain for sympathy and support. A correspondent writing in the *Port Phillip Gazette* in 1840 warned his contemporaries that the 'tale of Aboriginal wrongs' was well-known overseas. 'The eyes of England are upon us', he declared.[4] In the same year a South Australian clergyman wrote to members of the Anti-Slavery Society in London informing them that 'if there were not the dread of things being enquired into in England the Natives would be far worse treated than they are'.[5] Almost a hundred years later the feminist and human rights activist M.M. Bennett contacted the same organisation with the plea: 'The only help for our poor natives that there is comes from knowledge and public opinion in England. Australians are sensitive about that.'[6]

Since the Second World War specific concern about British opinion may have diminished but there remains a keen sense that the eyes of the world are upon us. It was a view expressed powerfully by Gough Whitlam in 1973 when he warned the community that: 'Australia's treatment of her Aboriginal people will be the thing upon which the rest of the world will judge Australia and Australians—not just now, but in the greater perspective of history.'[7]

With the establishment of the League of Nations after the First World War indigenous affairs began to move beyond the narrow valley of Imperial-Dominion relations and into the broad estuary of international politics. Article 236 of the League Covenant obliged member nations to undertake to secure just treatment of the native inhabitants of the territories under their control. Australia, however, used all its limited diplomatic clout to prevent the incorporation in the Covenant of further and more specific commitments to racial equality and the rights of indigenous minorities. In his Draft Covenant of January 1919, American President Woodrow Wilson included a paragraph which provided that the League would:

> require all new states to bind themselves as a condition precedent to their recognition as independent or autonomous states, to accord to all racial or national minorities within their jurisdiction exactly the same treatment and

security, both in law and in fact, that is accorded the racial or national majority of their people.[8]

The paragraph was ultimately rejected as a result of the strenuous opposition of the British delegation, which was caused in turn by 'the adamant stand' of the Australian and New Zealand prime ministers who were concerned that the 'propriety of the treatment of their Aboriginal and Maori population might come under scrutiny'.[9]

But while no general provision regarding racial equality was incorporated in the Covenant the League was interested in the general question of the rights of national minorities especially in central and eastern Europe, a concern which found expression in 25 so-called Minority Treaties signed between 1919 and 1934. In a recent study, W. McKean observed that as well as providing for non-discrimination 'racial, religious and linguistic minorities' were accorded special rights in the various treaties including the following:

(a) the right to use their own language in private inter-course, in commerce, in religion, in the press or in publications, or at public meetings;
(b) the right to have separate educational establishments;
(c) the right to possess their own religious and charitable institutions;
(d) the right to have an equitable share in the enjoyment of public funds;
(e) certain specific stipulations with regard to respect for the sabbath for Jews, family law, and rights for Muslims;
(f) certain traditional rights and, occasionally, a limited autonomy.[10]

Meanwhile, the International Court of Justice set down a number of basic principles concerning minority groups during the 1920s and 1930s. In the case *Minority Schools in Albania* of 1935 the court outlined the rights which should be accorded to national minorities (in this case Greek) which lived in enclaves within the boundaries of states dominated by a majority alien to them in language, culture and traditions. It was a classic statement of group rights emphasising that the idea underlying the Minority Treaties was to secure for certain elements incorporated in a State, the population of which differs from them in race, language or religion, the possibility of living peaceably alongside that population and in co-operating amicably with it, while at the same time preserving the characteristics which distinguish them from the majority, and satisfying the ensuing special needs.

In order to attain this object, two things were regarded as particularly necessary, and have formed the subject of provisions in these treaties.

The first is to ensure that nations belonging to racial, religious or linguistic minorities shall be placed in every respect on a footing of perfect equality with the other nationals of the State.

The second is to ensure for the minority elements suitable means for the preservation of their racial peculiarities, their traditions and their national characteristics.

These two requirements are indeed closely interlocked, for there would be no true equality between a majority and a minority if the latter were deprived of its own institutions, and were consequently compelled to renounce that which constitutes the very essence of its being as a minority.[11]

When the League was superseded by the United Nations the emphasis shifted from the group-rights approach to the protection of individuals on the basis of universal human rights. In his recent book *Group Rights and Discrimination in International Law*, N. Lerner observed that the new approach was that whenever someone's rights were violated or restricted 'because of a group characteristic' the matter could be dealt with by protecting the rights of the individual in question on 'a purely individual basis, mainly by the principle of non-discrimination'.[12]

Inevitably, however, issues arose which specifically affected indigenous and other minority groups. The Genocide Convention of 1948, for instance, embodied a right of physical and cultural survival. The UNESCO Convention Against Discrimination in Education of 1960 provided protection for the education of children of minority groups. Under Article 5 the member states agreed that:

- It is essential to recognize the right of members of national minorities to carry on their own educational activities, including the maintenance of schools and, depending on the educational policy of each State, the use or the teaching of their own language, provided however:
- That this right is not exercised in a manner which prevents the members of these minorities from understanding the culture and language of the community as a whole and from participating in its activities, or which prejudices national sovereignty;
- That the standard of education is not lower than the general standard laid down or approved by the competent authorities; and
- That attendance at such schools is optional.[13]

The United Nations moved closer to enunciating a more general inventory of group rights in Article 27 of the 1966 International Covenant of Civil and Political Rights, which reads:

> In those States in which ethnic, religious or linguistic minorities exist, persons belonging to such minorities shall not be denied the right, in community with the other members of their group, to enjoy their own culture, to profess and practice their own religion, or to use their own language.[14]

The International Labour Organisation (ILO) was the first body to directly address the issue of indigenous rights by way of Convention 107 of 1957 which recognised both the right to ownership over traditional lands and to compensation when it was expropriated. However, the document reflected the time of its creation and was strongly assimilationist in tone, Article 7 declaring that: 'These populations shall be allowed to retain their own customs and institutions where they are not incompatible with the national legal system or the objectives of integration programmes.'[15]

In 1989 the ILO significantly modified its view of the rights and standing of indigenous people and in Article 5 of Convention 169 recognised and respected the 'social, cultural, religious and spiritual values and practices' of both individuals and communities.[16]

By that time the question of indigenous rights had assumed a much higher profile in international law and practice. A 1978 United Nations Conference on Racism urged member states to recognise the following rights of indigenous people:

(a) To call themselves by their proper name and to express freely their ethnic, cultural and other characteristics;

(b) To have an official status and to form their own representative organisations;

(c) To carry on within their areas of settlement their traditional structure of economy and way of life; this should in no way affect their right to participate freely on an equal basis in the economic, social and political development of the country.

(d) To maintain and use their own language, wherever possible, for administration and education;

(e) To receive education and information in their own language, with due regard to their needs as expressed by themselves, and to disseminate: information regarding their needs and problems.[17]

The United Nations Sub-Commission on Prevention of Discrimination commissioned a report on discrimination against indigenous populations that was published in 1986 and included a widely used definition of indigenous groups as those which

having a historical continuity with pre-invasion and pre-colonial societies that developed on their territories, consider themselves distinct from other sectors of the societies now prevailing in those territories, or parts of them. They form at present non-dominant sectors of society and are determined to preserve, develop and transmit to future generations their ancestral territories, and their ethnic identity, as the basis of their continued existences as peoples, in accordance with their own cultural patterns, social institutions and legal systems.[18]

But the most important initiative of the United Nations was the establishment in 1982 of a Working Group on Indigenous Populations. From 1985 the Group has worked on the compilation of a Declaration on Indigenous Rights which was eventually finalised and presented to the UN Commission on Human Rights in July 1994. The Declaration still faces a rigorous process of assessment, however, as it passes slowly forward within the UN bureaucracy. The expectation is that a final draft will be passed by the General Assembly in 2002, the end of the International Decade of the World's Indigenous People. Despite the hurdles that remain to be overcome the draft Declaration is an important statement of indigenous rights. Australian international law expert Sarah Pritchard believes it represents 'the beginning of indigenous empowerment through international law'.[19]

The Declaration has 45 Articles covering a wide range of rights which are thought to constitute 'the minimum standards for the survival, dignity and well-being of the indigenous peoples of the world'. Among the more important Articles are the following:

Article 4

Indigenous peoples have the right to maintain and strengthen their distinct political, economic, social and cultural characteristics, as well as their legal systems, while retaining their rights to participate fully, if they so choose, in the political, economic, social and cultural life of the State.

Article 7

Indigenous peoples have the collective and individual right not to be subjected to ethnocide and cultural genocide, including prevention of and redress for:

(a) Any action which has the aim or effect of depriving them of their integrity as distinct peoples, or of their cultural values or ethnic identities;
(b) Any action which has the aim or effect of dispossessing them of their lands, territories or resources;
(c) Any form of population transfer which has the aim or effect of violating or undermining any of their rights;
(d) Any form of assimilation or integration by other cultures or ways of life imposed on them by legislative, administrative or other measures;

(e) Any form of propaganda directed against them.

Article 8

Indigenous peoples have the collective and individual right to maintain and develop their distinct identities and characteristics, including the right to identify themselves as indigenous and to be recognized as such.

Article 9

Indigenous peoples and individuals have the right to belong to an indigenous community or nation, in accordance with the traditions and customs of the community or nation concerned. No disadvantage of any kind may arise from the exercise of such a right.

Article 21

Indigenous peoples have the right to maintain and develop their political, economic and social systems, to be secure in the enjoyment of their own means of subsistence and development, and to engage freely in all their traditional and other economic activities. Indigenous peoples who have been deprived of their means of subsistence and development are entitled to just and fair compensation.

Article 26

Indigenous peoples have the right to own, develop, control and use the lands and territories, including the total environment of the lands, air, waters, coastal seas, sea-ice, flora and fauna and other resources which they have traditionally owned or otherwise occupied or used. This includes the right to the full recognition of their laws, traditions and customs, land-tenure systems and institutions for the development and management of resources, and the right to effective measures by States to prevent any interference with, alienation of or encroachment upon these rights.

Article 27

Indigenous peoples have the right to the restitution of the lands, territories and resources which they have traditionally owned or otherwise occupied or used, and which have been confiscated, occupied, used or damaged without their free and informed consent. Where this is not possible, they have the right to just and fair compensation. Unless otherwise freely agreed upon by the peoples concerned, compensation shall take the form of lands, territories and resources equal in quality, size and legal status.

Article 31

Indigenous peoples, as a specific form of exercising their right to self-determination, have the right to autonomy or self-government in matters relating to their internal and local affairs, including culture, religion, education, information, media, health, housing, employment, social welfare, economic activities, land and resources management, environment and entry by non-members, as well as ways and means for financing these autonomous functions.[20]

A central theme of the Declaration is the right of self-determination. It is such an important question that it demands closer investigation. This will take us across much disputed, frequently crossed terrain back to the foundation documents of the United Nations including the Charter which refers in Articles 1(2) and 55 to 'the principle of equal rights and self-determination of peoples'.[21] The matter was picked up again in General Assembly Resolution 1514 in 1960 which declared: 'All peoples have the right to self-determination; by virtue of that right they freely determine their political status and freely pursue their economic, social and cultural development.'[22]

The same wording was used in both the International Covenant on Civil and Political Rights and the International Covenant on Economic, Social and Cultural Rights adopted in 1966. But with such sweeping declarations many questions are left unanswered. Who in 1966 were the 'peoples' who could demand the right of self-determination? Who could the demand be directed against?

The target was the remnants of European empires; the beneficiaries the remaining colonies—territories which were 'geographically separate' and distinct 'ethnically and/or culturally' from the country administering them.[23] Self-determination was not designed for the great variety of 'peoples' who found themselves within the borders of the new states or for indigenous minorities in New World settler societies.

Existing borders were to be protected against would-be secessionists; stability was sacrosanct. This was made clear in numerous UN documents including the 1970 *Declaration on Principles of Internal Law Concerning Friendly Relations and Co-operation Among States*. The document declared that all people had the right to freely determine their political status and pursue their economic, social and cultural development, and called on all states to 'bring a speedy end to colonialism' bearing in mind that 'subjection of peoples to alien subjugation, domination and exploitation' constituted a violation of the principle of self-determination. For all the fine words about the rights of people, however, it was the needs of states which took precedence. Following on the heels of the declaration about the will of people came the crushing coda:

> Nothing in the foregoing paragraphs shall be construed as authorizing or encouraging any action which would dismember or impair, totally or in part the territorial integrity or political unity of sovereign and independent States conducting themselves in compliance with the principle of equal rights and self-determination of peoples as described above and thus possessed of a government representing the whole possible belonging to the territory without distinction as to race, creed or colour.
>
> Every State shall refrain from any action aimed at the partial or total disruption of the national unity and territorial integrity of any other State or country . . .
>
> The territorial integrity and political independence of the State are inviolable.[24]

How can the need of states for stability and secure borders ever be reconciled with the proclaimed right of peoples to self-determination? At first glance it appears to be an impossible task. There are, after all, so many more peoples than states. It is estimated that there are 5000 discrete ethnic or national groupings in the world and there are less than 200 states.[25] Leaders of states seek to contain demands for self-determination and to head off any attempted secession but the idea is igniting imaginations all over the world. 'The idea of a state for every people', M.D. Levin observed in his recent book *Ethnicity and Aboriginality*, 'is a prime mover in late twentieth century politics'. In uniting in one concept a goal of such apparent simplicity 'and an ideal of universal application', 'it has achieved an incomparable capacity to capture the popular imagination . . .'.[26] In all areas of the globe, the legal scholar S.J. Anaya noted, 'segments of humanity are clinging to bonds of race, language, religion, kinship and custom and are projecting those bonds into the political future'.[27] Those states which took their independence from the European empires, marching forward under the banner of self-determination, now find themselves the target of similar demands from behind their backs and made from within their own borders. Enclave indigenous populations rally to the same cry and call for decolonisation to pervade their domains. 'Indigenous people', the Canadian scholar Douglas Sanders argued, 'have some right to decolonisation'.[28] His Danish colleague Frederik Harhoff observed that at least a significant level of political autonomy for indigenous people was required for 'full and final completion of the post-war decolonization process'.[29]

Those who push the cause of self-determination forward seek to outflank the imposing road blocks of fixed borders, state sovereignty and international stability. They advance from the secure outpost of the need for cultural survival recognised in Article 27 of the Covenant of Civil and Political Rights and thrust forward the argument that political autonomy is essential for the preservation of cultures and traditions. 'Self-determination', the American legal scholar Mary Ellen Turpel insisted, was 'synonymous with self-preservation for indigenous people'.[30] Douglas Sanders agreed, arguing succinctly:

> Indigenous peoples are cultural minorities. Cultural minorities require some autonomy to maintain and develop their distinctiveness. Particularly for indigenous peoples, where cultural difference is often very great, this requires autonomy or self-government.[31]

The nexus lacing together self-government and cultural survival was drawn even more tautly by the United Nations 1987 paper by Jose Cobo entitled *Study of the Problems of Discrimination Against Indigenous Populations*. Cobo argued that self-government was

an inherent part of their cultural and legal heritage which
has contributed to their cohesion and to the maintenance
of their social and cultural tradition . . . Self-determination,
in its many forms, is thus a basic pre-condition if indigenous
peoples are to be able to enjoy their fundamental rights and
determine their future, while at the same time preserving,
developing and passing on their specific ethnic identity to
future generations.[32]

A minority of scholars and activists favour secession as a
solution to the vexed problem of nations and states and look
forward to the proliferation of many small new states. 'The
organization that endures best among human beings', Rudolph
Ryser argued, is the small group 'ranging in size from perhaps
four hundred individuals to not more than a few hundred
thousand'. Such small communities or nations are the 'most
successful unit of human organization'. Consequently, the
natural diversity of peoples should be reflected in the 'multi-
plicity of small states'.[33] In a similar vein, the philosopher T.W.
Pogge has recently spoken of the need to disperse political
authority widely 'over nested territorial units'. Borders could
be re-drawn to more easily 'accord with the aspirations of
peoples and communities'. As a consequence, the intensity of
the struggle for wealth and power between states would
decrease, thereby reducing the incidence of war, poverty, and
oppression.[34] The English scholar John Keane has pursued the
same theme of radical decentralisation in relation to Western
Europe but his ideas have implications for indigenous people
in other parts of the world. He called for a 'decentring' of
the nation state downwards and sideways, for a 'scattering' of
political power among a variety of smaller political units with
a return to the situation of the early modern period when
Western Europe contained 500 political units of varying types
and sizes.[35] In a recent book, Allen Buchanan has outlined a
liberal argument in favour of secession arguing that if we begin
'with a general presumption in favor of liberty' it carries with
it a presumption 'in favor of a right to secede'. Such a right
is the 'logical extension of liberty' it carries with it a presumption 'in favor of a principle of toleration thought to be central

to the liberal point of view'.[36] Following a similar line of thought the American scholar Robert McGee urged that the pertinent question was not whether secession was justified but rather: 'Does a group of individuals who dislike their present government ever *not* have the right to reject that government and form one that is more to the group's liking?'[37] [emphasis in the original]

Support for secession has come also from scholars adopting a communitarian rather than a liberal standpoint. In a recent article in the *Journal of Philosophy* Magalit and Raz argue that political independence is of critical importance for what they call 'encompassing groups' and the well-being of individuals depends in turn on the welfare of the collective. 'The importance of encompassing groups to the lives of their members', they argue, 'means that there is a strong, if indirect link between communal prosperity and individual well being'. As a result, any encompassing group should have the right to determine the status of a territory where it makes up a majority of the population.[38]

Relatively few commentators, however, are sanguine about the process or confident about the consequences of secession. The history of such movements teaches harsh and brutal lessons. Anthony Smith, the leading contemporary historian of nationalist movements, has written of the difficulties which confront emerging would-be nationalist movements. The world of nations, he argues, is 'a jealous one'. It is also pre-emptive. Earlier nationalisms 'do no easily tolerate derived or secondary nationalisms . . . within their desired borders'. Any 'late comer ethnic identity' faces great difficulties in gaining recognition and 'breaking out of the existing state system'. The fires of their nationalist aspirations 'waste themselves upon the iron grid of the inter-state system'.[39] Other writers offer an even grimmer prognosis about secessionist movements. In a recent book *Secessionist Movements in Comparative Perspective*, R.R. Primdas observed that the secessionists' demands for territorial autonomy 'is only reluctantly relinquished by an antecedent state. Bloodshed, chaos and suffering tend to accompany the birth of the secessionist child'. He argued:

Should it succeed, a secessionist movement legitimates its claim to an autonomous territorial survival on the 'natural right' as a unique nation to determine its destiny. Self-determination of nationality groups is an enshrined sacred right. But rights are never unequivocal and unrestrained. The right to secede and determine a group's destiny is asserted in diametrical opposition to another sacred right, that of a state to safeguard its sovereignty and territorial integrity. The latter is also a right sanctioned by the United Nations. Secession, then, is not an uncontested moral claim made in a vacuum and yielded to without argument and challenge. Its success, it seems, depends less on an inscrutable moral imperative and more on superior physical power and unsurrendering persistence. The right to secede is as valid as the capability of forcibly wresting territory and people from another state. No state dismembers itself willingly; no separatist movement has been proffered victory on a platter.[40]

Whether welcomed or not, few observers doubt the potent impact of what has variously been called the 'ethnic revival' or the rise of 'post-modern tribalism'. It contains, according to Walker Conner, the seeds 'of a radical re-drawing of today's political map'.[41] For Alfred Cobban the basic difficulty with self-determination is that if the world opens the door to secession 'even to a limited extent' how will it be possible to prevent it from being flung wide open? 'If self-determination means this kind of thing', he warned darkly, 'where, and with what unit, can the process possibly stop?'[42] Anthony Smith believes that ethnic conflicts 'are undoubtedly the most intractable of all' because they involve 'so much more than a mere redrawing of the political map'. To run with the cause of ethnic nationalism would leave 'no state untouched' and would 'drastically alter the composition and mode of governing most states in the modern world'.[43] Not all observers look on the ethnic revival with foreboding however. Rudolf Ryser welcomes the fact that:

a new international political order, based on concepts of diversity and decentralization, is evolving under the influence of a global political movement led by indigenous populations. Modern states are slowly, reluctantly, yielding to the increasing demands of the indigenous populations who seek to regain their natural place in the family of nations.

The desire of indigenous peoples to reclaim their nations as separate and distinct from neighbouring peoples has begun to shake the stability of many states. Some nationalist movements of indigenous peoples threaten to dismember the large artificial states that surround them, thus giving rise to the formation of many small states.

Through political activism and violent revolution, indig-enous peoples have come into direct confrontation with states on every continent to challenge their expanding economic, social, military, and political power. Such con-frontations, combined with increasing evidence that large states can no longer manage and control their domains, promise to alter boundaries, eliminate existing states, and change, once again, the structure of global human organi-zation.[44]

But prognosis on its own leaves many pertinent questions unanswered. Who, after all, are the people who have a now much proclaimed right to self-determination? Which groups, David Papineau asked recently, have the right to 'draw a line around themselves and constitute a sovereign state'. Although it was the 'most pressing of contemporary questions' it had been 'remarkably little discussed by political philosophers'.[45] Despite the lack of debate on the question its roots burrow down towards the mainstream of democratic theory. In his classic nineteenth-century study on *Representative Government* John Stuart Mill remarked:

> Where a sentiment of nationality exists in any force, there is a prima facie case for uniting all the members of the nationality under the same government, and a government to themselves apart. This is merely saying that the question of government ought to be decided by the governed. One hardly knows what any division of the human race should be free to do, if not determine, with which of the various collective bodies of human beings they choose to associate themselves.[46]

Many contemporary scholars merge theory with the practical problems attending secession as well as the rights of the states and people who are potential targets of secessionist movements. In an article on 'The Right to Rebel', Tony Honore, Oxford's Regius Professor of Civil Law, addressed the question of how to decide whether a group is entitled 'if it wishes to become a sovereign state', whether it, in fact constitutes what he calls a 'unit of self-determination'. If it does, all that its members need appeal to in order to establish their right to independence 'is their wish to be autonomous'. But conditions apply: to be a unit of self-determination a group must consciously possess 'a certain degree of separateness from its rulers or neighbours' as regards language, culture, religion, ethnicity, history and social mores. It must also be 'geographically coherent, sufficiently numerous, economically viable', and have the capacity to 'assume the responsibilities of a member of the international community'.[47] To the Canadian jurist Douglas Sanders the critical question is territorial. Dispersed minorities may claim educational, linguistic and cultural rights 'but any regime of political autonomy requires a jurisdictional boundary'. There can, therefore, be no meaningful political autonomy 'without a distinct territorial base for the population'.[48] In his book *The Self Determination of Minorities in International Politics*, A. Heraclides summarised the principal practical arguments against secession. They included:

1. the fear of Balkanization, the domino theory, or the spectre of the Pandora's Box;
2. the fear of indefinite divisibility, because very few states are ethnically homogeneous, and often neither are the secessionist territories themselves;
3. the fear of the effect such a right could have on the democratic system, by providing a minority with an opportunity for constant blackmail—threatening to secede if there is no conformity with its wishes;
4. the danger of giving birth to non-viable and particularly small entities which would rely on extensive international aid;
5. the fear of trapped minorities within the seceding state who presumably cannot themselves secede in their turn;

6. the fear of 'stranded majorities' in cases where the seceding territory is economically or strategically crucial to the original state.[49]

Most jurists and most indigenous leaders, however, steer a careful course between the rights of existing states and those of minority peoples. Geoff Clark, an Australian Representative at an ILO Conference in 1988, demanded the right 'to control our territories, the organization of our societies, our own decision making institutions', but added: 'We are not looking to dismember your States and you know it'.[50] Many commentators cluster around that position supporting the need for a redistribution of internal sovereignty within the boundaries of the host states. Heraclides argued that the best a secessionist movement can realistically hope for 'is some kind of autonomy or federated status and a degree of power sharing with the Centre'.[51] James Anaya observed that self-determination should not be equated with a right to independent statehood but should embrace a 'much more nuanced interpretation and applications'. Self-determination should be understood, he observed,

> as a right of cultural groupings to the political institutions necessary to allow them to exist and develop according to their distinctive characteristics. The institutions and degree of autonomy, necessarily, will vary as the circumstances of each case vary. And in determining the required conditions for a claimant group, decisionmakers must weigh in the human rights of others. While not precluded independent statehood will be justified only in rare instances. Such a formulation of self-determination, I believe, will advance global peace and stability consistent with international law's normative trends.[52]

The same points were powerfully argued by the Canadian legal scholar Brian Slattery in his article 'The Paradoxes of National Self-Determination', in which he asserted that advocates of secession did not consider the range of political options 'short of independence' that might satisfy a national group's need to survive and advance its welfare 'while avoiding the risks and disruptions associated with the breakup of a state'. Measures like regional autonomy or constitutional protection

171

of indigenous rights were a more satisfactory solution. Unless they could be shown to be inadequate national self-government could not be justified, particularly when the interests held by the larger body of citizens within the existing state were taken into account.[53]

The development of new political and constitutional arrangements between indigenous nations and their enfolding states has attracted considerable attention in many parts of the world both on the ground and in the academic literature. Some form of federalism is seen as the most appropriate vehicle to devolve power and re-distribute sovereignty. Writing of 'Ethnic Identity and Constitutional Design for Africa', Alemante Selassie observed that federalism allowed for local experimentation with different laws, for greater freedom from central control and, in effect, allowed for ethnic diversity to exist.[54] The English scholar Anthony Smith looks forward to the eventual creation of a world of nations whose identities 'are respected and protected by umbrella states'. Federalism, he believes, holds out much hope because

> in principle, the rise of federal and confederal states would make it possible to de-link ethnic and national aspirations from statehood and sovereignty, so permitting ethnic groups at present denied all social and political recognition to achieve a broad cultural and economic autonomy within 'joint' or 'overarching' states.[55]

As well as autonomy at home, many observers believe that peoples and nations also need some form of international standing. In his article 'Nations Without States' the American scholar Gideon Gottlieb argued that such nations should be granted 'a formal non-territorial status and a recognized standing internationally, albeit one that differs from the position of states'.[56] His colleague Howard Berman observed recently that direct access to international organisations was a vital necessity 'for the survival of indigenous societies'. History, he believed,

> has demonstrated tragically that indigenous rights cannot be left in the national context. Some form of continuing international supervision clearly would be warranted to

ensure the fairness of associational negotiations and the adherence of the state to terms of agreement.[57]

Frederik Harhoff linked the survival of indigenous cultures with both the need for internal self-government and the establishment of a secure and assured place in the international order. He wrote:

Dissolution of indigenous cultures would represent a tremendous loss of human values in our world, and the most effective legal means to avoid this would clearly be to involve the indigenous peoples themselves directly in the international society as entitled and obliged parties for all purposes of their optimal cultural survival. Thus, it seems clear that self-determination is more than just an internal, national rearrangement of domestic powers. It reflects new dimensions in the international society and requires new thinking in international law.[58]

But such an eventuality may be to the advantage of the international order and not just to the indigenous peoples of the world. The re-entry of the 'captive nations' onto the international stage could be 'vital to the reproduction of international society', which, like any other, 'relies on sources of difference for adaption and survival'.[59] The Vietnamese-American jurist M.C. Lâm looks to the United Nations, 'a pleasantly ambiguous term that covers both peoples and states', to bring the two together 'in their separate but intertwining identities'.[60]

With so much emphasis on international issues and overseas scholars it will appear that the focus has moved away from Australia. But as we saw at the beginning of the chapter there has always been an international dimension to the relations between the settler society and indigenous Australians and that at least some people have always been aware of it. It is time now to bring these many contentious questions back home.

CONCLUSION

AUSTRALIA IS CAUGHT AT THE CONFLUENCE of two powerful currents—one reaching us from the past, the other running off into an unglimpsed future. We are troubled by the turbulence whipped up in the wake of decolonisation. Like indigenous and tribal people all over the world Aborigines and Islanders seek to exercise their self-determination in order to craft a new relationship with the Australian state. The faltering cause of decolonisation merges with the upsurge of 'post-modern tribalism' which has followed the end of the Cold War. Two major questions entwine. How will the world manage the profound misfit between the more than 5000 cultural communities and the less than 200 states? Who will decide when the process of national liberation has 'proceeded far enough'?[1]

These matters evoke both enthusiasm and disquiet. The Canadian scholar Menno Boldt has written:

> Colonized aboriginal peoples such as Indians in Canada were bypassed by the 'wave' of third-world liberation from colonialism following the Second World War. Now, there is a new wave of liberation building worldwide. This time the energy is coming from ethnically defined 'peoples' who, not unlike Indians in Canada, are trapped against their will within the borders of larger nation-states. The world is

seething with such 'peoples', who are determined to achieve liberation.[2]

In his recent book *Autonomy, Sovereignty and Self-Determination*, H. Hannum argued that while the full exercise of self-determination might attract many minorities,

> the prospect of 5,000 homogeneous, independent statelets which define themselves primarily in ethnic, religious, or linguistic terms is one that should inspire at least as much trepidation as admiration. As frontiers are shifted and minorities displaced to make way for greater purity, a new age of intolerance is more likely to follow than an era of mutual respect and tolerance for all.[3]

States faced with demands for self-determination from within their borders search for solutions on the open ground between the extremes of secession and repression. Australia's difficulties are as much conceptual as practical. There is a great reluctance to recognise that Australia has played the role of an imperial power exercising authority over what have been called 'internal colonies' or 'nations within'. There has been resistance to any slippage between the two concepts of state and nation. Aren't they the same, synonymous, interchangeable, many people would ask? After all, that is the way they have characteristically been seen. Indeed it has been like that since the creation of federated Australia. The 'founding fathers' were spurred on both by the virulent racism of the time and the liberal nationalism of people like John Stuart Mill who argued, in his highly influential work *Representative Government*, that:

> Free institutions are next to impossible in a country made up of different nationalities. Among a people without fellow feeling, especially if they read and speak different languages, the united public opinion necessary to the working of representative government, cannot exist.[4]

The new Australia was to be populated by people with 'fellow feeling'; they were to be white and British in culture and ethnic affiliation. Ethnic cleansing would attend to the outsiders—all non-European migration was prohibited, Kanakas were deported, Aborigines were placed outside the circle of citizenship where, it was almost universally assumed, they would demographically wither away. The Commonwealth was custom-made to provide a very neat fit of race, state and nation. The constitutional tailors had, in Lord Acton's words, 'made the State and the nation commensurate with each other'. Writing 40 years before Federation he was prescient enough to see how such a situation would end, that it would reduce

> practically to a subject condition all other nationalities that may be within the boundary. It cannot admit them to an equality with the ruling nation which constitutes the State, because the State would then cease to be national, which would be a contradiction of the principle of its existence. According, therefore, to the degree of humanity and civilization in that dominant body which claims all the rights of the community, the inferior races are exterminated, or reduced to servitude, or outlawed, or put in a condition of dependence.[5]

For indigenous Australians exclusion, discrimination and deprivation provided the common experience which fostered the gradual emergence of Aboriginal and Islander nationalism. By the time that mainstream Australia offered full membership of the state and admission into the nation it was already too late.

If we are to assess the situation of the two indigenous communities it is important to specify what is actually meant by the term 'nation' and how a nation differs from a state. Definitions of nations have remained remarkably constant since the nineteenth century. They are concerned with culture, traditions, descent and identity. States, on the other hand, are legal, political and constitutional institutions. A selected cluster of definitions will clarify the situation. 'A portion of mankind may be said to constitute a Nationality', John Stuart Mill explained last century,

> if they are united among themselves by common sympathies which do not exist between themselves and any others— which makes them co-operate with each other more

willingly than with other people, desire to be under the same government, and desire that it should be government by themselves or a portion of themselves exclusively.[6]

Modern definitions are similar to Mill's. The American scholar Walker Connor declared that a nation was 'a self-conscious ethnic group',[7] while Alfred Cobban thought that any 'territorial community' the members of which were 'conscious of themselves *as* members of a community and wished to maintain that identity' was a nation.[8] The English sociologist Anthony Smith has stressed the close relationship between ethnicity and nationalism:

> An ethnic group, then, is distinguished by four features: the sense of unique group origins, the knowledge of a unique group history and belief in its destiny, one or more dimensions of collective cultural individuality, and finally a sense of unique collective solidarity.
>
> Nations are closely related to ethnic communities, often 'growing out' of the latter, or being 'constructed' from ethnic materials.[9]

Professor James Kellas defined a nation as, 'A group of people who feel themselves to be a community bound together by ties of history, culture and common ancestry'.[10] A nation exists, Professor Seton-Watson argued, if a significant number of people in a community consider themselves 'to form a nation, or behave as if they formed one'.[11]

When we bring these definitions of nationality back home their relevance immediately becomes apparent. They suggest that both the Aboriginal and Islander communities have the potential to become, or already are, nations—that there is not one but three nations encased within the Australian state, albeit two of them are very small. Such a proposition will not find easy acceptance but would be commonplace in similarly situated countries overseas. The American Indians have always been considered domestic dependent nations with their own remnant sovereignty. Canadians both commonly and officially refer to the Inuit, the Indians and the Métis as first nations. In Scandinavia, scholars explain that the Inuit, the Sami, the Greenlanders and Faroe Islanders are nations in their own right 'however small'; that as a result the Nordic region contains nine nations but only five states.[12] It is not an unusual situation because the condition of having more than one nation in the state is the common experience of human kind, very few states have only one. No more than 5 per cent of United Nations members would qualify on those grounds with experts referring variously to Poland, Portugal, Korea, Iceland, mainland Denmark and Japan which would, however, only qualify if the Ainu are overlooked.

We have never been one nation, popular rhetoric notwithstanding. We may never become one, at least not in the foreseeable future. We share a country, a continent and a state, but not a nation. Those commentators who expect us to become one nation in the near future display considerable conceptual confusion about what nations are and in the process help create quite unrealistic expectations. Indigenous people may never want to be absorbed in the Australian nation. Why should they give up, could they in fact surrender, what they have so recently achieved—a sense of nationhood which may be of critical importance in their survival as a distinctive people with a unique history and culture. A separate state may not be essential for cultural survival in the modern world but a sense of nationhood almost certainly is.

What would be the consequences of recognising the indigenous people as the first nations of Australia? Clearly it would enable indigenous and non-indigenous to meet on terms of greater equality than ever before. Individual equality would be bolstered by the equality of nations. Writing of such situations the Canadian scholar Patrick Macklem observed that 'a relationship between sovereigns' was a relation of equality in which 'each views itself and the other as independent and distinct'.[13] By more clearly defining what we mean by nation we can partially de-couple nation and state allowing for commitment to the state to be separated from emotional loyalty to the nation. But the process would have to work both ways. Indigenous Australians would have to accept that they might forever remain 'stateless' nations. The legal academic H. Hannum observed that many minority and indigenous groups were currently returning to the 'rhetoric of the ethnic-linguistic state of the nineteenth century'. But, he argued that they, too, 'may need to abandon the "nation-state" as an ideal, so long as their nation can otherwise be preserved'.[14]

Under the new dispensation indigenous communities may well come to see that the Australian state is the irreplaceable protector of their inescapably fragile nationhood and be able to join the rest of Australia on the common ground of civic identity and commitment to the institutional superstructure. Once the spheres of culture, internal self-government and national identity are placed securely in indigenous hands, once the areas of responsibility are clearly marked, indigenous leaders may welcome an even stronger state presence. This situation can be seen most clearly in the Torres Strait. No-one can doubt the determination that exists there to achieve regional self-government and political autonomy. But at the same time the new Torres Strait authority will seek a greater federal presence in matters of defence, quarantine, immigration, customs and environmental management. A strong federal state is required to underwrite their autonomy, to provide a secure arena in which they can operate.

With their nationhood respected indigenous Australians would be better able to accept overlapping loyalties and cultural exchange without fearing loss of identity. 'Political loyalty to an existing state', Hannum argued, 'does not necessarily imply national or cultural disloyalty'.[15] There would be less need to sharply differentiate between Aboriginal and non-Aboriginal, to dig a deep trench between indigenous and immigrant heritages. Cultural exchange could proceed without cries of 'sell-out', 'co-option' and take-over'. People could more readily embrace mixed descent and creole culture. The cultural merging and inter-communal co-operation common in our history could be freely accepted and even celebrated. Increasingly, Australians of all backgrounds could identify with a mixed or mestizo heritage. In the process we will not become one nation but slowly increasing numbers of people will come to identify with several.

By viewing Aborigines and Islanders as either actual or potential nations we can dispense with the concept of race. In doing so we can avoid those constant attempts to relate

Aboriginality to racial characteristics, to distinguish between 'real' Aborigines and the rest, to talk of people as being 'half-castes' or of 'mixed blood'. At the same time we can jettison the term 'black' which is so often used for people who everyone can see are not. It is, after all, politics not pigment that matters if it is nationality we are talking about. The distinguished Canadian jurist Thomas Berger insisted that the Indian nations were 'political communities, founded on tradition and culture, not on race'.[16] His colleague, the legal scholar Brian Slattery agreed, observing that Aboriginal nations were

> constitutional entities rather than ethnic or racial groups. Although a First Nation . . . may happen to be composed mainly of people of a certain stock, its status does not stem from its racial or ethnic makeup but from its political autonomy.[17]

Menno Boldt spoke out even more strongly against using the 'Indian-White' dichotomy despite the continuing presence of racism and the 'use' of race as a means of seeking legal protection against discrimination. Scholars, he observed,

> who legitimate a 'racism' analysis of injustice to Indians, by juxtaposing 'Indian' and 'White,' are not serving the interests of Indian peoples. A 'racism' paradigm robs Indians of the most significant elements of Indian identity—their history, nationhood, cultures, and languages—and thereby undermines their historical and moral claims to self-determination. In an enlightened world, peoples who are defined primarily in racial terms are not regarded as having a legitimate claim to nationhood.[18]

But further questions arise. How can indigenous autonomy be married to Australia's multicultural society? How can special rights be accorded indigenous people and not granted to other ethnic groups? If it is good for Aborigines why isn't it also good for Greeks, Italians or Vietnamese? How can indigenous people exercise self-determination without undermining the broad principles of equality? Shouldn't we all be treated equally? Although this question is frequently used by racists, that doesn't diminish its validity or importance. Will recognition of indigenous nationalism undermine the delicate multi-cultural balance? Will it provoke a resurgence of Anglo-Celtic ethnic nationalism which will have an impact on all non-British minorities?

The starting point must be that there is a fundamental difference in the circumstances of Aborigines and Islanders on the one hand, and immigrant minorities on the other. Ethnic minorities have rights of cultural preservation and can demand an end to discrimination but they have 'no clear, recognizable, or useful legal or theoretical foundation' available to them 'for demanding self-determination, but all Aborigines do'.[19] The status of indigenous people is now clearly recognised in international law. They are part of what has become known as the fourth world. The critical point is that they were 'here before', they were the original owners and sovereigns of the continent. Thomas Berger addressed the question of why Canada's First Nations should be given special consideration:

> No such consideration was made for the Ukrainians, the Swedes, the Italians, or for any other ethnic group of nationality. The Indians, the Inuit and the Metis did not immigrate to Canada as individuals or families who expected to be assimilated. Immigrants chose to come here and to submit to Canadian laws and institutions; their choices were individual choices. The Indians, the Inuit and the Metis were already here; they have been forced to submit to the laws and institutions . . . of the dominant White society. And they have never relinquished their claim to be treated as distinct peoples in our midst.[20]

An indigenous view of the same question was presented by the Grand Council of the Mikmaq Indian Nation in a submission to the UN Commission on Human Rights in 1982:

> If a people exercise their right to self-determination by incorporating themselves freely into another people—by immigration or voluntary cession—they surrender their separate status and become one, politically, with the host State. The right to self-determination persists, but ever after must be exercised in common with the host as one people with one voice. As a minority they may justly demand both non-discriminatory treatment under the host's laws, and

freedom to preserve and develop their culture within its general framework of laws and responsibilities . . .

The situation is different where no voluntary incorporation of peoples has occurred, and there has been no free consolidation of two peoples' political rights. A people lawlessly annexed or taken from their country by force do not thereby lose their separate voice or choice of destiny, but retain it until given an unrestrained opportunity for its exercise. They do not become, by force of seizure, colonization or enslavement, a minority, but remain a people still.[21]

While historically based rights and international legal precepts are one thing, finding a successful political formula for their articulation is quite another. Such outcomes do not unfold of their own accord. They will have to be argued about, agitated over, contended for and ultimately secured both in the cock-pit of politics and the wider arena of popular sentiment. Australia, however, has the advantage of a long and strong tradition of innovative political and social reform and a mature federal system. As H.C. Coombs observed, it has 'an incomparable range of experience in innovative federalism'. Flexibility and diversity were achievable, he believed, if the political will existed.[22] If sovereignty could be divided between the six colonies and the new Federal Government in the early twentieth century it can be cut again to accommodate emerging ethnic nationalism. Practical models already exist in the case of the external territories and particularly the Cocos Islands and Norfolk Island. In dealing with Norfolk Island Australian governments have conceded most of the things sought by Aborigines and Torres Strait Islanders. The 2000 to 3000 permanent residents have their own parliament, raise their own taxes and control all of those things accorded the state governments in the Constitution and many of the powers exercised by the Commonwealth. If effective autonomy can be conceded to the Norfolk Islanders, in recognition of their cultural and historic distinctiveness, there can be no in principle objection to the same rights being extended to indigenous communities.

There clearly are differences. Australia doesn't feel threatened by Norfolk Island assertiveness; to the extent that anyone knows about it, it appears quaint rather than confronting. But a major question arises in both cases. Does the grant of autonomy appease or sharpen the desire for independence? No-one really knows the answer. Experts are divided on the question. Walker Connor believed that ethnonationalism 'appears to feed on concessions' which provide 'constant reminders of separate identity and rallying points for further demands'.[23] In his 1991 study *The Self-Determination of Minorities in International Politics*, A. Heraclides argued to the contrary that 'once a separatist process has begun' it can only be arrested if the national government 'redefines its position and accords extended autonomy and power sharing to the regional separatist group'.[24] The truth may well be that, as in the relations between central and regional governments in a federation, the balance between indigenous and mainstream authority, between state and nation, will continue to fluctuate and be the occasion for constant negotiation. The celebrated jurist John Salmond glimpsed something of the likely circumstances in his 1902 study *Jurisprudence* when he observed:

> In every nation there is an impulse, more or less powerful to develop into a state—to add to the subsisting community of descent a corresponding community of government and political existence. Conversely every state tends to become a nation; that is to say, the unity of political organization eliminates in course of time the national diversities within its borders, infusing throughout all its population a new and common nationality, to the exclusion of all remembered relationship with those beyond the limits of the state.[25]

What of the process of reconciliation? It is manifestly a worthy objective but it is not completely clear who is to be reconciled to what or to whom. Presumably Aborigines and Islanders are to be reconciled to loss of land and sovereignty. If that is the case they have already delivered. The widespread support for the Mabo legislation represented an acceptance of the validity of all titles—and by implication of the dispossession and loss of sovereignty over the lands in question. It is not immediately apparent what non-indigenous Australians are expected to become reconciled with. It can't relate to the fact that they have started treating Aborigines with justice and fairness, that belatedly they have begun to do the right thing. What might be expected is an acceptance of the existence and validity of indigenous nationalism and a commitment to seek ways in which it can be accommodated beneath the overarching roof of the Australian state. That would be a gesture of appropriate gravity, magnitude and generosity.

Such acceptance will not come easily; it will be opposed by racists. That goes without saying. But to assume all opposition to Aboriginal self-determination is motivated by racism grossly distorts the true situation. Some opponents will hold strongly to basic principles of political philosophy, to some of our best ideas rather than the worst. Ethnic nationalism challenges the widespread belief that the state should be the sole repository of sovereignty and the individual citizen 'the sole vessel for political rights'.[26] It seeks to devolve sovereignty and to accord special rights to indigenous communities which occupy an intermediate place between the individual and the state.

So where will it all end? No-one can answer that at the moment. Will self-determination represent the maturing of the multicultural society, an enhancement of creative but cohesive diversity, or will it end up in a retreat into tribal enclaves and ethnic exclusiveness? The questions project Australian politics into the centre of a debate of world significance—about whether 'polyethnic' states like the United States, Canada and Australia will continue to thrive or whether they will be pulled apart by contending parties, identities and loyalties. Will postmodern tribalism overrun multiculturalism? The opposing visions have haunted western thinking for a long time now. They were outlined by two of the leading figures of mid-nineteenth century British intellectual life, John Stuart Mill and Lord Acton. Mill believed states should ideally be made up of people who were 'united among themselves by common sympathy' which did not exist 'between them and any others', that all members of the same nationality should be under the same government with a government 'to themselves apart'.[27]

Acton, on the other hand, thought that the combination of different nations in one state is as necessary a condition of civilised life as the combination of men in society. The 'fertilizing and regenerating process' of ethnic mixing could only be experienced by living under one government. It is, he argued,

> in the cauldron of the State that the fusion takes place by which the vigour, the knowledge, and the capacity of one portion of mankind may be communicated to another. Where political and national boundaries coincide, society ceases to advance, and nations relapse into a condition corresponding to that of men who renounce intercourse with their fellowmen. The difference between the two unites mankind not only by the benefits it confers on those who live together, but because it connects society either by a political or a national bond, gives to every people an interest in its neighbours, either because they are under the same government or because they are of the same race . . .[28]

It is doubtful if Australia has a choice. The die was cast when the British decided to plant a colony in an 'impure soil', in an already inhabited land, and in a part of the world where Europeans could never be more than a small minority. The heroic attempt to create a state which contained only one homogeneous nation was, in the long run, doomed to failure. The indigenous people survived and the perceived threat from the Asian environment provoked the desire for massive migration which eventually had to be drawn from all over the world.

Australia must make a success of the mixing of different cultures in the cauldron of the state. We must create a situation where nations and minorities feel no desire to lapse into a condition corresponding to that of men who renounce intercourse with their fellow men. There is no acceptable alternative scenario.

As we have already seen, Anthony Smith hoped that the rise of federal and confederal states would make it possible to de-link ethnic and national aspirations from statehood and sovereignty, so allowing ethnic nations at present denied all social and political recognition to achieve a broad cultural and economic autonomy within 'joint' or 'overarching' states. But he feared that a world of nations whose identities were respected and protected by umbrella states was a remote possibility; it was a 'utopian dream'.[29] Perhaps more than most societies Australia has a chance to pursue that dream. It is a goal worth seeking.

ENDNOTES

INTRODUCTION

1. F. Bacon, *Essays*, Dent, London, 1906, p.104.
2. W. Dampier, *A New Voyage Round the World* [1697], 2 vols, Israel, Amsterdam, 1970, 1, 465
3. J. Banks, *The Endeavour Journal*, 2 vols, Angus & Robertson, Sydney, 1962, 2, pp.122–23.
4. *Historical Records of NSW* (hereafter *HRNSW*), 1, no.2, Sydney, 1889, p.1.
5. W. Tench, *Sydney's First Four Years*, Angus & Robertson, Sydney, 1961, pp.51–52.
6. E. de Vattel, *The Law of Nations*, 3 vols, Carnegie, Washington, 1916, 3, p.84.
7. (1889) 14 AC, 46.
8. *Milerrprum v Nabalco* (1970), 17 FLR, 141.
9. N. Glazer & D. Moynihan, *Ethnicity*, Harvard, Cambridge, Mass., 1975, p.4.
10. 'The Warmth of Nationhood', *Times Literary Supplement*, 19 Feb. 1993.
11. R. Falk, 'Promise of Natural Political Communities', in R. Thompson, *The Rights of Indigenous People in International Law*, University of Saskatchewan, Saskatoon, 1987, p.60.
12. B. Slattery, 'Aboriginal Sovereignty and Imperial Claims', in B.W. Hodgens, et al, *Co-Existence? Studies in Ontario—First Nations Relations*, Trent University Press, Trent, 1992, pp.158–59.
13. A. Dickey, 'Law of the Worora Aborigines', *University of Western Australia Law Review*, 12, 1975–76, pp.361–63.
14. E. de Vattel, *The Law of Nations*, London, 1758, p.84.

CHAPTER 1

1. 107, *Australian Law Reports* (*ALR*), 1992, 92 (hereafter Mabo).
2. Ibid, pp.29–30
3. Ibid, p.27
4. Ibid, p.30
5. Ibid, p.179
6. Ibid, p.79
7. Ibid, p.121
8. *Salaman v Secretary of State for India, 1906 1 King's Bench* (*KB*), 639.
9. *The Fargernes*, 1927, p.324.
10. *NSW v the Commonwealth*, 135, Commonwealth Law Reports (CLR), 1975, 388.
11. Mabo, p.63.
12. 53, *Australian Law Journal and Reports* (*ALJR*), 1979, 403.
13. Ibid, p.404.
14. Ibid.
15. Ibid, p.411.
16. Ibid, p.408.
17. *Coe v the Commonwealth*, 118, *ALR*, 1993, 195.
18. Ibid, p.200.
19. Ibid, p.193.
20. 1976, *New South Wales Law Reports* (*NSWLR*), 581.
21. Ibid, p.586.
22. Ibid, p.587.
23. Ibid, p.584.
24. *Walker v NSW*, 126, *ALR*, 1994, 321.
25. 1847, 1, Legge, 320.
26. Mabo, pp.28–29.
27. 1976, 1, *NSWLR*, 584.
28. Supreme Court Papers 5/1161, NSW Archives, 24/48, p.211.
29. 1921, 2 Appeal Cases (AC), 402–03.
30. 17 Federal Law Reports (FLR), 1971, 267.
31. *Coe v the Commonwealth*, op.cit., p.403.
32. Ibid.
33. Mabo, pp.99–100.
34. Ibid, p.36.
35. Ibid, p.42.
36. Ibid.
37. Cambridge, 1904, p.107.
38. Mabo, p.29.
39. Ibid, p.30.
40. Ibid.

CHAPTER 2

1. 1836, 1, Legge, 72; 1889, 14, AC, 286.
2. Banks, op.cit., 2, p.122.
3. Ibid., 1, p.465.
4. J. King, 'Terra Australia' etc., *Journal Royal Australian Historical Society*, 72, 2, Oct. 1986, p.76.
5. Tench, op.cit., p.35.
6. *HRNSW*, 2, p.664.
7. J. Hunter, *An Historical Journal*, London, 1793, p.52.
8. Tench, op.cit., p.52.
9. *HRNSW*, 1, part 2, pp.287, 324.
10. Aberdeen, 1789, p.30.
11. E.J. Eyre, *Journals of Expeditions of Discovery*, 2 vols, London, 1845, 1, p.351.
12. *Aboriginal Protection Society, Report of Sub-Committee on Australia*, London, 1838, pp.17–18.
13. *HRNSW*, 1, part 2, pp.289–90.
14. Ibid., pp.302, 321.
15. Tench, op.cit., p.220.
16. *HRNSW*, 5, p.771.
17. Tuckfield Journal, La Trobe Library, MSS. 655, p.174.
18. G. Grey, *Journals of Two Expeditions of Discovery*, 2 vols, London, 1841, 2, p.263.
19. E.J. Eyre, op.cit., 2, p.247.
20. Hunter, op.cit., p.43.
21. L. Leichhardt, *Journal of an Overland Expedition in Australia*, London, 1847, pp.354–55.
22. T. Mitchell, *Journal of an Expedition into the Interior of Tropical Australia*, London, 1848, p.413.
23. 'Amacitia', 19 Aug. 1824.
24. *HRA*, 1, 1, p.160.
25. Hunter, op.cit., p.43.
26. *HRA*, 1, 1, p.160.
27. Tench, op.cit., pp.225–26; Mrs Macarthur to her friends, *HRNSW*, 2, p.504.
28. *HRNSW*, 2, p.718.
29. Tench, op.cit., p.226.
30. Calcutta, 1832, p.149.
31. Grey, op.cit., 2, p.252.
32. J.D. Lang quoted in *Tracts Relative to the Aborigines*, London, 1842, p.11.
33. Letters of James Backhouse, London, 1838, pp.40, 57.

34. W.H. Breton, *Excursions in New South Wales*, etc., London, 1833, pp.188–89.
35. Grey, op.cit., 2, p.236.
36. Henderson, op.cit., p.151.
37. C. Sturt, *Two Expeditions into the Interior of Southern Australia*, 2 vols, London, 1833, 2, pp.126, 212.
38. *South Australian Gazette*, 28 April 1838.
39. *Physical Description of New South Wales and Van Diemen's Land*, London, 1845, p.340.
40. Gawler to Angus, 10 Jul. 1840, Angus Papers, A461, PRG 174.
41. Walker to Watson, 5 Dec. 1821, Bonwick Transcripts, 52.
42. Ibid., 5 Nov. 1821.
43. S. Nind, *Journal of Royal Geographical Society*, 1, 1831, p.44.
44. G.F. Moore, *Perth Gazette*, 14 May 1836.
45. Aboriginal Protection Society Papers, 11, 1841, p.114.
46. C.P. Hodgson, *Reminiscences of Australia*, London, 1846, pp.73–74.
47. J. King, op.cit., p.77.
48. Tench, op.cit., p.285.
49. Hunter, op.cit., p.62.
50. T.F. Bride, *Letters from Victorian Pioneers*, Melbourne, 1898, p.398.
51. *Report on the Condition, Capabilities and Prospects of the Australian Aborigines*, Melbourne, 1845, p.19.
52. *Brief Notes of the Aborigines of New South Wales*, Geelong, 1845, p.6.
53. Eyre, op.cit., 1, p.317.
54. *Aborigines of South Australia*, Adelaide, 1841, p.6.
55. *Australian Aborigines*, Melbourne, 1881, p.5.
56. Quoted by E. Curr, *The Australian Race*, 4 vols, Melbourne, 1886–87, 1, p.52.
57. Ibid.
58. *Two Representative Tribes of Queensland*, London, 1910, p.129.
59. London, 1904, pp.295–96.
60. Tench, op.cit., p.285.
61. Strzelecki, op.cit., p.340.
62. Eyre, op.cit., p.384.
63. Grey, op.cit., 2, pp.216, 219, 223.
64. Curr, op.cit., 1, p.51.
65. Ibid., p.54.
66. Howitt, op.cit., p.296.
67. McMillan, London, pp.11, 46.
68. See for instance: E. Curr, op.cit.; G. Taplin, ed., *The Folklore, Manners, Customs and Languages of the South Australian Aborigines*, Adelaide, 1879; R.B. Smyth, *The Aborigines of Victoria*, 2 vols, Melbourne, 1876.
69. L. Fison & A.W. Howitt, *Kamilaroi and Kurnai*, London, 1880.
70. *The Aborigines of Australia*, Melbourne, 1854, p.12.

71. J. Dredge, *Brief Notes on the Aborigines of New South Wales*, Geelong, 1845, p.6.
72. Curr, op.cit., 1, p.69.
73. *Transactions of the Royal Society of Victoria*, 1, 2, 1889, p.101.
74. *The Tribe, and Intertribal Relations in Australia*, London, 1910, p.46.
75. Quoted by R.M. & C.H. Berndt, *The World of the First Australians*, Ure Smith, Sydney, 1964, p.303.
76. Angus & Robertson, Sydney, 1962, p.242.
77. 'Indigenous Forms of Government Among the Australian Aborigines', in J. Hogbin & L.R. Hiatt, *Readings in Australian and Pacific Anthropology*, Melbourne University Press, 1968, p.71.
78. Ibid., pp.250, 251.
79. Ibid., p.242.
80. 'People with "Politiks": Management of Land and Personnel on Australia's Cape York Peninsula', in N. Williams & E.S. Hunn, *Resource Managers*, AIATSIS, Canberra, 1982, p.155.
81. 'The Cultural Basis of Politics in Pintupi Life', *Mankind*, 12, 3, June 1980, p.208.
82. 17 FLR, 1971, p.265.
83. Ibid., p.266.
84. Ibid., p.267.
85. 53 *ALJR*, 1979, pp.409–10.

CHAPTER 3

1. Lindley, op.cit., p.11.
2. Ibid., p.20.
3. 1836, 1, Legge, 73.
4. NSW Supreme Court Papers, 5/1161, p.210.
5. C50/1564/1851, S.Aus. Archives 6R6 24/1.
6. 1964, *Oceania*, New York, p.32.
7. Vattel, op.cit., 3, p.11.
8. Carnegie, Washington, 1916, p.157.
9. 2 vols, London, 1743, 1, p.169.
10. NSW Supreme Court Papers, op.cit., p.211.
11. Ibid.
12. *De Jure Naturae Et Gentium*, [The Law of Nations, 1749] Oxford, Clarendon, 1934, p.968.
13. Vattel, op.cit., 3, p.7.
14. Wolff, op.cit., p.15.
15. 4th ed., London, 1873, p.239.
16. NSW Supreme Court Papers, op.cit., p.239.
17. E. R77, 397.

18. *De Indis* [1532] Carnegie, Washington, 1917, pp.128–29.

19. Oxford University Press, New York, 1916, pp.13, 19.

20. Wolff, op.cit., p.89.

21. Justice Burton, NSW Supreme Court Papers, op.cit., p.211.

22. Wheaton, op.cit., p.18.

23. Vattel, op.cit., 1, p.1.

24. Wolff, op.cit., p.157.

25. Wheaton, op.cit., p.18.

26. J. Bentham, *A Fragment of Government*, Oxford, 1894, p.141.

27. Blackstone, op.cit., 1, pp.26, 27.

28. Austin, op.cit., pp.226, 233.

29. Ibid., pp.88–89.

30. Wheaton, op.cit., p.18.

31. NSW Supreme Court Papers, op.cit., p.210.

32. Wolff, op.cit., pp.144, 445.

33. G.F. Von Martens, *The Law of Nations*, 4th ed., London, 1829, p.64.

34. Von Savigny, *Treatise on Possession*, 6th ed., London, 1848, pp.10, 143,149–51.

35. F. Schulz, *Classical Roman Law*, Clarendon, Oxford, 1951, p.442. See also J.A.C. Thomas, *Text Book of Roman Law*, North Holland, Amsterdam, 1976, pp.145–46.

36. Quoted by J. Goebel, *The Struggle for the Falklands*, Yale, New Haven, 1927, p.115.

37. 2 vols, London, 1743, 1, p.179.

38. Wolff, op.cit., pp.157–58.

39. Ibid.

40. Ibid., p.159.

41. Ibid., pp.140–41.

42. Ibid., p.141.

43. Ibid., p.160.

44. R. Wildman, *Institutes of International Law*, London, 1849, quoted in Vattel, op.cit., 3, XLIV.

45. Vattel, op.cit., 3, p.143.

46. Ibid., p.142.

47. Ibid., p.91.

48. Ibid., p.85.

49. Ibid., p.48.

50. E. de Vattel, *The Law of Nations*, 1st English edition, London, 1760, p.150.

51. J. Salmond, *Jurisprudence*, London, 1902, p.185.

52. *The Principles of International Law*, 4th ed., London, 1914, p.160.

53. Ibid., p.57.

54. Ibid., p.107.

55. Cambridge, 1904, pp.105,107.

56. Ibid., p.148.
57. Ibid., p.151.
58. P. Fiore, *Nouveau Droit International Public*, Paris, 1868, p.379.
59. Paris, 1889, p.206.
60. Lindley, op.cit., p.20.
61. Ibid., p.22.
62. Ibid.
63. M. Shaw, *Title to Territory in Africa*, Clarendon, Oxford, 1986, pp.36–37.
64. Ibid.
65. Mabo, pp.181–82.
66. Ibid., p.41.
67. Lindley, op.cit., p.21.

CHAPTER 4

1. W. Tench, op.cit., pp.51, 285.
2. *HRNSW*, I, p.485.
3. *HRA*, 3, 1, p.529.
4. Ibid., 1, 9, pp.142–43.
5. Ibid.
6. *Sydney Gazette*, 16 Jun. 1829.
7. *NSW Supreme Court Papers*, op.cit., p.234.
8. Ibid.
9. Ibid., p.239.
10. Ibid.
11. Ibid., p.245.
12. Cooper to Robe, n.d. but received 27 March 1847, CSO 1564/1851 SAA, 6R6 24/1.
13. Ibid.
14. *West Australian Gazette*, 8 Jan. 1842.
15. *The Inquirer*, 12 Jan. 1842.
16. Ibid., 19 Jan. 1842.
17. E.W. Landor, op.cit., pp.192–93.
18. 1, Legge, p.72.
19. 'Aborigines: Australian Colonies', *BPP*, op.cit., p.148.
20. Ibid., p.153.
21. Ibid., p.151.
22. Ibid.
23. Ibid., p.144.
24. Vattel, op.cit., pp.94, 100–08.
25. Ibid., p.84.

26. Ibid.
27. *The Argus*, 29 Jun. 1860.
28. Ibid., 7 Sep. 1860.
29. *R v Cobby*, NSWP, IV, 1883, p.356.
30. M. Hale, *The History of the Common Law*, 2 vols, 5th ed., London, 1794, 2, pp.7, 9.
31. T. Carson, *Prescription and Custom*, London 1907, p.113.
32. Lambert, J. in *Delgamuukw v British Columbia*, 104, DLR, 4th, 1993, p.651.
33. *ER*, 112, p.1265.
34. C.K. Allen, *Law in the Making*, 6th ed., Clarendon, Oxford, 1958, p.127.
35. Carson, op.cit., p.119.
36. T.O. Elias, *British Colonial Law*, Stevens, London, 1962, p.101.
37. W. Holdsworth, *A History of English Law*, vol. XI, London, Methuen, 1938, p.129.
38. *ER*, 77, p.398.
39. *ER*, 90, p.1089.
40. 4 vols, 4th ed., London, 1876, I, p.81.
41. Holdsworth, op.cit., XI, p.239.
42. *Khoo Hooi Leong v Khoo Chong Yeok*, *AC*, 1930, p.355.
43. 2nd ed., London, Stevens, 1915, p.451.
44. C.K. Allen, op.cit., p.150.
45. T.O. Elias, op.cit., p.80.
46. J. Wu, 'Towards Legal Pluralism in Australia? The Malaysian Experience', *Australian Journal of Public Administration*, 31, 2, Jun. 1992, p.238.
47. Quoted by A. Frame, 'Colonising Attitudes Towards Maori Custom', *New Zealand Law Journal*, 17, March 1981, p.107.
48. J. Wu, op.cit., p.239.
49. M.B. Hooker, *Legal Pluralism*, Clarendon, Oxford, 1975, p.128.
50. Frame, op.cit., p.106.
51. The Law Reform Commission, *The Recognition of Aboriginal Customary Laws*, 2 vols, AGPS, Canberra, 1986, 1, p.42.
52. Ibid.
53. A.P. Elkin, 'Aboriginal Evidence and Justice in North Australia', *Oceania*, 17, 3, March 1947, p.201.
54. E. Eggleston, *Fear, Favour or Affection*, ANU, Canberra, 1976, pp.284–85.
55. *Recognition of Aboriginal Customary Laws*, 1, op.cit., p.3.
56. Ibid., p.94.
57. Ibid., 2, p.253.
58. *Aboriginal Customary Law*, AGPS, Canberra, 1994, p.III.

59. M. Kirby quoted by R. Johnstone, 'Aboriginal Issues in Australian Legal Scholarship', in M.P. Ellinghaus, et.al., eds, *The Emergence of Australian Law*, Butterworth, Sydney, 1989, p.26.
60. Ellinghaus, op.cit., pp.66–69.
61. Ibid.

CHAPTER 5

1. F. Wharton, *A Digest of the International Law of the United States*, 3 vols, Washington, 1886, 3, p.840.
2. J. Story, *Commentaries on the Constitution of the United States* [1832], 5th ed., Boston, 1891, p.6.
3. *Worcester v Georgia*, 1831, quoted in M.F. Lindley, *The Acquisition and Government of Backward Territory in International Law*, London, 1928, p.29.
4. Ibid., pp.26–27.
5. *The Freedom of the Seas*, New York, 1916, p.11.
6. J.G. Heineccius, *A Methodical System of Universal Law*, 2 vols, London, 1743, 1, p.182.
7. 8th ed., Oxford, 1924, pp.129–30.
8. 16 CLR, 1913, 439.
9. *Commonwealth and Colonial Law*, Stephen & Co., London, 1966, p.631.
10. H.S. Maine, *Ancient Law*, London, 1861, p.246.
11. C. Wolff, op.cit., p.157.
12. 90 ER, 1089 (K.B.).
13. 1 ER, 21.
14. Published as footnote to Calvin's Case in ER, 77, 398.
15. London, 1820, p.29.
16. G. Clark, *A Summary of Colonial Law*, London, 1834, p.4.
17. 2 vols, 18th ed., London, 1823, 1, p.104.
18. J.L. Klueber, *Droit de Gens Moderne de l'Europe*, Paris, 1831, pp.209–10.
19. A.W. Heffter, *Das Europaische Volkrrecht* [1844], as quoted in P. Fiore, *Nouveau Droit International Public*, Paris, 1868, p.379.
20. *HRA*, 4, 1, p.330.
21. Ibid., p.414.
22. *Wilson v Terry*, 1, Legge, 1849, p.508.
23. *McHugh v Robertson*, 1886, 11 VLR, 431.
24. 14 AC, 1889, p.291.
25. Lindley, op.cit., p.41.
26. J.L. Stokes, *Discoveries in Australia*, 2 vols, London, 1846, 2, p.464.
27. 2 vols, Stevens, London, 1970, 1, p.409.
28. The Acquisition of Territory in Australia and New Zealand, *Grotian Society Papers*, 1968, pp.18–19.

29. 'The Concept of Statehood and the Acquisition of Territory in the Nineteenth Century', *Law Quarterly Review*, 94, 1978, p.415.
30. Clarendon, Oxford, 1979, p.180.
31. Lindley, op.cit., p.45.
32. L. Hanke, *Aristotle and the American Indians*, London, 1959, p.88.
33. *Queenslander*, 6 Dec. 1890.
34. G.F. Bowen, *Thirty Years of Colonial Government*, 2 vols, London, 1889, 1, p.214.
35. S. Kittle, *A Concise History of the Colony and Natives of New South Wales*, Edinburgh, 1816, p.7.
36. 53 *ALJR*, 408.
37. 14 AC 1889, 291.
38. *Sunday Telegraph*, 13 Feb. 1994.
39. 13 Feb. 1994.
40. *Kamilaroi and Kurnai*, Melbourne, 1880, p.182.
41. E. Curr, op.cit., 1, pp.100–06.
42. *Courier-Mail*, 12 Feb. 1994.
43. *Launceston Advertiser* 26 Sep. 1831.
44. *Hobart Town Gazette*, 23 Jul. 1824.
45. 14 Dec. 1827.
46. Van Diemen's Land Co. Letterbook, 1931/1.
47. *The Colonist*, 4 May 1839.
48. T. Bartlett, *New Holland*, London, 1843, p.78.
49. *Extracts from the Letters of James Backhouse*, 3rd ed., London, 1838, p.80.
50. 9 Dec. 1848.
51. 23 Oct. 1875.
52. *South Australia Parliamentary Papers*, 2, 1890, no.28. p. 9.
53. Tasmanian Governor's papers, 60, 33/7, p.27.
54. *HRA*, 1, 12, p.21.
55. *The Bushman*, London, 1847, pp.187–89.
56. 12–13 Feb. 1994.
57. Wheaton, op.cit., p.363.
58. G. Henderson in *Courier-Mail*, 12 Feb. 1994.
59. *HRNSW*, 1, p.39; 2, p.411.
60. S. Zavalia, *The Political Philosophy of the Conquest of America*, Editorial Culture, Mexico City, 1953, p.35.
61. A. Atkinson, 'The Ethics of Conquest', *Aboriginal History*, 6, 1982, p.87.
62. *Courier-Mail*, 12 Feb. 1994.
63. Quoted by R.J. King, op.cit., p.77.
64. *HRA*, 1, 1, p.161.
65. 'Mabo, International Law, Terra Nullius', *Melbourne University Law Review*, 19, June 1993, pp.208–09.
66. *Two Hundred Years Later*, AGPS, Canberra, 1983, p.45.

67. Y. Blum, *Historical Titles in International Law*, Nijhoff, Hague, 1965, p.100.
68. R. Phillimore, *Commentaries on International Law*, 4 vols, London, 1854, I, pp.265, 272, 279.
69. Vattel, op.cit., 1, 158.
70. *Two Hundred Years Later*, op.cit., p.10.
71. T. Twiss, *The Oregon Question Examined*, New York, 1840, p.24.

CHAPTER 6

1. A.G. Price, *The Explorations of Captain James Cook*, Angus & Robertson, Sydney, 1958, p.19.
2. *The Voyage of the Resolution and Discovery, 1776–80*, Cambridge University Press, 1967, p.CCXXIII.
3. *House of Commons Journals*, 40, 1785, p.1164.
4. T. Twiss, *The Oregon Question Examined*, New York, 1846, pp.85, 90.
5. Colonial Office, CO 202/5, 26 Feb. 1800.
6. Quoted in R. King, op.cit., p.77.
7. Banks, op.cit., 2, p.122.
8. *HRA*, 4, 1, p.330.
9. Ibid., p.414.
10. 14 AC 1889, 291.
11. Evatt, op.cit., pp.18–19.
12. O'Connell, op.cit., 1, p.409.
13. Quoted by R. King, op.cit., p.77.
14. A. Frost, *Botany Bay Mirages*, Melbourne University Press, Melbourne, 1994, pp.184, 189.
15. D. Collins, *An Account of the English Colony of New South Wales, 1798–1804*, 2 vols, London, 1802, 1, pp.118, 497, 546.
16. *HRA*, 3, 1, p.529.
17. Vattel, London, 1760, pp.91, 180, 152.
18. Huskisson to Arthur, 6 May 1828, Governor's Office Papers, G.O. 1/7, vol. 2.
19. Murray to Arthur, 20 Feb. 1829, G.O. 1/9.
20. Arthur to Goderich, 10 Jan. 1829, Military Operations . . . against the Aboriginal Inhabitants of Van Diemen's Land, *BPP*, 1831, 19, no.259, p.5.
21. Parramore to Surveyor General, 4 Dec. 1827, Colonial Secretary, CSO 38/1.
22. Arthur to Goderich, 10 Jan. 1828, *Military Operations*, op.cit., p.4.
23. Ibid., pp.4,5.
24. H. Melville, *A History of Van Diemen's Land (1835)*, Sydney, Horwitz, 1965, p.76.

25. 24 Sep. 1830.
26. 3 Apr. 1830.
27. 24 Sep. 1832, Colonial Office, C.O. 280/35.
28. 27 Jan. 1835, 'Select Committee on Aboriginal Inhabitants', *BPP*, 1837, 7, no.425, p.126.
29. *The State and Position of Western Australia*, London, 1835, p.28.
30. 'Select Committee on Aboriginal Inhabitants', op.cit., p.176.
31. Arthur to Glenelg, 22 Jul. 1837, Colonial Office, C.O. 280/84.
32. *South Australian Register*, 3 Oct. 1840.
33. J. Dredge, *Brief Notes of the Aborigines of New South Wales*, Geelong, 1845, p.26.
34. *ALRC*, Aboriginal Customary Law, Public Hearings, 1446, 15 Apr. 1981.
35. 'Select Committee on Aboriginal Inhabitants', 1837, op.cit., p.83.
36. Memo of James Stephen, 10 Dec. 1835, Colonial Office, 13/3.
37. *The Adelaide Chronicle*, 4 Nov. 1840.
38. *The South Australian Register*, 19 Sep. 1840.
39. Blackstone, op.cit., 1, p.9.
40. H.S. Maine, *International Law*, London, 1890, p.58.
41. London, 1894, pp.212, 218, 223, 224.
42. Ibid., p.228.
43. Ibid., p.230.
44. 6 PET.515, 540.
45. B. Slattery, *Ancestral Lands: Aliens Laws*, University of Saskatchewan, Saskatoon, 1983, p.6.
46. 8 Wheaton, 574, 603.
47. *Worcester v Georgia*, op.cit., p.517.
48. U.S. Reports, 34, Peters, 9, 712.
49. *Worcester v Georgia*, p.519.
50. Peters, 5, 7, p.16.
51. *Worcester v Georgia*, p.580.
52. 118 U.S., 380.
53. B. Slattery, *The Land Rights of Indigenous Canadian People*, University of Saskatchewan, Saskatoon, 1979, p.20.
54. Ibid., p.44.
55. 107 U.S., 1883, 571.
56. B. Slattery, *Ancestral Lands*, etc., p.14.
57. *Crowe v Eastern Band of Cherokee Indians*, 506, F.2d., 1231.
58. *Iron Crow v Oglala Sioux Tribe*, 231, F.2d., 90.
59. *McClanachan v Arizona Tax Commissioner*, 411 United States Law Reports (US) 1973.
60. 104 D.L.R. (4th) 1993 at 470.
61. Ibid., p.640.
62. Ibid., p.655.

63. Ibid.
64. Ibid.
65. B. Slattery, 'Aboriginal Sovereignty and Imperial Claims', *Osgoode Hall Law Journal*, 29, no.4. 1991, p.701.
66. *Delgamuukw v British Columbia*, op.cit., p.472.
67. Royal Commission on Aboriginal People, *Partners in Confederation*, Ottawa, 1993, p.9.
68. Ibid.
69. P. Macklem, 'First Nations Self Government and the Borders of Canadian Legal Imagination', *Revue De Droit De McGill*, 46, no.1, 1991, p.389.
70. *Partners in Confederation*, op.cit., p.3.
71. Ibid., p.36.
72. *Delgamuukw v British Columbia*, op.cit., p.642.
73. B. Slattery, 'Understanding Aboriginal Rights', *Canadian Bar Review*, 66, 1987, p.738.
74. M. Asch and P. Macklem, 'Aboriginal Rights and Canadian Sovereignty', *Alberta Law Review*, 29, no.2, 1991, pp.499–517.
75. *Mabo v Queensland*, op.cit., pp.28–29.
76. P. Macklem, 'Indigenous Peoples and the Canadian Constitution: Lessons for Australia', Paper given to Conference on Indigenous People in National Constitutions, Canberra, May 1993, p.41.

CHAPTER 7

1. ATSIC, *Reconciliation, Social Justice and ATSIC*, ATSIC, Canberra, 1992, p.7.
2. The Constitutional Settlement: An address to conference on position of indigenous people in national constitutions, Canberra, 4–5 June 1993, p.9.
3. Ibid., p.4.
4. Ibid.
5. Aboriginal/T.S. Islander Social Justice Commissioner, 1st Report, 1993, p.41.
6. M. Mansell, 'Tomorrow: The Big Picture', *The Future of Australia's Dreaming*, Australian Museum, Sydney, 1992, p.17.
7. Ibid.
8. Ibid.
9. 'Towards Aboriginal Sovereignty', *Chain Reaction*, 62, p.4.
10. Legislative Review Committee, *Towards Self Government*, Canberra, 1991, p.3.
11. Ibid., pp.1–2.
12. *Land Rights News*, Aug. 1993.

13. H.C. Coombs, *Aboriginal Autonomy*, Cambridge University Press, Melbourne, 1994, p.182.
14. *Townsville Bulletin*, 30 Aug. 1993.
15. Quoted in Council for Reconciliation, *Agreeing on a Document*, AGPS, Canberra, 1994, p.19.
16. Ibid.
17. B. Galligan, 'Public Attitudes to Aboriginal Issues', in C. Fletcher, ed., *Aboriginal Self Determination in Australia*, AIAS, Canberra, 1994, p.102.
18. Coombs, op.cit., p.220.
19. Ibid., p.228.
20. R. Mathews, 'Towards Aboriginal Self Government', *CEDA Public Information Paper*, 46, July 1993, pp.10–11.
21. Reconciliation Council, *Going Forward*, Commonwealth of Australia, 1995, p.37.
22. F. Brennan, *Securing a Bountiful Place for Aborigines*, Constitutional Centenary Foundation, Melbourne, 1994, pp.20–21.
23. Ibid., p.43.
24. S. Harris, *It's Coming Yet*, Aboriginal Treaty Committee, Canberra, 1979, p.12.
25. *Two Hundred Years Later*, AGPS, Canberra, 1983, p.50.
26. *Sydney Morning Herald*, 13 Jun. 1988.
27. Council for Aboriginal Reconciliation, *Addressing the Key Issues for Reconciliation*, AGPS, Canberra, 1993, p.50.
28. G. Nettheim & T. Simpson, 'Aboriginal Peoples and Treaties', *Current Affairs Bulletin*, 65, no.12. May 1989, p.23.

CHAPTER 8

1. 53 *ALJR*, 1979 403.
2. See generally H. Reynolds, *The Law of the Land*, Penguin, Ringwood, 1992.
3. See, P. Biskup, *Not Slaves, Not Citizens*, University of Queensland Press, St Lucia, 1973.
4. 22 Apr. 1840.
5. R.W. Newland to Anti-Slavery Society, 18 Dec. 1840, Anti-Slavery Papers, Rhodes House, Oxford, MSS British Empire, S22.
6. Ibid., 10 Feb. 1934.
7. Quoted in H. Reynolds, *The Law of the Land*, p.183.
8. W. McKean, *Equality and Discrimination Under International Law*, Clarendon, Oxford, 1983, p.14.
9. Ibid., p.15.
10. Ibid., p.22.
11. Minority Schools in Albania (6 Apr. 1935) 64 PCIJ, p.17.

12. Nijhoff, Dordrecht, 1991, p.14.
13. P. Thornberry, *Minorities and Human Rights Law*, Minority Rights Group, London, 1991, p.14.
14. Ibid., p.13.
15. Ibid., p.18.
16. Ibid.
17. D. Sanders, 'Aboriginal Rights', in M. Boldt and J.A. Long, eds, *The Quest for Justice*, University of Toronto, Canada, 1988, p.301.
18. UN Document, E/CN 4/Sub 2/1986/7.
19. *Land Rights Queensland*, Nov–Dec, 1995, p.6.
20. Unpublished draft of UN Declaration on Indigenous Rights provided by Aboriginal and Torres Strait Islander Commission.
21. Thornberry, op.cit., p.9.
22. UN Document, A/4684 (1960).
23. Quoted in R. McCorquodale, 'Self-Determination Beyond the Colonial Context', *African Journal of International and Comparative Law*, 4, 1992, p.601.
24. UN Document, A/5217 (1970).
25. S. James Anaya, 'The Capacity of International Law to Advance Ethnic or Nationality Rights Claims', *Iowa Law Review*, 75, 1990, p.839.
26. University of Toronto, 1993, p.3.
27. Anaya, op.cit., p.3.
28. 'Self-Determination and Indigenous Peoples', in C. Tomuschat, ed., *Modern Law of Self-Determination*, Nijhoff, Dordrecht, 1993, p.79.
29. F. Harhoff, 'Constitutional and International Legal Aspects of Aboriginal Rights', *Nordic Journal of International Law*, 57, 1988, p.290.
30. M.E. Turpel, 'Indigenous Peoples' Rights', *Cornell International Law Journal*, 25, 1992, p.593.
31. D. Sanders, op.cit., p.80.
32. Quoted by S.J. Anaya, op.cit., p.842.
33. R. Ryser, 'Fourth World Wars: Indigenous Nationalism and the Emerging New International Political Order', in M. Boldt and J.A. Long, *The Quest for Justice*, University of Toronto, 1985, pp.305–15.
34. T.W. Pogge, 'Cosmopolitanism and Sovereignty', *Ethics*, 103, Oct. 1992, p.48.
35. J. Keane, 'Democracy's Poisonous Fruit', *Times Literary Supplement*, 21 Aug. 1992, p.10.
36. A. Buchanan, *Secession*, Westview Press, Boulder, 1991, p.29–31.
37. R. McGee, 'The Theory of Secession and Emerging Democracies', *Stanford Journal of International Law*, 28, 1992, p.452.
38. A. Magalit and J. Raz, 'National Self-Determination', *Journal of Philosophy*, 87, 199, pp.439, 457.
39. A.D. Smith, *The Ethnic Origin of Nations*, Blackwell, Oxford, 1986, pp.224–25.

40. St Martin's Press, New York, 1990, p.13.

41. W. Connor, 'The Politics of Ethnonationalism', *Journal of International Affairs*, 27, no. 1, 1973, p.1.

42. A. Cobban, *The Nation State and National Self-Determination*, Crowell, New York, 1970, p.137.

43. A.D. Smith, *The Ethnic Revival*, Cambridge University Press, 1981, p.196.

44. Ryser, op.cit., p.304.

45. D. Papineau, 'The Warmth of Nationhood', *Times Literary Supplement*, 19 Feb. 1993, p.14.

46. J.S. Mill, *Consideration on Representative Government*, Oxford University Press, London, 1963, p.381.

47. T. Honore, 'The Right to Rebel', *Oxford Journal of Legal Studies*, 8, no.1, 1988, pp.44–45.

48. As quoted in J. Dahl, 'From Ethnic to Political Identity', *Nordic Journal of International Law*, 57, 1988, p.312.

49. A. Heraclides, *The Self-Determination of Minorities in International Politics*, Cass, London, 1991, p.28.

50. *Aboriginal Law Bulletin*, 2, no. 34, October 1988, p.13.

51. Op.cit., p.211.

52. S.J. Anaya, op.cit., p.842.

53. B. Slattery, 'Paradoxes of National Self-Determination', *Osgoode Hall Law Journal*, 32, no.4, 1994, p.725.

54. *Stanford Journal of International Law*, 29, no.1, 1992, p.43.

55. *The Ethnic Origins of Nations*, op.cit., p.225.

56. *Foreign Affairs*, 73, no.3, May–Jun. 1994, p.107.

57. 'Are Indigenous Populations Entitled to International Juridical Personality?' Proceedings of American Society of International Law 79th Annual Meeting, 1985, pp.190, 195.

58. 'Constitutional and International Legal Aspects of Aboriginal Rights', *Nordic Journal of International Law*, 57, 1988, p.290.

59. Ibid.

60. M.C. Lâm, 'Making Room for Peoples at the United Nations', *Cornell International Law Journal*, 25, 1992, p.602.

CONCLUSION

1. H. Hannum, op.cit., p.454.

2. M. Boldt, op.cit., p.47.

3. Hannum, op.cit., pp.454–55.

4. Mill, op.cit., p.382.

5. J.M.E. (Lord) Acton, *The History of Freedom and Other Essays*, Macmillan, London, 1922, pp.297–98.

6. Mill, op.cit., p.380.
7. W. Connor, 'The Politics of Ethnonationalism', *Journal of International Affairs*, 27, no.1, 1973, p.3.
8. A. Cobban, *The Nation State and National Self-Determination*, Crowell, New York, 1970, p.107.
9. A. Smith, *The Ethnic Revival*, Cambridge University Press, 1981, pp.66, 85.
10. J. Kellas, *The Politics of Nationalism and Ethnicity*, Macmillan, London, 1991, p.2.
11. H. Seton-Watson, *Nations and States*, Methuen, London, 1977, p.5.
12. A. Grahl-Madsen, 'Introduction', *Nordic Journal of International Law*, 55, 1986, p.2.
13. P. Macklem, 'Distributing Sovereignty: Indian Nations and Equality of Peoples', *Stanford Law Review*, 45, May 1993, p.1350.
14. Hannum, op.cit., p.454.
15. Ibid.
16. As quoted by Macklem, 'Distributing Sovereignty', p.1325.
17. Ibid.
18. Boldt, op.cit., p.XV.
19. G. Werther, *Self-Determination in Western Democracies*, Greenwood Press, Westport, Connecticut, 1992, p.24.
20. As quoted in Macklem, 'Distributing Sovereignty', p.1329.
21. As quoted in R.L. Barsh, 'Indigenous North America and Contemporary International Law', *Oregon Law Review*, 62, 1983, p.94.
22. H.C. Coombs, op.cit., p.229.
23. W. Connor, op.cit., p.21.
24. A. Heraclides, op.cit., p.210.
25. J. Salmond, *Jurisprudence*, Sweet & Maxwell, London, 1902, p.197.
26. G. Werther, op.cit., p.87.
27. J.S. Mill, op.cit., p.380.
28. Lord Acton, op.cit., p.290.
29. p.225.

BIBLIOGRAPHY

Aborigines Protection Society, *Report of Sub-Committee on Australia*, London, 1838

Action, J.M.E. (Lord), *The History of Freedom and Other Essays*, MacMillan, London, 1922

Allen, C.K., *Law in the Making*, 6th ed., Clarendon Press, Oxford, 1958

Amos, S., *Lectures on International Law*, London, 1874

An Authentic and Interesting Narrative of the Late Expedition to Botany Bay, Aberdeen 1789

Anaya, S.J., 'The capacity of international law to advance ethnic or nationality rights claims', *Iowa Law Review* 75, 1990, pp. 837–44

Andrews, J.R., 'The concept of statehood and the acquisition of territory in the nineteenth century', *Law Quarterly Review* 94, 1978

Asch, M. and Macklem, P. , 'Aboriginal rights and Canadian sovereignty', *Alberta Law Review* 29:2, 1991

Atkinson, A., 'The ethic of conquest, *Aboriginal History* 6, 1982

ATSIC, *Reconciliation, Social Justice and ATSIC*, ATSIC, Canberra, 1992

Austin, J. *Lectures on Jurisprudence* 4th ed., London, 1873

Australian Law Reform Commission, *The Recognition of Aboriginal Customary Law*, 2 vols, AGPS, Canberra, 1986

Backhouse, J., *Extracts from the Letters of James Backhouse* 3rd ed., London, 1838

Bacon, F., *Essays*, Dent, London, 1966

Banks, J., *The Endeavour Journal 1768–1771*, 2 vols, Angus & Robertson, Sydney, 1962

Bannister, S., *Humane Policy or Justice to the Aborigines*, London, 1830

Barsh, R.L., 'Indigenous North American and contemporary international law', *Oregon Law Review* 62, 1983, pp. 73–125

Bartlett, T., *New Holland*, London, 1843

Bentham, J. A. *A Fragment on Government*, Oxford, 1894

Beran, H., 'A liberal theory of secession', *Political Studies* 32, 1984, pp. 22–31

Berman, H.R., 'Are indigenous populations entitled to international juridical personality?', *Proceedings American Society of International Law*, 1985, pp. 189–204

Binder, G., 'The case for self-determination, *Stanford Journal of International Law* 29, 1993, pp. 225–70

Birch, A.H., 'Another liberal theory of secession', *Political Studies* 32, 1984, pp. 596–601

Blackstone, W., *Commentaries on the Laws of England*, 2 vols, 18th ed., London, 1823

Boldt, M., *Surviving as Indians*, University of Toronto Press, Toronto, 1993

Boldt, M. and Long, J.A., *The Quest for Justice*, University of Toronto Press, Toronto, 1988

Bouvier, J., *A Law Dictionary*, 2 vols, 11th ed., Philadelphia, 1866

Bowen, G.F., *Thirty Years of Colonial Government*, 2 vols, London, 1889

Bowyer, G., *Commentaries on Universal Public Law*, London, 1884

Brennan, F., *Securing a Bountiful Place for Aborigines*, Constitutional Centenary Foundation, Melbourne, 1994

Breton, W.H., *Excursions in New South Wales*, London, 1833

Bride, T.F. (ed.), *Letters from Victorian Pioneers*, Melbourne, 1898

Brierly, J.C., *The Law of Nations*, Clarendon Press, Oxford, 1928

Brolmann, C., et. al. (eds), *People and Minorities in International Law*, Kluwer, Amsterdam, 1993

Broms, B., 'Identity and equality: Co-existence of separate sovereignties in the same territory', *Nordic Journal of International Relations* 57, 1988, pp. 301–10

Broom, H., *Constitutional Law*, 2 vols, 2nd ed., London, 1885

Buchanan, A., *Secession*, Westview Press, Boulder, 1991

Carson, T.H., *Prescription and Custom*, Sweet & Maxwell, London, 1907

Castles, A.C., 'The reception and status of English law in Australia', *The Adelaide Law Review*, 1963, pp. 1–31

Clark, C., *A Summary of Colonial Law*, London, 1834

Cobban, A., *The Nation State and National Self-Determination*, Crowell, New York, 1970

Cobbett, P., *Leading Cases and Opinions on International Law* 2nd ed., London, 1892

Cohen, F., 'The Spanish origin of Indian rights in the law of the United States', *The Georgetown Law Journal* 31, Nov. 1942, pp.1–21

Collins, D., *An Account of the English Colony in New South Wales*, 2 vols, Reed, Sydney, 1975

Connor, W., 'The politics of ethnonationalism', *Journal of International Affairs* 27:1, 1973

Cook, J., *The Voyage of the Resolution and Discovery 1776–1780*, ed. J.C. Beaglehole, Cambridge University Press, 1967

Coombs, H.C., *Towards Self Government*, University of Queensland Press, Brisbane, 1991

Council for Reconciliation, *Agreeing on a Document*, AGPS, Canberra, 1994

Cranston, R., 'The Aborigines and the law', *University of Queensland Law Journal* 8, 1973, pp. 62–78

Crawford, J., *The Creation of States in International Law*, Clarendon, Oxford, 1979

——(ed.), *The Rights of Peoples*, Clarendon, Oxford, 1988

Dahl, J., 'From ethnic to political identity', *Nordic Journal of International Law* 57, 1988

Dawson, J. *Australian Aborigines*, Melbourne, 1881

Dench, G., *Minorities in the Open Society*, Routledge & Kegan Paul, London, 1986

Despagnet, *Cours de Droit International*, Paris, 1910

Dickey, A., 'Law of the Worora Aborigines', *University of Western Australia Law Review*, 12, 1975–76

Dinstein, Y. and Tabory, M. (eds), *The Protection of Minorities and Human Rights*, Nijhoff, Dordrecht, 1992

Dredge, J., *Brief Notes on the Aborigines of New South Wales*, Geelong, 1845

Eggleston, E. *Fear, Favour or Affection*, ANU, Canberra, 1968

Elias, T.O., *British Colonial Law*, Stevens, London, 1962

Elkin, A.P., 'Aboriginal Evidence and Justice in North Australia', *Oceania* 17:3, March 1947

Ellinghaus, M.P., et al. (eds), *The Emergence of Australian Law*, Butterworth, Sydney, 1989

Else-Mitchell, R., 'Territorial conquest—Phillip and afterwards', *Victorian Historical Journal* 43, Aug. 1975, pp. 429–46

Emerson, R., 'Self-determination', *The American Journal of International Law* 65, 1971, pp. 459–75

Evatt, E., 'The acquisition of territory in Australia and New Zealand', *Grotian Society Papers*, 1968, pp. 16–45

Evatt, H.V., 'The Legal Foundation of New South Wales', *Australian Law Journal* II, Feb. 1938, pp. 409–24

Eyre, E.J., *Journals of Expeditions of Discovery*, 2 vols, London, 1845

Fiore, P., *Nouveau Droit International Public*, Paris, 1868

Fison, L. and Howitt, A.W., *Kamilaroi and Kurnai*, London, 1880

Fletcher, C. (ed.), *Aboriginal Self-Determination in Australia*, AIATSIS, Canberra, 1994

Frame, A., 'Colonising attitudes towards Maori custom', *New Zealand Law Journal* 17, March 1981

Frost, A., *Botany Bay Mirages*, Melbourne University Press, Melbourne, 1994

Gilbert, K., *Aboriginal Sovereignty: Justice, the Law and Land*, Barrambunga Books, Canberra, 1993

Glazer, N. and Moynihan, D., *Ethnicity*, Harvard University Press, Cambridge, 1975

Goebel, J., *The Struggle for the Falkland Islands*, Yale University Press, New Haven, 1927

Gottlieb, G., 'Nations without states', *Foreign Affairs* 73:3, 1994, pp. 100–12

Grey, G., *Journals of Two Expeditions of Discovery*, 2 vols, London, 1841

Grotius, H. *The Freedom of the Seas*, Oxford University Press, New York, 1916

——*The Rights of War and Peace*, London, 1738

——*De Jure Belli Ac. Pacis Libri Tres*, 2 vols, 1646, facsimile ed., Oxford, Clarendon Press, 1935

Hale, Sir Matthew, *The History of the Common Law*, 5th ed., 2 vols, London, 1794

Halifax, S., *An Analysis of the Roman Civil Law Compared with that of England*, Cambridge, 1774

Hall, W.E., *A Treatise on International Law*, 8th ed., Clarendon Press, London, 1924

Halleck, H.W., *International Law*, 2 vols, London, 1878

Hanke, L., *Aristotle and the American Indians*, Hollis & Carter, London, 1959

Hannum, H., *Autonomy, Sovereignty and Self-Determination*, University of Pennsylvania Press, 1990

Harhoff, F., 'Constitutional and international legal aspects of Aboriginal rights', *Nordic Journal of International Law* 57, 1988

Harring, S.L., 'The killing time', *Ottawa Law Review* 26:2, 1994

Harris, S., *'Its Coming Yet . . .' Aboriginal Treaty Within Australia Between Australians*, Aboriginal Treaty Committee, Canberra, 1979

Heineccius, J.G., *A Methodical System of Universal Law*, 2 vols, London, 1743

Henriksen, G., 'Cultural plurality and social organization', *Nordic Journal of International Law* 57, 1988, pp. 316–24

Heraclides, A., *The Self-Determination of Minorities in International Politics*, Cass, London, 1991

Heydte, F.V.D. 'Discovery and visual effectiveness in international law', *The American Journal of International Law* 29, 1935

Hodgens, B.W. et al. (eds), *Co-Existence? Studies in Ontario-First Nations Relations*, Trent University, Peterborough, 1992

Hodgson, C.P., *Reminiscences of Australia*, London, 1846

Hogbin, J. and Hiatt, L.R. (eds), *Readings in Australian and Pacific Anthropology*, Melbourne University Press, Melbourne, 1968

Holdsworth, W., *A History of English Law* XI, Methuen, London, 1938

Holland, T.E., *The Elements of Jurisprudence*, Oxford, 1880

——*Lectures on International Law*, Sweet & Maxwell, London, 1933

Honore, T., 'The right to rebel', *Oxford Journal of Legal Studies* 8:1, 1988

Hooker, M.B., *Legal Pluralism*, Clarendon, Oxford, 1975

Howitt, A.W., *The Native Tribes of South-East Australia*, London, 1904

Hunter, J., *An Historical Journal*, London, 1793

Hutchinson, J. and Smith, A.D. (eds), *Nationalism*, Oxford University Press, 1994

Irwin, F.C., *The State and Position of Western Australia*, London, 1835

Jezè, G., *Etude Theorique et Pratique*, Paris, 1896

Kellas, J., *The Politics of Nationalism and Ethnicity*, Macmillan, London, 1991

Kelleher, J., *Possession in the Civil Law*, Calcutta, 1888

Keller, A.S., Lissitzyn, O.J. and Mann, F., *Creation of Rights of Sovereignty through Symbolic Acts, 1400–1800*, Columbia University Press, New York, 1938

Kent, J., *Commentaries on American Law* 11th ed., 4 vols, 1867

King, R.J., 'Terra Australis: terra nullius aut terra aboriginum', *Journal Royal Australian Historical Society* 72:2, Oct. 1986, pp. 75–91

Kingsbury, 'Claims by non-state groups in international law', *Cornell International Law Journal* 25, 1992, pp. 481–513

Kittle, S., *A Concise History of the Colony and Natives of New South Wales*, Edinburgh, 1816

Klueber, J.L., *Droit de Gens Moderne de L'Europe*, Paris, 1831

Kymlicka, W., *Multicultural Citizenship*, Clarendon, Oxford, 1995

——(ed.), *The Rights of Minority Cultures*, Oxford University Press, 1995

Lâm, M.C., 'Making room for peoples at the United Nations', *Cornell International Law Journal* 25, 1992

Landor, E.W., *The Bushman*, London, 1847

Latham, J., 'The migration of the common law: Australia', *The Law Quarterly Review* 76, 1960, pp. 54–8

Lawrence, T.J., *The Principles of International Law* 4th ed., Macmillan, London, 1910

Ledrum, S.D., 'The "Coorong Massacre": natural law and the Aborigines at first settlement', *Adelaide Law Review* 6, Sept. 1977, pp. 26–43

Legge, J.G. (ed.), *A Selection of Supreme Court Cases*, 2 vols, Sydney, 1891

Leichhardt, L., *Journal of an Overland Expedition in Australia*, London, 1847

Lerner, N., *Group Rights and Discrimination in International Law*, Nijhoff, Dordrecht, 1991

Levin, M.D., *Ethnicity and Aboriginality*, University of Toronto Press, Toronto, 1993

Lightwood, J.M., *A Treatise on Possession of Land*, Stevens & Sons, London, 1894

Lind, M., 'In defence of liberal nationalism', *Foreign Affairs* 73:3, 1994, pp. 87–99

Lindley, M.F., *The Acquisition and Government of Backward Territory in International Law*, Longmans, London, 1928

Lorimer, J., *The Institutes of the Law of Nations*, 2 vols, Edinburgh, 1883

McCorquodale, R., 'Self-determination beyond the colonial context', *African Journal of International & Comparative Law* 4, 1992

MacDonnell, J., 'Occupation and *Res Nullius*', *Journal of the Society of Comparative Legislation* 1, 1899, pp. 276–86

McGee, R.W., 'The Theory of Secession and Emerging Democracies', *Stanford Journal of International Law* 28, 1992, pp. 451–76

McKean, W., *Equality and Discrimination Under International Law*, Clarendon, Oxford, 1983

Macklem, P., 'Distributing sovereignty: Indian nations and equality of peoples', *Stanford Law Review* 45, May 1993

——'First nations, self government and the borders of Canadian legal imagination', *Revue de Droit de McGill* 46:1, 1991

Magalit, A. and Raz, J., 'National self determination, *Journal of Philosophy* 87, 1993

Maine, H.S., *Ancient Law*, London, 1861

——*International Law*, London, 1890

Mansell, M. 'Tomorrow: the Big Picture', *The Future of Australia's Dreaming*, Australian Museum, Sydney, 1992

Marshall, J., *The Constitutional Decisions of John Marshall*, 2 vols, Da Capo Press, New York, 1969

Matthew, J., *Two Representative Tribes of Queensland*, London, 1910

Matthews, R., 'Towards Aboriginal self government', *CEDA Public Information Paper* 46, July 1993

Melville, H., *A History of Van Diemen's Land* [1835], Horwitz, Sydney, 1965

Mill, J.S., *Considerations on Representative Government*, Oxford University Press, 1963

Mitchell, T.L., *Journal of an Expedition into the Interior of Tropical Australia*, London, 1848

Myers, F., 'The cultural basis of politics in Pintupi life', *Mankind* 12:3, June 1980

Nettheim, G. and Simpson, T., 'Aboriginal peoples and treaties', *Current Affairs Bulletin* 65:12, May 1989

Nind, S., 'Description of the Natives of King George's Sound', *Journal Royal Geographical Society* 1, 1831

Nys, E., *Les Origines du Droit International*, Paris, 1894

O'Connell, D.P., *The Law of State Succession*, Cambridge University Press, 1958

——*International Law*, 2 vols, Stevens & Co., London, 1970

Oppenheim, L., *International Law* 8th ed., Longmans, London, 1967

Papineau, D., 'The warmth of nationhood', *Times Literary Supplement* 19 Feb. 1993

Phillimore, R., *Commentaries upon International Law*, 4 vols, London, 1854

Pogge, T.W., 'Cosmopolitanism and sovereignty', *Ethics* 103, 1992, pp.48–75

Polson, A., *Principles of the Law of Nations*, London, 1848

Price, A.G. (ed.), *The Explorations of Captain Cook*, Angus & Robertson, Sydney, 1958

Primdas, R.R., *Secessionist Movements in Comparative Perspective*, St Martins Press, New York, 1990

Pufendorf, S., *De Jure Naturae Et. Gentium* 1688 facsimile ed., Clarendon Press, Oxford, 1934

Queensland Legislative Review Committee, *Towards Self Government*, Brisbane, 1991

Rachel, S., *Dissertation on the Law of Nations* facsimile ed., 2 vols, Carnegie Corp., Washington, 1916

Reconciliation Council, *Going Forward*, Commonwealth of Australia, Canberra, 1995

Roberts-Wray, K., *Commonwealth and Colonial Law*, Stevens & Co., London, 1966

Salmond, J., *Jurisprudence* 10th ed., Sweet & Maxwell, London, 1947

Salomon, C., *L'Occupation des territoires Sans Mâitre*, Paris, 1889

Sanders, D., 'Is autonomy a principle of international law?', *Nordic Journal of International Law* 55, 1986, pp. 17–21

——'The re-emergence of indigenous questions in international law', *Canadian Human Rights Yearbook*, 1983, pp. 3–30

Schulz, F., *Classic Roman Law*, Clarendon, Oxford, 1951

Selden, J., *Of the Dominion or Ownership of the Sea*, London, 1652

Senate Standing Committee on Constitutional and Legal Affairs, *Two Hundred Years Later*, AGPS, Canberra, 1983

Seton-Watson, H., *Nations and States*, Methuen, London, 1977

Shaw, M., *Title to Territory in Africa*, Clarendon, Oxford, 1986

——'The Western Sahara case' in *The British Year Book of International Law*, Clarendon Press, Oxford, 1979

Simpson, G., 'Mabo, international law, terra nullius', *Melbourne University Law Review* 19, June 1993

Simsarian, J., 'The acquisition of legal title to terra nullius', *Political Science Quarterly* 53, 1938, pp.111–28

Slattery, B., 'Aboriginal sovereignty and imperial claims', *Osgoode Hall Law Journal* 29:4, 1991

——*Ancestral Land: Alien Laws*, University of Saskatchewan, Saskatoon, 1983

——*Land Rights of Indigenous Canadian People*, University of Saskatchewan, Saskatoon, 1979

——'Paradoxes of National Self-Determination', *Osgoode Hall Law Journal* 32:4, 1994

——'Understanding Aboriginal Rights', *Canadian Bar Review* 66, 1987

——*Canadian Native Law Cases* 2, 1870–1890, University of Saskatchewan, Saskatoon, 1981

Smith, A.D., *The Ethnic Origin of Nations*, Blackwell, Oxford, 1986

——*The Ethnic Revival*, Cambridge University Press, Cambridge, 1981

Symth, R.B., *The Aborigines of Victoria*, 2 vols, Melbourne, 1876

Stokes, J.L., *Discoveries in Australia*, 2 vols, London, 1846

Stuart, C., *Two Expeditions into the Interior of Southern Australia*, 2 vols, London, 1833

Sutton, P. S. and Rigsby, B., 'People with "Politiks", etc.' in N. Williams and E.S. Hunn (eds), *Resource Managers*, AIATSIS, Canberra, 1982

Taplin, G. (ed.), *The Folklore, Manners, Customs and Languages of the South Australian Aborigines*, Adelaide, 1879

Taylor, H., *A Treatise on International Public Law*, Callaghan, Chicago, 1901

Teichelmann, G.C., *Aborigines in South Australia*, Adelaide, 1841

Tench, W., *Sydney's First Four Years*, Angus & Robertson, Sydney, 1961

Textor, J.W., *Synopsis of the Law of Nations*, facsimile ed., Carnegie Institute, Washington, 1916

Thomas, J.A.C., *Text Book of Roman Law*, North Holland, Amsterdam, 1976

Thompson, R., *The Rights of Indigenous People in International Law*, University of Saskatchewan, Saskatoon, 1987

Thornberry, P., *Minorities and Human Rights*, Minority Rights Group, London, 1991

——'Self-determination, minorities, human rights', *International and Comparative Law Quarterly* 38, October 1989, pp. 867–89

Tomuschat, C. (ed.), *Modern Law of Self-Determination*, Nijhoff, Dordrecht, 1993

Turpel, M.E., 'Indigenous peoples' rights', *Cornell International Law Journal* 25, 1992

Twiss, T., *The Oregon Question Examined*, New York, 1846

Van Dyke, V., 'Collective entities and moral rights', *Journal of Politics* 44, 1982, pp.21–40

——'Human rights and the rights of groups', *American Journal of Political Science* 18, 1974, pp.725–41

Vattel, E. de, *The Law of Nations* [1760], 3 vols, Carnegie Institute, Washington, 1916

Victoria, F. de, *De Indis*, Carnegie Institute, Washington, 1917

Von Martens, G.F., *The Law of Nations* 4th ed., London, 1829

Von Savignys Treatise of Possession 6th ed., London, 1848

Ward, R., *An Enquiry into the . . . Law of Nations in Europe*, 2 vols, London, 1795

Warkoenig, L.A., *Analysis of Savigny's Treatise on the Law of Possession*, Edinburgh, 1839

Werther, G., *Self-Determination in Western Democracies*, Greenwood Press, Westport, Conn., 1992

Westgarth, W., *Report on the Condition, Capabilities and Prospects of the Australian Aborigines*, Melbourne, 1845

Westlake, J., *International Law*, Cambridge University Press, 1904

Wheaton, H., *Elements of International Law* [1836], Clarendon Press, Oxford, 1936

Wheeler, G., *The Tribe, and Inter-tribal Relations in Australia*, London, 1910

Wildman, R., *Institutes of International Law*, London, 1849

Wilson, G.G. and Tucker, G.F., *International Law* 5th ed., Harrap, London, 1909

Wolff, C., *The Law of Nations* [1750], Clarendon Press, Oxford, 1934

Woolsey, T.D., *Introduction to the Study of International Law*, Boston, 1860

World Council of Churches, *Justice for Aboriginal Australians*, ACC, Sydney, 1981

Wright, J., *We Call for a Treaty*, Collins/Fontana, Sydney, 1985

Wu, J., 'Towards legal pluralism in Australia?', *Australian Journal of Public Administration* 31:2, June 1992

Zavalia, S., *The Political Philosophy of the Conquest of America*, Editorial Culture, Mexico City, 1953

INDEX